This terrific and engaging new introduction to philosophy will help Christian readers better understand philosophy and how to use it to explore and strengthen their faith. It can also help the philosophically inclined to better grasp the full nature of real Christian faith. It is wise and engaging to read, and it will spark great conversations for a very long time. It's a superb introduction to many basic philosophical concepts and proceeds with a generosity of spirit that matches its care.

—**Tom Morris,** public philosopher and author of *True Success*, *If Aristotle Ran General Motors*, *Philosophy for Dummies*, *Plato's Lemonade Stand*, and *The Oasis Within*

For several decades now there has been a significant and discouraging gap in depth and quality between the best Christian philosophy and the most popular and accessible offerings from the "Christian apologetics" industry. This book is a welcome breath of fresh air. Clear and accessible yet rigorous and philosophically sensitive, Dolores Morris's *Believing Philosophy* is the best introduction to Christian philosophical thinking for a broad, popular readership that I have encountered. Youth and adults, lay readers and experts will all find something of value here, and the book is a particularly helpful resource for people looking for serious yet highly readable treatment of the problem of suffering—the most important and pastorally difficult objection to Christian faith.

—**Michael Rea,** Rev. John A. O'Brien Professor of Philosophy, University of Notre Dame

I am so glad that Dolores Morris wrote this book and so glad to have read it. The first part is a wonderful introduction to philosophy, much of which will be helpful to any introductory philosophy student. Morris's treatment of complex philosophical questions of interest to Christians in the second part perfectly balances accessibility and nuance. She is especially insightful about the power and the limits of arguments. I will definitely read and discuss this book with Christian undergraduates, and I know that we will all benefit tremendously.

—**Kyla Ebels-Duggan,** associate professor of philosophy, Northwestern University

Dolores Morris's accessible book on Christian philosophy is a wonderful gateway to understanding the relationship between faith and reason. Morris works through caricatures and misrepresentations about philosophy, and she presents important arguments and analyzes issues to show how philosophy under the lordship of Christ can be a vital, faith-shaping tool both for individual Christians and the overall well-being of the church.

—**Paul Copan,** Pledger Family Chair of Philosophy and Ethics, Palm Beach Atlantic University, and author of *Loving Wisdom: A Guide to Philosophy and Christian Faith*

Dolores Morris's *Believing Philosophy* is an achievement and a lifeline. Deploying a rich array of argument, anecdote, and illustration, this outstanding book meets a vital but neglected need. Morris provides an accessible, trustworthy, and well-stocked outpost from which to explore and enjoy the wealth of Christian philosophical resources. She throws a ready lifeline to those who feel forced to choose between faith and intellectual integrity. Morris dismantles the myth that philosophy is a luxury for those with spare time for pointless speculation about unanswerable questions. She shows that philosophy, far from being irrelevant or hostile to faith, can be good—even invaluable—for one's faith. For all those who seek a more mindful faith: take up and read!

—**Robert Garcia,** associate professor of philosophy, Baylor University

Believing Philosophy is a gift to the church. Dr. Morris exhorts Christians to pursue wisdom as part of their discipleship into Christlikeness. She argues compellingly that philosophy provides one avenue for that pursuit. Incredibly accessible, this work introduces the reader to the resources of philosophy (logic, argumentation, clarity, and charity) and then models how to apply those resources to the problem of evil. *Believing Philosophy* is a must-read for Christians who want to have tools to think more deeply about their faith and to engage charitably in the face of disagreements.

—**Christa L. McKirland,** lecturer in systematic theology at Carey Baptist College in Auckland, New Zealand, and founder and executive director of Logia International

Dr. Morris does so many things so well in this book. Christians who love philosophy, as well as those who are unsure or even skeptical about its value, should read *Believing Philosophy*. The practical guidance, sustained look at the problem of evil, and rare combination of boldness and humility will be useful to anyone in search of wisdom.

—**Michael W. Austin,** professor of philosophy,
Eastern Kentucky University

"Christians should work to understand what they believe and why they believe it. This quest for understanding does not mean that Christians must replace their faith with reason. On the contrary, a well-reasoned faith pursues wisdom with the confidence that comes from knowing that God himself is the source of wisdom." With these incisive and challenging words philosopher Dolores Morris opens up a new and hopeful invitation for Christians to reconsider their avoidance of philosophy and to develop instead a cogent, reasonable basis for our faith. I appreciate that the very subject can be intimidating to many, but Morris has succeeded where many have failed. She writes not only as a Christian and as a philosopher but also significantly as a wise instructor. Beginning with the essentials she builds a case for this essential discipline while providing the tools needed to develop philosophical muscles. This is a needed work and one I will be commending to many. Christ, the "Wisdom of God," is glorified when his people learn to love the Lord with our minds, renewed in the truth that Jesus himself came to bear witness to. Get this book. Read it. Work with it. Share it.

—**David Cassidy,** lead pastor, Christ Community Church,
Franklin, Tennessee

Dolores Morris gives her readers clear and persuasive arguments for the value of Christian philosophy and then demonstrates that value with an evenhanded treatment of one of the most powerful objections to Christian faith—the problem of suffering. She also makes the case that objective moral values are better explained on a Christian worldview than on a secular one. Her writing is accessible and compelling, and she instructs her readers in the tools of philosophical reasoning that are invaluable for any serious engagement with life's hardest questions. Most importantly, Morris does all this by modeling the virtues of thought and character that I want to develop in myself and help form in my students—intellectual honesty and deep respect for those with whom she reasons.

—**Faith Pawl,** St. Agnes School, St. Paul, Minnesota

Believing Philosophy is the antidote for those who think reason and Christian belief are at odds. The book provides a clear, rigorous, and engaging invitation to thinking about God, suffering, objective values, and other critical, challenging topics.

Many recent popular books treat religion as a superstitious intellectual wasteland. Christian apologetics books often tell readers *what* they should believe about topics related to Christianity. *Believing Philosophy* instead shows readers *how* to reason carefully and rigorously, and it demonstrates the intellectual integrity of Christian faith. Students, lay Christians, and atheists alike will benefit enormously from the valuable, accessible volume.

—**Michael Murray,** president, Arthur Vining Davis Foundations

Believing
Philosophy

—

A Guide
to Becoming a
Christian Philosopher

DOLORES G. MORRIS

ZONDERVAN
ACADEMIC

ZONDERVAN ACADEMIC

Believing Philosophy
Copyright © 2021 by Dolores G. Morris

Requests for information should be addressed to:
Zondervan, *3900 Sparks Dr. SE, Grand Rapids, Michigan 49546*

Zondervan titles may be purchased in bulk for educational, business, fundraising, or sales promotional use. For information, please email SpecialMarkets@Zondervan.com.

ISBN 978-0-310-10952-5 (hardcover)

ISBN 978-0-310-10954-9 (ebook)

Cover design: Emily Weigel
Cover art: Bonnie Van Voorst
Interior design: Kait Lamphere

Printed in the United States of America

21 22 23 24 25 26 27 28 29 30 31 /LSC/ 15 14 13 12 11 10 9 8 7 6 5 4 3 2 1

Contents

Acknowledgments

I must begin by thanking the John Templeton Foundation and the University of South Florida for their generous support, without which this book would not have been possible. *Believing Philosophy* is, in many ways, the culmination of a series of classes that I taught at Tampa Covenant Church. I am immensely grateful to all those who attended those classes and encouraged me to continue the process of bringing philosophy into the church. I am especially thankful to my pastor Lou Kaloger for his persistent question, "How's the book coming?"—a question which he began asking long before I ever agreed to write such a book. (My other pastors—Eric Meyer and Mark Farrell—were equally encouraging, but Lou gets credit for being the most dogged in his efforts!) Many thanks as well for the helpful comments from the following early readers: Kyle Barrington, Paul Copan, Robert Garcia, Angela Knobel, Chelsie Morris, Josh Morris, Michael Morris, Michael Murray, Michael Rea, and Wes Skolits. In the same vein, I am thankful to Christa McKirland, who asked me frankly, "Do you think you have a book to write?" and when I answered, "Someday!" replied, "Why not now?" Finally, I am tremendously grateful for the editorial work and encouragement of Katya Covrett. This book is much better than it would have been without her input.

This book is the culmination of my experience as a Christian and, eventually, a philosopher. In that respect, I am immensely grateful to my parents, Jack and Kathy Griffin; my childhood pastor, Rev. Charles Drew; and my first philosophy professor, Michael Murray, all of whom encouraged me to keep seeking answers to my questions. My parents in particular led me to believe that I really could do anything that I set my mind to. I'm not sure that this is factually correct, but it certainly has been a powerful encouragement throughout my life! Further thanks are due, as well, to my in-laws, Terry and David Morris, who allowed our family to take up residence during the great pandemic of 2020. I can't imagine having completed this book without that help.

Finally, I could not have pulled this off without the support of—and the countless conversations with—my husband, fellow philosopher Michael Morris. Michael and our children, David, Kathleen, and Samuel, have been exceedingly patient with me as I have continued to insist that the book is *almost* done. We are all very glad to see it *actually* done.

The painting featured on the cover of this book is the beautiful *Transfiguration* by Bonnie Van Voorst. This is just one of my many favorites of Bonnie's work, and I highly recommend checking out her page at www .bonnievanvoorst.com.

Introduction

I am a Christian philosopher. Being both a Christian and a philosopher means that I occasionally am subjected to suspicious attitudes from two fronts: Christians who are skeptical of philosophy and philosophers who are skeptical of Christianity. This book is designed to answer both kinds of skepticism. It is a defense of Christianity and a defense of philosophy; more specifically, it is an introduction to and a defense of Christian philosophy.

Part 1, "Christian Philosophy: What, Why and How?" introduces the discipline of philosophy and defends it from some common objections. The first four chapters answer the following questions: What is philosophy? And why does it matter? Chapter 5 is a response to the commonly asked question, Isn't the Bible enough? In chapter 6, I lay out some practical guidance for learning how to read philosophy. Finally, chapters 7 and 8 include a basic introduction to philosophical arguments. These last two chapters of part 1 can be tricky, especially if you are reading this book on your own. I recommend working through them with a teacher or a group of friends, if possible. You may also choose to skip them and go straight from chapter 6 to chapter 9 if you are reading this alone.

In part 2, I put these tools and resources to work. This second part, "Philosophy in Action," includes a detailed examination of the problems of evil and suffering. In chapter 9, I introduce the philosophical problem known as the "problem of evil." In chapters 10 and 11, I present two theistic responses to the problem, two ways of defending belief in the existence of God in light of the suffering in this world: skeptical theism and the free will defense. As we will see, the problem of evil is largely a problem of suffering; despite its name, the philosophical problem of evil does not require the existence of moral evil. In response, chapters 12–14 offer a different perspective on evil, turning the existence of moral evil into an argument for the existence of God.

This "moral argument" takes as its starting point the reality of evil—that is, not merely suffering, but genuine, objective, moral wrongdoing. Chapter 12 is a defense of the objectivity of evil and other moral values and an overview of the moral argument. In chapter 13, I consider the resources available to the atheist for making sense of morality. In chapter 14, I consider the resources available to the theist for doing the same. Ultimately, I conclude that theism is a better explanation of objective moral values than atheism. As such, the existence of objective moral values, including moral evil, are evidence of the existence of God.

To be clear, this book does not contain any knock-down arguments guaranteed to prove the existence of God to the ardent atheist. I believe the world contains a great deal of evidence of the existence of God, and some of that evidence can be useful in philosophical arguments. On the whole, however, philosophy rarely delivers such decisive proof. Instead, as you will see throughout this book, philosophical arguments help us to see how our beliefs are related to one another—how one belief can lead to or rule out another. Good arguments should be persuasive, but they almost never eliminate disagreement entirely.

In addition to being an introduction to the discipline of philosophy, this book is also intended to introduce readers to a wealth of Christian philosophers. Throughout this book you will encounter Christian thinkers who have a great deal to offer the church at large. Some of these figures are historical philosophers; others are alive and well, teaching and writing today. The thinkers introduced in this book are a tiny sample of the historical and contemporary community of Christian philosophers. It is my hope that you will move on from this book to their works and from their works to the writings of still more Christian philosophers. We are called to seek wisdom, to pursue it as treasure. Philosopher means "lover of wisdom." The study of philosophy is, of course, not the only way to pursue wisdom, but the tools and resources of philosophy, coupled with the accumulated works of the community of believing philosophers, is a resource that should not be ignored.

Indeed, the questions of philosophy cannot be ignored. At some point in the life of every believer, difficult questions will arise: What exactly do I believe? Why do I believe it? Are those reasons good reasons for that belief? Should I believe something different instead? What if I am wrong? How would I know? If I am right, how can I explain the fact that so many people disagree with me? Why is life so difficult? If God really does exist, then why hasn't he made his existence more obvious? And why do so many of my prayers seem to go unanswered? These are just a tiny sampling of the questions of philosophy. In light of the inevitability of these questions, it is imperative that believers proactively seek the tools and resources best equipped to help them find answers. To anticipate a common reply: yes, of course, Scripture can answer many of these questions. Nevertheless, finding answers requires careful reasoning, and philosophical reasoning is careful reasoning.

I was introduced to philosophy at an immensely difficult time in my life. Reading philosophical texts by Christian authors did not eliminate my grief or despair, but it was instrumental in the preservation and perseverance of my faith. Careful reasoning enabled me to reconcile the reality of human suffering with the goodness and providential control of a loving God. Furthermore, the discipline of philosophy and the writings of other Christian philosophers have enhanced my ability to read Scripture, to pray, to wait on God, to meditate on the goodness of God, and to "grow in the grace and knowledge of our Lord and Savior Jesus Christ" (2 Peter 3:18). Becoming a Christian philosopher radically transformed my life as a believer. It is my sincere hope that the rich resources of Christian philosophy will do the same for you.

PART 1

Christian Philosophy

———

What, Why, and How?

Why Philosophy?

Mamaw was dead, and without a church or anything to anchor me to the faith of my youth, I slid from devout to nominal, and then to something very much less. By the time I left the Marines in 2007 and began college at The Ohio State University, I read Christopher Hitchens and Sam Harris, and called myself an atheist. I won't belabor the story of how I got there, because it is both conventional and boring. A lot of it had to do with a feeling of irrelevance: increasingly, the religious leaders I turned to tended to argue that if you prayed hard enough and believed hard enough, God would reward your faith with earthly riches. But I knew many people who believed and prayed a lot without any riches to show for it.

—*J. D. Vance, "How I Joined the Resistance"*[1]

If this book works as I intend, religious readers who open it will be atheists when they put it down.

—*Richard Dawkins,* The God Delusion[2]

I t is a story that has become alarmingly familiar: a young Christian, raised in the church, discovers the work of a popular atheistic author with some philosophical training. Typically, this begins with one of the "four horsemen of new atheism": Sam Harris, Daniel Dennett, Christopher Hitchens, or Richard Dawkins. Before long, this Christian is reading that her belief in God is foolish and irrational—the intellectual equivalent of believing in Zeus, fairies, or a Flying Spaghetti Monster. Dawkins decries belief in God

---

1. J. D. Vance, "How I Joined the Resistance," *The Lamp* 1 (2020), https://thelampmagazine
.com/2020/04/01/how-i-joined-the-resistance/.
2. R. Dawkins, *The God Delusion* (Boston: Houghton Mifflin, 2006), 52.

as "a pernicious delusion."[3] Hitchens blithely claims that "the incompatibility of reason and faith has been a self-evident feature of human cognition and public discourse for centuries."[4] Sam Harris describes religion as "violent, irrational, intolerant, allied to racism and tribalism and bigotry, invested in ignorance and hostile to free inquiry, contemptuous of women and coercive toward children."[5] Dennett agrees, writing that "I think that there are no forces on this planet more dangerous to us all than the fanaticisms of fundamentalism."[6] The message is clear: belief in God is akin to a particularly dangerous form of mental illness, wholly irrational and utterly harmful to all involved. These are weighty, emotionally charged accusations. Is it any wonder that Dawkins's goal is so often successful? Many religious readers who open his book, or books like it, do indeed find themselves atheists at the end of their inquiries.

What is happening? Why, after a lifetime in the church, do some Christians find these writings so persuasive? Well, part of what is happening is that inquisitive Christian congregants are discovering philosophy without the help and guidance of the Christian philosophical community. In reading the "new atheists," they are introduced to the basic ideas of logically structured thought and the critical evaluation of fundamental beliefs. (That is, they are introduced to philosophical thinking.) Because they have had no experience with Christian philosophy, they come to associate careful thinking and rational evaluation with atheism. Perhaps they will talk to their parents and friends about the challenges raised in these arguments; if they are particularly diligent, they may consult their pastors. Unfortunately, unless their parents, friends, or pastors have the conceptual resources fostered by philosophy, they may have a difficult time explaining where and why they disagree with the atheists' arguments. That they disagree is clear; articulating the reasons for their disagreement can be a substantial challenge. As a result, these intellectually curious Christians conclude that atheism is the thoughtful and intelligent choice and that Christianity is the stuff of blind faith.

---

3. Dawkins, *The God Delusion*, 52.

4. C. Hitchens, *God Is Not Great : How Religion Poisons Everything*, 1st ed. (New York: Twelve, 2007), 56.

5. S. Harris, "An Atheist Manifesto," SamHarris.org, December 7, 2005, https://samharris.org/an-atheist-manifesto/.

6. D. Dennett, *Darwin's Dangerous Idea : Evolution and the Meanings of Life* (New York: Simon & Schuster, 1995), 515.

In reality, Christianity and the discipline of philosophy have a long, rich, shared history. The apostle Paul makes frequent references to the Greek philosophy of his time; many of the early church fathers were themselves philosophers. For a long time philosophy was, by default, at least theistic, if not explicitly Christian in nature. That is, for quite a lot of the history of philosophy, most philosophers believed in the existence of God and the reality of his creative activity in our world. In the last three centuries, all of that changed. This is not to say that all philosophers ceased believing in God, or even that all Christians abandoned the field of philosophy—not at all! But the general attitude toward the existence of God became increasingly skeptical as the intellectual attitudes of the Enlightenment took hold.[7] As a result, many Christians today are suspicious of the discipline of philosophy.

Philosophy and the Church

What exactly is philosophy? I will say more about this in chapter 2, for an adequate answer to this question requires more than a brief definition. Still, the word *philosophy* means "love of wisdom," and that is as good a place to start as any. The study of philosophy is, or ought to be, the pursuit of wisdom. The method of philosophy is the asking of big questions: Why are we here? Why is there something rather than nothing? Is there a God? If so, what is God like? Do people have souls? How should we live? What makes one choice good and another bad? What is a good life, and how can I best achieve it? This is just a small sampling of the questions of philosophy. At the same time, philosophy demands that you do more than merely ask these questions. Instead, philosophical reasoning requires that you spend some time determining not only what you believe but also why you believe it, and whether or not your reasons are good reasons for that belief. Very simply stated, philosophy asks you to think more carefully about what you believe. This is the core of philosophy.

---

7. To be sure, there were Enlightenment-era Christian philosophers. Still, the emphasis on gaining knowledge through human reason alone resulted in increased suspicion of religious belief—especially belief which rested on any kind of divine revelation. For a powerful reflection on the influence that the enlightenment has had on evangelical Christianity, I recommend M. A. Noll, *The Scandal of the Evangelical Mind* (Grand Rapids: Eerdmans, 1994). For more on the historical trajectory of Christian philosophy, see C. G. Bartholomew and M. W. Goheen, *Christian Philosophy: A Systematic and Narrative Introduction* (Grand Rapids: Baker, 2013); and: J. A. Simmons, *Christian Philosophy: Conceptions, Continuations, and Challenges* (Oxford: Oxford University Press, 2019).

So why would philosophy be good for the Christian church? At the most basic level, it is good for the church to be equipped with believers who know what they believe! It is good for believers to develop the skills of thinking clearly, reading clearly, and working through the reasons they have for the beliefs they hold. In my own life, the study of philosophy absolutely transformed my ability to read Scripture with a careful eye. Furthermore, the long history of Christian philosophical writings provides a rich resource for believers. Many of the doctrines central to Christianity are rooted in the philosophical writings of Augustine, Aquinas, or other early philosophers. At the same time, the last fifty years have seen a tremendous resurgence of Christian philosophers. You do not need to turn to Medieval thinkers to find thoughtful Christians giving careful reflections on core Christian doctrines; such reflections abound today.

Still, it cannot be denied that a great deal of recent philosophical writing is explicitly designed to undermine the Christian faith. (Dawkins wasn't joking; his aim really is to make atheists out of theists.) The last twenty years have given rise to this new kind of atheistic philosophy—the so-called new atheists referenced above. The newness of the new-atheist movement is largely a matter of style. Where the "old" atheistic philosophers wrote largely for other philosophers, the "new" ones write and speak primarily to a popular audience. Their approach has been quite successful. New atheism sets out to convert philosophically curious religious believers into atheists, and it manages to do so far more often than it should. In response, the church must rise to the challenge—encouraging and equipping philosophically capable, prepared, intellectually resilient believers.

The Antiphilosophical Response

Of course, I am a philosopher. It is perhaps not surprising that I would respond to a problem generated by philosophy with the prescription "more philosophy!" In contrast, a very common response to the worrying trend instigated by the new atheists is to blame philosophy itself. ("That's what happens when you read worldly philosophy!") I believe that this is a mistake, and a dangerous one at that. It is a mistake for at least three reasons: it comes from a place of fear, it is almost never effective, and we can do better. What message do we send when we tell people that the answer to their doubts is to stop asking questions? I will tell you what message that sends: it says, "We don't have the answers. If you must insist on finding them, you will have to look elsewhere."

To illustrate, consider this online review of *The God Delusion*:

> I had been a Christian for many years in my youth, but began to question things and was told not to seek answers basically. But I was not ok with that and so I set out to educate myself. Long story short I went from Christian to agnostic and finally atheist. This book was wonderful and the last little nudge I needed to complete my transition into the logical and rational world I now live in. Highly recommend this book.[8]

Note the tragic trajectory of this reader's life. As a longtime believer, she found herself asking some hard questions. Rather than working alongside her to understand and address those questions, her Christian community urged her simply not to think about them. Unwilling or unable to ignore her concerns, she turned to the one community that she knew of that was willing to address them—the new atheists.

Perhaps some of you are thinking something like the following: "Yes, well, let that be a warning to the rest of us! She should not have spent so much time asking hard questions and should have just trusted God. She should have 'believed harder.' She replaced faith with philosophy and is now paying the price." The first thing to note about this response is that it often comes from a place of fear, not faith. The very notion that asking questions will lead a believer away from God rests on the presumption that Christian answers to these questions are not available. This is not faith in the truth of Christianity; it is fear that Christianity won't hold up to intellectual scrutiny.

The second problem with the antiphilosophical response is that it almost never works; telling a person to ignore her concerns does very little to alleviate those concerns. Here is an analogous story from my own life. In the thirty-fifth week of pregnancy with my first child, I developed preeclampsia, a very serious complication involving, among other things, dangerously high blood pressure. The baby and I both made it through all right, but because

---

8. SLbond (Sheila Bond), https://www.amazon.com/God-Delusion-Richard-Dawkins/product-reviews/0618918248/ref=cm_cr_arp_d_paging_btm_next_2?ie=UTF8&reviewerType=all_reviews&pageNumber=2.

there is a risk of recurrence, I was cautious during my second pregnancy. Naturally, when my blood pressure began to rise in the thirty-fifth week of that pregnancy, I raised my concerns with my doctor. She responded by telling me to stop checking my blood pressure. In my doctor's mind, I was worrying too much, and worrying can increase blood pressure. Far better, she thought, to just stop checking and stop worrying about it! I hope that you can see that this was foolish advice. When my blood pressure readings were normal, I was not worried. When they began to rise, I was worried, but I was worried for a reason. I was worried because I had encountered some troubling evidence; telling me not to worry was essentially telling me to ignore that evidence. This was the wrong response for a lot of reasons, and my daughter was indeed born (early, but healthy) within the week. The Christian concerned with hard questions has already encountered some troubling evidence; telling her to stop thinking about that evidence is unwise and ineffective.

What kind of evidence am I referring to here? Perhaps she has begun to worry about the prevalence of evil and suffering in this world, the spiritual fate of those born into cultures with little knowledge of Christianity, or how it can be true that God is in control and yet people have free will. In short, perhaps she has begun to grapple with a philosophical question. Each of these questions brings with it some worrying piece of evidence: this world contains a great deal of suffering and evil; a lot of people live without access to or knowledge of the gospel; the concept of freedom is difficult to understand, particularly in light of the sovereignty of God. The Christian who has encountered and been moved by this evidence is unlikely simply to forget about it.

Fortunately, the third problem with the antiphilosophical attitude under discussion is one that ought to give us hope: we can do better! We can do better than to tell our fellow Christians not to worry about intellectual challenges to their faith; we can do better than to tell them to avoid philosophy. Instead, we can work with them and alongside them to work through these questions in ways that will strengthen their faith and our own. We can choose to engage these challenges together, seeking insight and guidance from our shared experiences, from the Bible, from the church fathers, and from a source that is, I think, currently neglected in the church worldwide: the vast, rich network of Christian philosophers.

The Case of J. D. Vance

We can see the spiritual benefits of philosophical study by turning to the story of author J. D. Vance, quoted in the epigraph above. Vance's life followed a path similar to the one described at the beginning of the chapter, but where I have characterized this trend as "alarmingly common," Vance decries his experience as "both conventional and boring." We can learn a lot from Vance's account, for his path did not end in atheism. Instead, he persisted in the pursuit of truth, continuing to examine what he believed, why he believed it, and whether or not those beliefs seemed to match the world as he knew it. On this last question, Vance describes reading a passage in *City of God*, written by the church father and early Christian philosopher Augustine. In this passage, Augustine detailed "the debauchery of Rome's ruling class." Vance writes, "It was the best criticism of our modern age I'd ever read. A society entirely oriented towards consumption and pleasure, spurning duty and virtue."[9] In the writings of a fifth-century philosopher, Vance found the words to describe his concerns about contemporary culture. He did not stop there. Instead, Vance persisted in his efforts to examine his beliefs critically, finally beginning what he describes as "a more serious period of study" with a Dominican friar. Though he could have run from the philosophical questions that had undermined his early faith or run from the spiritual truths which had grounded that same faith, J. D. Vance leaned into both, working toward a resolution.

Ultimately, Vance returned to Christ, becoming a devout, committed member of the Catholic Church. He describes his move toward Catholicism in the following passage, beginning with a reference to his beloved grandmother's "deep, but completely de-institutionalized faith":

> I slowly began to see Catholicism as the closest expression of her kind of Christianity: obsessed with virtue, but cognizant of the fact that virtue is formed in the context of a broader community; sympathetic with the meek and poor of the world without treating them primarily as victims; protective of children and families and with the things necessary to ensure they thrive. And above all: a faith centered around a Christ who demands perfection of us even as He loves unconditionally and forgives easily.[10]

---

9. Vance, "How I Joined the Resistance."
10. Vance, "How I Joined the Resistance."

The arguments of the new atheists convinced Vance to abandon Christianity in favor of atheism. The careful, thoughtful reflections of faithful, philosophically trained Christians helped bring him back. There is a lesson here.

But there is also a lesson in why he left. By Vance's own account, his initial departure from Christianity had more to do with unmet expectations than it did careful argumentation. He writes:

> A lot of it had to do with a feeling of irrelevance: increasingly, the religious leaders I turned to tended to argue that if you prayed hard enough and believed hard enough, God would reward your faith with earthly riches. But I knew many people who believed and prayed a lot without any riches to show for it.[11]

If faith is supposed to be a pathway to earthly comfort, and earthly comfort remains out of reach, then what is the point of going on believing? I mean no harm to the religious leaders in Vance's life, but the hard truth is that they failed him. They gave him the wrong reasons for persisting in faith, promising things that God himself never promised. Instead of working with him to find good reasons to believe the truth of Christianity, they simply suggested that he believe harder. "Just keep believing and God will make you rich!" is neither biblical nor rational; this combination of injunctions is especially likely to fail a struggling believer.

Feel-Good Faith

The fault does not really lie with these particular religious leaders. Their approach is symptomatic of a growing trend in our culture, both inside and outside of Christianity, to treat religious belief as a kind of self-help manual. On this view, all that really matters is the role that faith plays in your life. If it makes you happy, that's great! If it doesn't, ditch it! Of course, people are all very different, so what makes one person happy may not make another person happy. If my faith makes me happy but also makes you uncomfortable, then you should allow me to practice my faith in my private life, and I should do what I can to keep from imposing my faith upon you. As long as we all

---

11. Vance, "How I Joined the Resistance."

feel good about the role of religion in our lives, we don't need to worry about disagreements or difficult questions.

This general attitude is the core of what we might call feel-good faith.[12] The tricky thing about feel-good faith is that it is pervasive in our world today, and pervasive views have a tendency to spread unnoticed. What do I mean by this? Well, I'm sure some of you would admit to holding something like the feel-good approach to faith, but I suspect not the majority. More of you—more of us—would not explicitly accept this attitude, but may have nevertheless internalized some of its features: that belief in God should always be comforting, never challenging or uncomfortable; that what matters is what some verse of the Bible means to me, or how it makes me feel; that God wants his people to be healthy, prosperous, and powerful; that God will never give you more than you can handle—and that means that the thing you most fear could never happen to you. To be clear, I am fairly confident that the religious leaders in Vance's early life would have wholeheartedly denied the core claims of feel-good faith, but aspects of this feel-good approach were present—in particular, the belief that earthly comfort is so highly valued as to be promised to the faithful by God himself.[13]

Perhaps the most pervasive feature of the feel-good approach to faith is the tendency not to think deeply about what you believe, why you believe it, and whether those beliefs are compatible with Scripture, with the history of Christian thought, and with truths made evident in the world around us. The result is a flimsy faith, a faith with very little substance at all. We should be concerned about the growing tendency of young people to abandon the Christian faith, but perhaps we should not be surprised. All children eventually outgrow their security objects; the overwhelming majority of self-help manuals end up on the trash heap. A faith focused on how a believer feels is likely to be given up—when it stops providing comfort, when a new source of comfort is found, or when the believer is told that real maturity requires that you not need any comfort objects at all.

---

12. For a robust, historically grounded account of the societal trends that have led to the prevalence of feel-good faith, see C. Taylor, *A Secular Age* (London: Harvard University Press, 2007), especially chapter 6 on "Providential Deism." For a more recent treatment of a similar account, see Rod Dreher's discussion of "moral therapeutic deism" in *The Benedict Option: A Strategy for Christians in a Post-Christian Nation* (New York: Penguin, 2017).

13. This view, *prosperity theology* in its most extreme form, will feature significantly in subsequent chapters.

This attitude toward faith is well-captured in an analogy penned by Sam Harris. Curiously enough, Harris introduces this analogy not as an attack on or criticism of religious belief, but rather as an attempt to defend religious believers from a certain kind of scorn. Writing to his atheistic peers, Harris poses the following challenge: Why are these believers so incapable of being persuaded by our clear, effective arguments for atheism? Are they really all that foolish? Perhaps not! Perhaps we too have beliefs we would rather hold on to, even in the face of clear evidence to the contrary! More simply stated, Harris's "Fireplace Delusion" is an attempt to help the committed atheist to understand why some believers have a hard time "seeing the light of reason," so to speak, and walking away from their faith.

Harris writes:

> On a cold night, most people consider a well-tended fire to be one of the more wholesome pleasures that humanity has produced. A fire, burning safely within the confines of a fireplace or a woodstove, is a visible and tangible source of comfort to us. We love everything about it: the warmth, the beauty of its flames, and—unless one is allergic to smoke—the smell that it imparts to the surrounding air.[14]

But here is where the trouble begins. Harris continues:

> The unhappy truth about burning wood has been scientifically established to a moral certainty: That nice, cozy fire in your fireplace is bad for you. It is bad for your children. It is bad for your neighbors and their children.

So there you have it. Wood fires are a historical tradition, a comforting ritual, an actual source of warmth on a cold day—and they are bad for the environment, bad for your lungs, and bad for the lungs of those around you. What's a reasonable person to do?

Well, it's tricky! When confronted with these challenging facts about wood fires, Harris has found that his (rational, atheistic) friends immediately jump to denial, justifications, and bad arguments. They scramble for reasons

---

14. S. Harris, "The Fireplace Delusion," SamHarris.org, February 2, 2012, https://samharris .org/the-fireplace-delusion/.

to believe that Harris's careful, factually supported case against wood fires just must be wrong. So desperate are they to hold on to the comforting ritual of a wood fire that they become incapable of or unwilling to face the facts—and in this way, he suggests, they are exactly like those foolish religious believers. Even the most serious of atheists are subject to the basic human tendency to protect their prized sources of comfort and good feelings—even at the cost of rationality. Yes, it is delusional; yes, it is irrational. Harris is clear that this is something that we all ought to work to overcome. But in this one small way, he also asks the atheist to be a little more gracious to the delusional Christian. After all, he notes, we all have our happy delusions. Right?

The church must do better than to content ourselves with a comforting delusion. Fortunately, the church can do better. The actual truth or falsity of the claims of Christianity have nothing whatsoever to do with how those claims make you feel. Christian doctrine, like all claims about reality, should be judged by what it says, not whether it works as a source of comfort and familiarity. To that end, Christian believers should work to know what they believe. It is not enough to merely identify as a Christian without further reflection on what that means. We need to become a people who are unafraid to think about what we believe and why we believe it. We need to become a church of Christian philosophers.

A Better Way: Embracing Philosophy

When we turn to the resources found in Christian philosophy, we will find another source of encouragement: the challenges raised by the new atheists are not, in fact, new challenges at all. They are among the oldest topics of philosophical discourse. For that reason, there is a great deal of careful, clear writing on these topics by faithful, philosophically gifted believers. Furthermore, the recent formulations of these challenges by the new atheists are philosophically weaker, not stronger, than their predecessors. You need not take my word for this; consider the words of the atheistic philosopher Michael Ruse:

> Unlike the new atheists, I take scholarship seriously. I have written that *The God Delusion* made me ashamed to be an atheist and I meant it.

Trying to understand how God could need no cause, Christians claim that God exists necessarily. I have taken the effort to try to understand what that means. Dawkins and company are ignorant of such claims and positively contemptuous of those who even try to understand them, let alone believe them. Thus, like a first-year undergraduate, he can happily go around asking loudly, "What caused God?" as though he had made some momentous philosophical discovery.... There are a lot of very bright and well-informed Christian theologians. We atheists should demand no less.[15]

New atheism is bad philosophy. It may be accessible and engaging, but to a philosophically trained reader it smacks of sophism—clever, compelling wordplay with very little philosophical substance.[16] There are, to be sure, more careful philosophical thinkers who are also atheists, but they tend not to be nearly as dismissive of those with whom they disagree. Ruse, for example, concludes by noting that "I don't think I am wrong [about atheism], but the worth and integrity of so many believers makes me modest in my unbelief." It takes philosophical training to see the distinction between good and bad philosophical argumentation. For this reason alone, the church needs more philosophically trained believers.

Recall those parents, pastors, and friends who were unable to construct a well-reasoned response to the challenges raised by the new atheists' writings. As I noted, this often leads a questioning Christian to conclude that Christianity is not as reasonable as atheism. The truth is, these parents, pastors, and friends just don't know the rules of engagement. They do not yet have the language or conceptual tools to respond to these arguments in a substantive way. Now imagine if those parents, pastors, or friends could point their inquisitive child (or friend, or spouse) toward the works of a reputable Christian philosopher. Better still, imagine if they offered to read those philosophical works together. Suppose we fill our churches with people who are willing to train their minds for precisely these kinds of discussions. Instead

---

15. M. Ruse, "Dawkins et al. Bring Us into Disrepute," *The Guardian*, November 2, 2009, https://www.theguardian.com/commentisfree/belief/2009/nov/02/atheism-dawkins-ruse.

16. This is particularly striking in the cases of Dennett and Dawkins. Both Dennett and Dawkins, unlike Harris and Hitchens, have contributed quite *good* philosophical works in areas other than philosophy of religion. They are capable of better. In matters pertaining to God, they seem not to hold themselves to their usual standards of intellectual rigor.

of waiting for more inquisitive brothers and sisters to discover philosophy as an atheistic endeavor, we could equip fellow believers with the philosophical resources needed to understand and defend their faith—to each other, to those with whom they disagree, and to themselves. Let the church, young and old, discover philosophy not as the pull toward atheism but as the godly pursuit of wisdom. Above all, let us not abandon the realm of philosophy— "The logical and rational world"—to the atheists.

When we proactively pursue philosophical study, we equip ourselves not only for the needs of others but also for the challenges we will most certainly encounter. Consider just a few of the "big questions" raised in philosophical discourse:

How can a good God exist when there is so much evil in the world?
How can we reconcile human free will with the sovereignty of God?
If God is all-knowing and all-powerful, then why should we pray for anything or anyone?
How ought we to understand unanswered prayer?

It is easy to imagine that we have answers to these questions when those answers have not yet been tested. A person who has not yet experienced genuine trauma might believe she is reconciled to the idea of God's allowance of evil and yet find her faith shaken when evil hits too close to home. Likewise, casually held beliefs about free will, divine sovereignty, and the nature of prayer may suddenly feel deeply insufficient when praying for a dearly loved friend who has left the faith. In general, when the best we can do to ground our religious beliefs is to gesture toward the beliefs of our community, we may find that we have not yet secured those beliefs in a meaningful way. Any substantial challenge to an unexamined belief has the potential to undermine it entirely. Flimsy faith is easily shaken.

We will all face challenges of this sort. Philosophical reasoning helps prepare us for such challenges by seeking and securing good reasons for our fundamental beliefs. By critically examining our fundamental beliefs before they are challenged, we are better able to evaluate these beliefs calmly and rationally. It takes time and careful thought to secure a foundation, whether conceptual or physical. It is always better to do so before the foundation is under threat of collapse.

Conclusion

I hope that I have persuaded you of the value of philosophy for the Christian church. I want to end with this. There are at least two ways of understanding the charges that Sam Harris and the rest of the new atheists have raised against the Christian faith: (1) that faith must always be irrational, and (2) that faith is often irrationally held. More plainly stated, the new atheists claim that there are no good reasons to believe in Christianity and plenty of good reasons to reject it. They gesture toward arguments claiming to show that God does not exist, that if he did exist he would not be good, and that belief in God is harmful for individuals and the world at large. All of these arguments are, I think, quite weak; there are good, well-thought-out, carefully defended responses to every one of these charges—many of which you will encounter in this book.

In the second place, however, the new atheists also claim that Christian believers don't hold their beliefs on the basis of good reasons. Instead, like the fire-loving friends who refuse to acknowledge the troubling facts about wood fires, Christians put too great a value on how they feel and too little value on evidence and reason. This second charge is sometimes true. In fairness, I think it is equally true for many atheists. Despite what the new atheists suggest, atheism is at least as likely to be a source of comfort as theism. The person who wishes to live as she pleases will take far more comfort in the belief that there is no ultimate judge, no Creator to whom she will be called to account, than she would take in Christian theism. Others may seek comfort in atheism after a period of pronounced suffering; it can be emotionally easier to believe that there is no God than to work to understand why God would allow you to face profound suffering. Similarly, some Christians follow Christ largely because their parents did; some atheists reject God for precisely the same reason. People, Christian or otherwise, do not always hold their religious (or areligious) beliefs on the basis of good reasons.

The good news is, the tools and resources of Christian philosophy are just exactly what the Christian needs in order to respond to both of these charges. There are good reasons to believe in the reality and goodness of God; there are substantive, powerful answers to the hard questions. There are better foundations for faith than good feelings, and philosophy is all about finding secure foundations for beliefs. In short, Christian philosophy can provide a powerful, fitting, appropriate response to both of the accusations levied by the new atheists.

What Is Philosophy?

It is an assured truth and a conclusion of experience, that a little or superficial knowledge of philosophy may incline the mind of man to atheism, but a farther proceeding therein doth bring the mind back again to religion.

—*Sir Francis Bacon*[1]

In chapter 1, I said that the wealth of Christian philosophical resources available to us are often neglected by the church worldwide. This is something of an understatement. I have been shocked by the number of serious, thoughtful Christians who are wholly unaware of the writings, teachings, and indeed the very existence of contemporary and historical Christian philosophers. This is a shame, for Christian philosophy is a thriving academic field with a rich history and a tremendous spiritual resource. The primary purpose of this book is to bridge this gap between the church at large and Christian philosophy. Taking my cue from Dawkins, I offer the following goal: if this book works as I intend, religious readers who open it will be Christian philosophers when they put it down.

But we have still not answered the question, What is philosophy? As I said in chapter 1, this question is not so easily answered. The field of philosophy is incredibly wide-ranging, spanning topics in nearly every other discipline—mathematics, theology, physics, biology, anthropology, sociology, psychology, history, cognitive science, and more. Symbolic logic certainly falls under the category of philosophy, but so does the study of morality, questions about the existence of God, reflections on the nature of the mind, careful interpretation of historical and political texts written in centuries past—and that is just the beginning!

---

1. F. Bacon, *The Major Works*, ed. Brian Vickers (Oxford: Oxford University Press, 1996), 125–26.

Just a few years ago, the following joke made its way around social media:

"Why does philosophy matter?"
    "I don't know, why does science matter?"
    "Well because scie-"
    "Annnnnnnd you are doing philosophy."[2]

Philosophers *love* this joke. So what is the point? I do not believe it is an exaggeration to say that for every area of inquiry, there are questions about that area that are, at their core, inescapably philosophical. Philosophy isn't just another area of inquiry; it is a way of inquiring. For that reason, reading and practicing the discipline of philosophy is the best way of coming to understand what philosophy is. A definition is a helpful starting point, but I encourage the reader to consider this book as a whole as a response to the question, What is philosophy?

With that in mind, here is our helpful starting point: I propose that we understand philosophy as the use of reason to raise highly general and highly fundamental questions with the goal of acquiring wisdom. Perfectly clear, right? Perhaps not, but in the remainder of this chapter we will unpack each aspect of this definition. In the end, we will see that a Christian philosopher is any Christian who is willing and able to be equipped for such a task—that is, for the use of reason in the pursuit of wisdom.

But perhaps you are suspicious of this endeavor. Maybe you believe that wisdom can only be found in the Scriptures, and that the Scriptures can only be understood through revelation. That is, perhaps you believe that reason is the wrong tool for the pursuit of wisdom. If so, you are not alone! This is a common worry—so common, in fact, that the entirety of chapter 5 will be devoted to addressing it. For now, I ask only that you be willing to set those worries aside for a little while. After all, my goal is not to convince you that reason alone is the path to true wisdom; neither do I wish to deny that all wisdom comes from God. I mean only to say that the careful use of reason is one more tool for the Christian in the pursuit of wisdom.

---

2. Although this joke is sometimes attributed to other people, the origin is the twitter account "Existential Comics." Existential Comics (@existentialcoms), Twitter, August 4, 2015, 8:42 p.m., https://twitter.com/existentialcoms/status/628727755794821120?lang=en.

Christian Philosophers

If that's what philosophy is, then what is a philosopher? More to the point, what do I mean by *Christian philosophers*? When I say that I wish to make Christian philosophers out of all of you, what exactly am I proposing?

Let me begin with a story: My own life is a testament to the importance of Christian philosophers. I was raised in a devout family and took delight in my faith from a very early age. My parents never shied away from the hard questions, but those questions never felt very difficult to me as an early adolescent. I felt certain of the truth of Christianity, loved God deeply, and was completely confident in God's love for me too. By my sophomore year of college, a series of tragedies—each somehow worse than the last—had left me reeling. It wasn't so much that I didn't believe in God, but I just could not believe that he loved me and that his plans for me were good. I could not reconcile the circumstances of my life and the lives of those I loved with what I believed about God.

At that time, I was attending a small liberal arts college. Although I loved the school, there were very few religious believers on the faculty. When I learned that one professor was a Christian and that he taught a class titled "Reason and Religion," I knew I had to enroll. That class was a pivotal event in my life for two reasons: I fell in love with philosophy, a discipline I had somehow managed to avoid entirely up to that point, and I found a Christian mentor in my professor. In that classroom, the nagging doubts and worries I'd been struggling with became the subject of classroom discussions, carefully written texts, and thoughtful arguments. In the process, I was able to parse the difference between how I was feeling and what those feelings actually meant for the truth of Christianity. Although many of the students in the class were atheists, and I myself was wrestling with God, I found that my concerns seemed weaker, not stronger, once they were fully on the table for discussion. In fact, the readings I encountered in that class—both for and against belief in God—strengthened my faith immensely. To be clear, I do not mean to say that philosophy will always be the best tool for making Christians out of skeptics. In my own life, however, subjecting my faith to the rigors of reason gave me the resources to think through my doubts in a way that lead to a deeper, firmer foundation for my Christian faith.

This professor, Michael Murray, is a *Christian philosopher* in the narrowest sense of the term: a professional academic philosopher who is a Christian. He introduced me to the writings of countless other (professional, academic) Christian philosophers. Many of those who are Christian philosophers in this sense work on topics directly relevant to their faith. Often, but certainly not always, these topics fall under the heading of "philosophy of religion." These Christian philosophers, contemporary and historical, have so much to offer the church, and we will consider some of their writings in the second half of this book. Nevertheless, I do not expect, or even hope, that most readers of this book will become Christian philosophers in this sense.

On a slightly broader conception, the term *Christian philosopher* applies also to those who use the tools and resources of philosophy to publicly defend the Christian faith, but who do so largely or entirely outside of academic philosophy. C. S. Lewis is one such example. When I was grappling with questions about love, justice, and biblical teachings on hell, Dr. Murray handed me a short novella by C. S. Lewis. This book, *The Great Divorce*, is at once a creative, rich, and compelling piece of fiction and a careful philosophical reflection on human freedom and divine love. C. S. Lewis did not work in the field of academic philosophy and did not have a PhD in philosophy, but he was, without a doubt, a Christian philosopher—as evidenced both in his fiction and nonfiction writings. The whole field of Christian apologetics is philosophical, and its practitioners are Christian philosophers—whether or not they hold academic degrees in philosophy.[3] But again, as with the first understanding of this term, I neither expect nor hope that all readers of this book will become Christian philosophers in this sense.

My goal in this book is not to create professional Christian philosophers —though if you see yourself pursuing such a career, I certainly wouldn't object! My goal is to do for you what Michael Murray, C. S. Lewis, Alvin Plantinga, Eleonore Stump, Thomas Flint, Marilyn McCord Adams, William Lane Craig, and so many others did for me: to strengthen and deepen your faith, to enrich your understanding of Scripture, to increase your ability to reflect on what you believe, to equip you to engage in meaningful and beneficial ways with others who do not share your beliefs, and to do it all through the discipline of philosophy. When I say that I hope for my

---

3. To be more precise, *good* Christian apologetics is philosophical. Like most things, the full range of those who call themselves "Christian apologists" is broad, and many invoke arguments and rhetorical attacks that rely more on emotional rhetoric than on reasoned arguments.

readers to become Christian philosophers, I mean this in the broadest use of the term: Christians who draw on the tools and resources of philosophy to examine, deepen, and strengthen the foundations of their faith. My intention is not to make academic Christian philosophers, but to make Christians more philosophical. In the remainder of this chapter, this is how I will use the term. By *Christian philosopher*, I mean "a philosophically minded Christian."

The Questions of Philosophy: General and Fundamental

We can now, at last, turn to a more detailed introduction to the discipline of philosophy, beginning with the kinds of questions that philosophy asks. You have already been introduced to a range of examples of philosophical questions, but what do they all have in common? In *Philosophical Thinking: An Introduction*, Monroe and Elizabeth Beardsley suggest that the features that distinguish philosophical questions from the rest are that philosophical questions tend to be highly general or highly fundamental.[4] (They might, of course, be both.) For that reason, we have defined philosophy as "the use of reason to raise highly general and highly fundamental questions with the goal of acquiring wisdom."

Consider the following example: Suppose that a friend promised to give you a ride to work and then failed to arrive at the agreed-upon time. It would be reasonable to ask your friend why she did not arrive. You might say something like: "What happened? Were you unable to get me? Is everything okay?" In asking these questions, you would very likely be trying to determine whether she had been free to pick you up as planned. If she had been free, then your reaction would probably be one of anger and frustration, coupled with some kind of moral judgment against your friend. After all, she promised to pick you up, and she could have picked you up, so she ought to have done so! She is blameworthy; you would be right to think that she had done you wrong. On the other hand, if you learned that she had not been free to pick you up, you would likely be more understanding of the broken promise. Suppose she told you that her car had broken down or that she had

---

4. M. C. Beardsley and E. L. Beardsley, "What Is Philosophy?," *The World of Philosophy : An Introductory Reader*, ed. Steven M. Cahn, 2nd ed. (Oxford: Oxford University Press, 2019), 2.

been the victim of an armed robbery. In either case, she could hardly be held responsible for failing to keep her promise. We don't ordinarily blame people for failing to do what they were—through no fault of their own—incapable of doing.

At this point, we have already begun to move in the direction of philosophical reasoning. The example began as a story about two people: you and your friend. Then I asked you to think about what people in general ought to do when they make a promise. That is, the question moved from a specific case about two friends to the general tendencies among people. In suggesting that you would be more understanding if your friend had been detained involuntarily, I again noted that, as a rule, we don't judge people for failing to do what they could not have done. In both cases, the conversation shifted from one case of human interaction to the general discussion of promises, freedom, and moral responsibility. This move from the specific to the general is one of the hallmarks of philosophical reasoning.

In addition to generality, we noted that philosophical questions often focus on matters that are fundamental. Fundamental beliefs are foundational. They provide the foundation on which many other beliefs come to rest. This may sound complicated, but it is actually fairly straightforward. Indeed, we have already begun to discuss some commonly held fundamental beliefs in the example above. For instance, you expected your friend to arrive at the promised time because you believed that friends keep promises. Your belief that friends keep promises gave you reason to believe that your friend would pick you up; the former belief gave support for the latter. A quick test of whether one belief provides support for another belief is the following: Ask yourself why you think the latter belief is true. If the former is a good answer to that question, then it is the more fundamental belief. So when asked why you believed that your friend was going to pick you up as promised, "because friends keep promises" is a perfectly sensible response. Your belief that friends keep promises provides support for your belief that this friend will pick you up as promised; the former is more fundamental than the latter.[5]

In addition to this belief about friends keeping promises, you probably

---

5. Note, also, that the test does not work in reverse. If I asked you, "Why do you believe that friends keep promises?" a response of "because she is going to pick me up as promised" would be nonsensical. Just as is the case with physical foundations, if one belief is more fundamental than another, the reverse cannot also be true.

also believe that all people should keep promises whenever they are able, regardless of whether the promise was made to a friend. This belief is even more fundamental than the last, for it grounds both (1) your belief that friends keep promises and (2) your belief that this friend was going to pick you up as promised. To see the fundamental nature of this belief more clearly, consider the following exchange:

You: Is everything okay?

Friend: Yes, fine! Why?

You: You didn't pick me up this morning. Did you forget?

Friend: No, I didn't forget. I was just really enjoying my coffee and didn't want to leave.

You: But you promised!

Friend: I know, but then I changed my mind. What's the problem?

You: You said you'd pick me up, and then you didn't pick me up.

Friend: Yeah, we've been over this. What's the problem though? I already explained why, what more do you want from me?

You: How about an apology?

Friend: What for?

You: For breaking a promise and making me late to work!

Friend: Hey, it's your responsibility to get to work on time, not mine.

You: But you promised to get me—

Friend: Look, I don't know why you keep going on and on about this "promise." You're starting to sound like a broken record.

You: I'm going on and on about it because *you're not supposed to break promises.* You made a promise and you didn't keep it, so you owe me an apology.

Friend: Oh! Yeah, I don't see promises that way. When I said I promised to pick you up, I just meant that at the time I was pretty sure I'd pick you up. I just don't think breaking promises is a big deal. As far as I'm concerned, there's nothing wrong with breaking a promise!

In this exchange, a fundamental belief plays a central role: the belief that people ought to keep their promises whenever possible. This belief is fundamental because its truth provides the foundation for the truth of many other beliefs: that your friend ought to have kept her promise, that it was reasonable to expect her to arrive as planned, that she shares some responsibility for your tardiness at work, that she owes you an apology, and that you were wronged. If it is true that people ought to keep their promises whenever possible, then each of these beliefs is true as well.

If, however, your friend is correct that there is no moral requirement to keep promises, then the truth of these claims is less secure. Indeed, if it is not true that people ought to keep their promises, then it may be that your friend had no obligation to keep her promise, it was not reasonable for you to expect her to arrive as planned, she bears no responsibility for your tardiness at work, she owes you no apology, and you were not wronged.[6] The truth of the more general belief about promises provides support for the truth of the more specific beliefs about this case. Absent that support, we would no longer have reason to believe in these claims. For that reason, we call this a fundamental belief; in questioning the truth of that belief we are asking a fundamental question.

There is another fundamental belief at play in the above discussion: the belief that moral responsibility is dependent upon freedom. To return to our example, suppose instead that the exchange had gone as follows:

You: Is everything okay?
Friend: No, I've had a terrible car accident, and I'm in the hospital. It happened while I was on my way to get you this morning.
You: I'm sorry to hear that, but you should know that I am very angry with you. You promised to take me to work, and then you didn't. It's not okay to break a promise to a friend!
Friend: Didn't you hear me? I tried to get you, but I had a car accident—
You: Well, you should have thought of that before promising to pick me up. A car accident hardly absolves you of your responsibility to me as a friend.
Friend: I don't understand. How could I have picked you up? My car was wrecked, and I was taken to a hospital. I was totally unable to get you!

---

6. It must be noted that this discussion centers upon the actual truth or falsity of these beliefs, not the mere acceptance or rejection of them by some individual. This crucial distinction will be addressed in detail in chapter 4. For now, it will suffice to say that simply *not believing* that promises ought to be kept is not enough to absolve one of moral responsibility.

You: That isn't the point. The point is that you promised to and
then you didn't.

Friend: How can you blame me for something I couldn't control?

You: Oh, it's easy! I make no exceptions for promises. It's always
wrong to break a promise—even if you're not able to keep it.
So . . . where's my apology?

What is the fundamental belief under discussion here? This is a belief
that philosophers sometimes summarize as "ought implies can."[7] According
to this principle, a person can only be held morally responsible for something
that was within her power. We do not blame people for failing to do something that they were incapable of doing. In the dialogue above, your friend
clearly believes this to be true. You do not. This belief is foundational because
its truth or falsity determines who is in the right. If "ought implies can," then
you are owed no apology. If you are right, and moral responsibility does not
depend upon ability, then you have been wronged. The truth or falsity of the
fundamental belief is the deciding factor.

As a final illustration of fundamentality, note that this discussion could
go deeper still. Suppose that your friend's initial response was something like
the following:

Was I able to get you? Well, it's complicated. I've been studying physics,
and I've come to believe that the physical world is entirely mechanistic and
deterministic—like fate, but without all that spiritual stuff. The universe
is just one giant piece of clockwork, and my body—brain included—is but
a tiny gear. I don't even think we *have* free will! I meant to pick you up, but
I got distracted with Netflix. Still, the world being what it is, I couldn't
have done otherwise, and you really can't blame me!

Aside from the fact that this sort of reasoning is what gives philosophy
a bad name, there is one obvious sense in which your friend's defense has

---

7. This view is commonly attributed to Immanuel Kant. For example, in *Religion within the
Bounds of Mere Reason*, Kant wrote: "We *ought* to conform to it, and therefore we must also be *able*
to." Kant, *Religion within the Boundaries of Mere Reason and Other Writings*, ed. G. Di Giovanni
and A. W. Wood, Cambridge Texts in the History of Philosophy (New York: Cambridge
University Press, 1998), 81.

taken a philosophical turn. Instead of wondering under what circumstances we ought to judge a person for breaking a promise, we find ourselves asking whether we can judge a person for anything at all! Furthermore, we have to consider the very nature of the universe: Is it deterministic? (That is, have all future events already been determined by the laws of nature?) If so, does that mean that we lack free will? If we do, must we then abandon moral responsibility? These are profoundly fundamental questions, for they address beliefs that form the basis for a whole host of other beliefs. Philosophers ask these sorts of questions (though, to be fair, they don't typically ask them in the context of justifying their own broken promises). They are general in that they apply not only to one person or event but to persons and events; they are fundamental in that they concern the foundation of our conception of reality. These are philosophical questions.

Applying the Questions of Philosophy

Philosophical questions often look something like this:

What precisely do I believe about this?
Why do I believe it?
Are those reasons good reasons for that belief?

Philosophical questions clarify concepts and evaluate the rational justification and the truth of beliefs. Each of these types of activities will become clearer as they become our focus in chapters 3 and 4. For now, consider the application of these questions to one of the charges raised by the new atheists at the outset of chapter 1. Christopher Hitchens wrote, "The incompatibility of reason and faith has been a self-evident feature of human cognition and public discourse for centuries."[8] By applying our first question to this claim, we can ask precisely what Hitchens was claiming here. (What, exactly, did he believe about this?)

There seem to be two main accusations: (1) faith and reason are incompatible, and (2) this fact has been self-evident for centuries. Why might

8. S. Harris, "An Atheist Manifesto," SamHarris.org, December 7, 2005, https://samharris.org/an-atheist-manifesto/.

Hitchens have held the first belief? Perhaps he thought that all faith must be blind and unreflective. Sam Harris, Hitchens's friend and cohort, defines religious faith as "simply unjustified belief in matters of ultimate concern."[9] If "faith" means "belief on the basis of no reasons whatsoever," then faith and reason are indeed incompatible. It would be very odd to attempt to use reason to understand belief on the basis of no reason whatsoever. But this is not at all what most people mean by the word *faith*. Furthermore, there is an extensive tradition, both historical and contemporary, of rigorous religious scholarship. The fields of philosophy and theology are rife with examples of well-reasoned faith; entire university departments are dedicated to applying reason to questions of faith. If faith and reason are incompatible—if the two cannot be made to work together—then what exactly are they doing? These scholars certainly don't believe that faith and reason are incompatible.

How about the second accusation? What was Hitchens saying when he claimed that the incompatibility of faith and reason "has been a self-evident feature of human cognition and public discourse for centuries"? In ordinary language, to say that something is self-evident is to say that its truth is obvious. The philosophical use of the term is more specific: a self-evident claim is one whose truth can be known solely on the basis of the meaning of the terms involved. For example, "all unjust war is wrong" is a self-evident claim. Why? Because anything that is unjust is, in virtue of its being unjust, also wrong. In order to see the truth of this claim, one need only to understand the meaning of its terms. Now consider Hitchens's proposal: "The incompatibility of reason and faith has been a self-evident feature of human cognition and public discourse for centuries." Is this incompatibility obvious? If it were obvious, then quite a lot of university professors, writers, and public speakers would be out of a job. Is it true in virtue of the meaning of its terms? Not on most definitions of the word *faith*. Yes, if you define *faith* as unreasonable, then reasonable faith is a contradiction. One could just as easily define *atheism* as the "unjustified belief that God does not exist" with the result that reasonable atheism is impossible. This is wordplay, not argument. On neither use of the term *self-evident* is it true to say that "the incompatibility of reason and faith has been a self-evident feature of human cognition and public discourse for centuries."

---

9. S. Harris, *The End of Faith : Religion, Terror, and the Future of Reason*, 1st ed. (New York: Norton, 2004).

That final clause matters as well. Hitchens did not merely claim that the incompatibility of faith and reason was self-evident; he maintained that this had been the case "for centuries." On this final point, it is not difficult to see what Hitchens meant, so we should focus largely on our second question: On what basis was he making this claim? (Why did Hitchens believe this?) Consider the last three centuries of the philosophical tradition. In a historical survey of Christian philosophy, Craig G. Bartholomew and Michael W. Goheen write that in the late eighteenth and early nineteenth century, the Christian philosopher Thomas Reid was "probably the most popular philosopher in the United States and the United Kingdom, and he enjoyed considerable popularity in France."[10] Reid was also a Presbyterian minister. He was sincere in his faith and his dedication to reason. The nineteenth century also brought us Kierkegaard, another tremendously influential Christian philosopher. It is true that Reid and Kierkegaard were in the minority as Christian or otherwise theistic philosophers—in contrast to centuries past, the eighteenth and nineteenth centuries tended toward atheistic and naturalistic philosophy. Still, they were then and remain now widely influential thinkers who were also people of faith. The twentieth century saw a powerful resurgence of Christian philosophers, with one major pivot point typically attributed to the work of Alvin Plantinga. In 1969, a group of committed Christian philosophers founded the Society of Christian Philosophers, now a thriving professional society. I know this community well. I was fortunate enough to have Dr. Plantinga as a dissertation advisor and am fortunate enough to call him a friend, and this present book is largely the result of my attendance at the Society of Christian Philosophers' recent fortieth anniversary conference. The fellowship and activities of philosophers of faith shows no signs of stopping. More to the point, this is not a secret society. It is one of the largest professional organizations in the philosophical community, and I am confident that Hitchens knew of its existence.

Let me be as clear as possible about this: there has been a great deal of discussion about the apparent tension between faith and reason, and this discussion has been present for many, many centuries. There is, however, nothing like consensus about its incompatibility. On the contrary, the thriving

---

10. C. G. Bartholomew and M. W. Goheen, *Christian Philosophy: A Systematic and Narrative Introduction* (Grand Rapids: Baker, 2013), 138.

fields of philosophy of religion and analytic theology demonstrate the utter absurdity of Hitchens's claim. No professional philosopher, neither theistic nor atheistic, should accept the claim that the incompatibility of faith and reason is "self-evident"—not now, and certainly not "for centuries." If this incompatibility were obvious, if it were true in virtue of the meanings of *faith* and *reason*, these discussions would have long since died out. The only possible construal of Hitchens's claim on which he is not revealed to be deeply ignorant of such matters is this: what he really means by *faith* is wholly unreflective, "blind" faith. If that is what he means, then that is what he ought to say. Clarity matters. Perhaps it is true that wholly unreflective, blind faith is incompatible with reason. But if so, so what? The vast, rich, extensive history of Christian thinkers reveals that faith need not be blind.

In one small way, we have already begun to use the methods of philosophy in order to articulate and defend the Christian faith. Hitchens claimed that "the incompatibility of reason and faith has been a self-evident feature of human cognition and public discourse for centuries." Had we merely read these words and tried to forget them, they might have taken on a power far greater than they actually merit. Nagging doubts can erode a person's faith, and these kinds of challenges are best faced head-on rather than buried. By facing Hitchens's claim head-on—by asking what he meant, why he believed it to be true, and whether or not those were good reasons for that belief—we were able to demonstrate the utter indefensibility of his claim. There is simply no reasonable, educated conception of *faith*, *reason*, and *self-evidence* on which faith and reason are self-evidently incompatible. It isn't true now, and it has not been the case for centuries.

The Aim of Philosophy: Wisdom

We come now to the second important feature of philosophy: it is not enough that you raise philosophical questions; you must raise them for the right reasons. Returning to our previous fictitious examples, consider once again the friend who appealed to the deterministic nature of the universe in order to justify her broken promise:

> Was I able to get you? Well, it's complicated. I've been studying physics, and I've come to believe that the physical world is entirely mechanistic and

deterministic—like fate, but without all that spiritual stuff. The universe is just one giant piece of clockwork, and my body—brain included—is but a tiny gear. I don't even think we have free will! I meant to pick you up, but I got distracted with Netflix. Still, the world being what it is, I couldn't have done otherwise, and you really can't blame me!

I said that there was one obvious sense in which this final dialogue took a philosophical turn. There is, however, another sense in which this example did not involve true philosophy. Recall our definition of philosophy: the use of reason to raise highly general and highly fundamental questions with the goal of acquiring wisdom. In this imagined scenario your friend was raising questions that were highly general and highly fundamental, but it is unlikely that she was doing so with the goal of acquiring wisdom. Instead, her goal was to avoid moral responsibility for her failings. Her aim was not the truth, it was moral exoneration. Similarly, any person whose primary aim is to publicly undermine others and to promote her own intellectual reputation is not, on our definition, doing philosophy. Such a person might find the puzzles of philosophy interesting, but true philosophy requires more than that. As I noted in chapter 1, the etymological origins of the word *philosophy* are the Greek words *philo* (to love) and *sophia* (cleverness, wisdom, intelligence.) The word *philosophy* means "love of wisdom." The true philosopher must be a lover of wisdom.

What is wisdom? The Bible tells us that wisdom begins with the fear of the Lord, that wisdom is displayed by obeying God's law (Prov 9:10; Deut 4:6). Throughout Scripture wisdom is associated with knowledge, understanding, age, humility, self-restraint, righteousness, and justice. Wisdom comes from God. Like philosophy, wisdom may be better known by acquaintance than by definition; to really understand wisdom, we should look to the wise. I do not have much to add to the biblical conception of wisdom, but I will note this: the person who seeks wisdom must, at the very least, seek the truth. Whatever else wisdom is, it cannot be founded on falsehood; neither can it be founded on good feelings alone. Wisdom ought always to be a goal of the Christian; we are biblically enjoined to pursue it as we would a treasure.

The pursuit of wisdom is the primary activity of philosophy, and the next several chapters will be devoted to articulating and defending what we might call "the rational pursuit of wisdom." The goal of these chapters is not to replace the tools that you currently use in the pursuit of wisdom but to add to their number. As Christian philosopher Kyla Ebels-Duggan wrote, "Used properly, reason is a perfectly good tool in the pursuit of wisdom.... But [the tools of philosophy] are not always the best tools. Progress towards wisdom makes use of other tools as well."[11] I encourage you not to reject the tools of philosophy out of the fear that they will usurp or interfere with your established spiritual practices. Philosophy is certainly not the only way to pursue wisdom, but it is one important and oft-neglected method of doing so.

With that in mind, the remainder of part 1 will introduce the core conceptual resources, or "tools," that are central to philosophy: conceptual clarity, the consistency and reasonability of beliefs, the distinction between truth and provability, the distinction between truth and reasonability, and the incoherence of relativism with respect to truth. In chapter 6, we will put these ideas together in the practice of reading Scripture like a philosopher. I have already hinted at the dangers of feel-good faith and the benefits of adopting a philosophically minded approach to faith. In chapter 6 the dangers of the former and the benefits of the latter will be on full display. Still, I know that in the mind of many Christians—perhaps you included—I am already in dangerous waters. After all, the Bible tells us that wisdom comes from God, not from human beings. Accordingly, shouldn't prayer and Scripture be enough? This is a question I encounter frequently, but it is difficult to address this objection in full without first introducing some of the fundamental aspects of philosophical thought. For that reason, I will return to this objection in chapter 5.

---

11. K. Ebels-Duggan, "Christian Philosophy and the Christian Life," *Christian Philosophy: Conceptions, Continuations, and Challenges*, ed. J. A. Simmons (Oxford: Oxford University Press, 2019), 70.

Clear and Reasonable Beliefs

3

But even if you should suffer for the sake of righteousness, you are blessed.
And do not fear their intimidation, and do not be troubled, but sanctify
Christ as Lord in your hearts, always *being* ready to make a defense to
everyone who asks you to give an account for the hope that is in you,
yet with gentleness and reverence.

—*1 Peter 3:14–15*

Good philosophy must exist, if for no other reason because bad philosophy
must be answered.

—C. S. Lewis[1]

For two chapters now I have been exhorting Christians to take up the tools of philosophy. In this chapter, we will finally begin to examine some of those tools in detail. In particular, the practice of philosophy involves the clarification and justification of belief. Philosophy encourages a person to ask: What is it, exactly, that you believe? And why do you believe it? Are those reasons good reasons for that belief? By considering these questions, the philosophically minded Christian will glean the benefits of the increased clarity and reasonability of her beliefs.

Clarity of Concepts

Perhaps the most fundamental tool of philosophy is that of conceptual clarity. Conceptual clarity is exactly what it sounds like—it is the practice

---

1. C. S. Lewis, "Learning in War-Time," in *Weight of Glory* (San Francisco: HarperOne, 2009), 28.

of clarifying concepts. Before embarking on any kind of serious discussion or disagreement about a topic, philosophers typically begin by defining and articulating their key terms. For example, in chapter 1, I went through several iterations of what the term *Christian philosopher* can mean before finally settling on the usage that I found most appropriate for this text. In doing so, I was clarifying my usage of the term. I began with the three most general ways of understanding the term and explained which one was best suited for our purposes. Had my intended audience been other academic philosophers, those three iterations of the concept would have been woefully inadequate. I recently reviewed a three-hundred-page collection of essays on the question "What is Christian philosophy?" I can assure you that there were more than three proposals in those three hundred pages! Why, you might ask, would anyone devote three hundred pages to the task of clarifying a concept? Because words matter; meanings matter. This is particularly important in cases where disagreement is likely to arise; in such cases, getting clear about the meaning of the relevant concepts is the crucial first step toward navigating disagreement.

Suppose that I told you that the goal of this book was to increase the number of Christian philosophers, but I did not tell you what I meant by *Christian philosophers*. You might respond along the following lines:

> Look, I understand that you love being a Christian philosopher, but I hate being stuck at a desk, and I hate the idea of teaching even more. Plus, I love my job! I'm great at what I do, I'm successful, and I have no interest in a career change. I am just not the least bit interested in becoming a Christian philosopher, and nothing you put in this book could possibly change my mind.

Note how the ambiguity of my language gave rise to your objection. I said that I wanted to increase the number of Christian philosophers, and you heard that as me wanting to increase the number of professional academic philosophers who are Christian. This was a reasonable interpretation, for that is certainly one way of using the term *Christian philosophers*. Further, if that had been what I meant, then your objection would have been right on the mark! It would be terribly misguided of me—ridiculous, really—to suggest that every reader of this book would be better off working in academic philosophy. You and I were appealing to two completely different conceptions of "Christian philosopher," and as a result we were essentially talking past one another.

In this exchange, my failure to clarify my terminology led you to believe that we disagreed about something fairly important. Upon further examination, you and I may not disagree at all! You may agree that Christians ought to learn to be philosophically minded about their faith; I may agree that relatively few Christians should pursue a career in academic philosophy. That is, once we clarify our use of the term *Christian philosopher*, we may find agreement where we took ourselves to disagree. The same can happen in reverse; ambiguous terminology can lead two people to falsely conclude that they are of the same opinion when, in fact, they disagree significantly. A British expatriate and an American Southerner might take themselves to be in wholehearted agreement about the fact that biscuits and coffee are the very best of breakfasts. If the British person takes *biscuit* to mean cookie, and the American believes it to be a savory baked good, then they are wrong to think that they agree.

In each fictitious example, the conceptual ambiguity is easily resolved; a quick clarifying note would easily set things right. There is very little at stake, and no real cost to the confusion. In reality, the stakes can be quite high and the confusion more substantial; ambiguity about important concepts can lead people to believe that they disagree when they do not, and it can lead people to mistakenly conclude that they agree—even on matters of real significance.

There is a third difficulty as well: ambiguous concepts can perpetuate disagreement, making it difficult or impossible to hold a rational dialogue among people who disagree. This is especially true in cases where the concept under discussion is difficult to articulate. In such cases, we may find ourselves disagreeing about the application of the concept (over and over and over again) when, in reality, our disagreement lies within the boundaries of the concept itself. For example, we all agree that terrorism is wrong, but what counts as terrorism? We all agree that racism is wrong, but what counts as racism? We all agree that cults are dangerous, but what counts as a cult? Examples like these abound. Because it is difficult to define the parameters of these concepts, it will be difficult to reach agreement on specific problem cases. Such difficulties are intensified by the fact that we are all, to varying degrees, inclined to give grace to those we value and swift justice to those we do not. There are no easy answers here, but philosophical training can provide guidance. In thinking philosophically, we should strive to understand the concepts upon which we rely. Further, we should keep those concepts in mind, aiming to use them consistently—particularly in cases where we might be prone to bias or hypocrisy.

We have already begun the practice of conceptual clarification in this book. In addition to our discussion of the term *Christian philosopher*, we also worked to clarify *faith* and *self-evidence*. By getting clear about the ways that those words can be used, we were able to find the source of our disagreement with Hitchens. At first it appeared that we disagreed only about whether faith is incompatible with reason. On examination, however, we discovered a deeper disagreement about what *faith* means. If *faith* means "belief on the basis of no reasons whatsoever," then it may very well be incompatible with reason; on that much, at least, we can agree with Hitchens. Faith of the sort endorsed by Christian scholars throughout the world is a different thing entirely. In this case, we were not able to resolve our disagreement merely by clarifying our concepts, but we were able to find the real source of disagreement. This is important progress. In many ways, clarification of this sort is the primary task of philosophy.

Of course, this is not to say that terms and concepts can mean whatever we want them to mean. On the contrary, language is a shared enterprise. If I decided to use the term *Christian philosopher* to mean "a horse with the ability to leap tall fences," I would not be clarifying a concept; I would be fabricating it. The proper response to such a misuse of language would be to reject it. *Christian philosopher* does not mean "a horse with the ability to leap tall fences," and declaring it so does not make it so.[2] When we work to clarify a concept, we begin with the regular usage of that concept, and then we refine it. Sometimes, as was the case with *Christian philosopher*, the process of refining is merely a matter of narrowing down a particular application.

---

2. Is it in any way conceivable that these words could come to have such a surprising and unusual meaning? Of course! If, for example, an equestrian named her horse "Christian Philosopher," and that horse earned an international reputation for his ability to leap tall fences, then we might find ourselves describing other horses as "a Christian Philosopher." For example, "Did you see that horse jump? He's a regular Christian Philosopher!" The point here is not that words can't ever be used in surprising ways. Instead, I mean only to note that there are limits to how far a concept can be stretched before it breaks, and those limits are typically set by a community, not an individual.

Thus, while I chose one usage of *Christian philosopher* for my purposes, I did not in any way suggest that it was the best definition. Instead, my point was that it was better for this particular application. Conceptual clarification is not always so egalitarian. Often, the goal of clarifying a concept is to find the right way of understanding something important. It is not enough, for instance, that we find *some* way of understanding free will that is compatible with divine sovereignty; the *right* way of understanding free will must be compatible with divine sovereignty. That is, we want real freedom to be the sort of thing that is not endangered by the sovereignty of God.

Learning to think philosophically involves, in the first place, learning to think about what your words mean. When doing so, you also ought to think about whether you are using concepts consistently. In cases of disagreement or other forms of dialogue, it is essential that you come to understand how other people are using those same words. Until this has been done, meaningful and productive conversations about controversial topics will be impossible.

Clarity of Beliefs

Clarity is especially important as it pertains to questions of religious belief. Here it can be easy to believe that you agree with another person when, in fact, conceptual clarification would reveal deep and substantial disagreement. Consider the term *Christian*. There are a number of divergent ways of understanding this term. Accordingly, there is substantial disagreement about what it means to be a Christian. For this reason, there is also a great deal of disagreement about which other beliefs are compatible or incompatible with Christianity. This is not surprising, for if we cannot agree about what it means to be a Christian, how can we begin to agree about what Christianity includes or precludes?

By way of illustration, consider the case of Serene Jones—a Protestant pastor and the president of Union Theological Seminary. Jones is, by her own account, a Christian minister. On April 20, 2019, she was interviewed by Nicholas Kristoff for the *New York Times*. Over the course of this interview, Jones dismissed the doctrine of the virgin birth as "bizarre." She denounced the notion of a literal hell and expressed doubts about heaven. Yet most striking were her claims about the atonement and the nature of God, respectively:

Crucifixion is not something that God is orchestrating from upstairs. The pervasive idea of an abusive God-father who sends his own kid to the cross so God could forgive people is nuts.

At the heart of faith is mystery. God is beyond our knowing, not a being or an essence or an object. But I don't worship an all-powerful, all-controlling omnipotent, omniscient being. That is a fabrication of Roman juridical theory and Greek mythology.[3]

In Serene Jones we find a Christian minister who does not believe in a traditional personal God, rejects the atonement story, denies the virgin birth, casts doubt upon the bodily resurrection of Christ, is skeptical about heaven, and outright dismissive of hell. In what sense, you might ask, is this Christian minister Christian?

This is not a rhetorical question; it is a question we should ask both of Jones and of ourselves. What does it mean to be a Christian? What does it mean to believe that Christianity is true? To be clear, Serene Jones does take herself to be a Christian, and she has, presumably, spent a good deal of time thinking about what that means. Jones is both a pastor and the president of a seminary. Christianity is no small part of her identity. It is therefore critical that we ask these fundamental questions. It is not enough that we profess to be Christians; we must also be clear about what we mean by that. We must be willing to ask others to do the same. Until we do so, we can have no real discourse on the matter, for there will be no shared concept of Christianity about which to agree or disagree.

At the risk of sounding pedantic, we should begin by clarifying the basic concept of a belief. I recognize that this question seems a bit silly—surely we all know what it is to have a belief! But we actually have to do a bit of work to get clear about how we ought to use the term. To see why, note that the verb *believe* can mean very different things. There is a significant difference, for example, between believing in (1) Santa Claus, (2) gun control, and (3) your favorite politician. In the first case, *believing in* means "believing in the existence of." In the second case, it means "believing in the morality of." In the

---

3. N. Kristoff, "Reverend, You Say the Virgin Birth is 'a Bizarre Claim'?," *New York Times*, April 20, 2019, https://www.nytimes.com/2019/04/20/opinion/sunday/christian-easter-serene-jones.html.

third case, it means "believing in the value/capability of." Each is a different sort of claim. (It would be odd for the person who did not believe in your favorite politician to deny their existence!)

For this reason, it will be helpful to focus on what we believe, not what we believe in. That is, we will conceptualize beliefs as beliefs *that* rather than beliefs *in*. To see what I mean, we can rewrite each of the above beliefs accordingly: (1) "I believe in Santa Claus" means "I believe that Santa Claus exists"; (2) "I believe in gun control" means "I believe that gun control is morally right"; and (3) "I believe in my favorite politician" means, roughly, "I believe that my favorite politician will do good things." In reconceiving these as beliefs *that*, we make explicit the commitments of the claim that had been implicit. The belief in Santa Claus was always about existence; now it is explicitly about existence. The belief in gun control was always a moral claim; now it is clear that it is such.[4] The belief in your favorite politician was always a claim about the likelihood of her future success; now that likelihood is stated outright. This is a crucial first step in clarifying beliefs; it helps us understand what we mean when we say that we do or do not believe something.

As a final illustration, we can apply this distinction between *belief in* and *belief that* to the case of Serene Jones. Jones believes in Christianity, but does she believe that the orthodox doctrines of Christianity are true? More specifically, does she believe that Jesus was God incarnate? Does she believe that Jesus is now still God incarnate? Does she believe that sin is something for which atonement must be made? Does she believe that this atonement is beyond our reach and requires divine intervention? My aim here is not to pick on Serene Jones. Rather, my goal is to demonstrate the dialectical usefulness of asking the right questions—of ourselves and of those with whom we find ourselves in conversation. The first step is clarifying what you believe. It can be beneficial as well to use these questions to clarify what others believe. In the process, we can come to see more clearly where we agree and disagree with one another.

---

4. Note: sometimes, the *belief in* gun control may be more about legality than morality. In that case too, appropriately conceptualizing this belief will help us disambiguate the two. One person might believe that gun control is morally right. Another might merely believe that it is legally permissible. Both might express those (different) beliefs as the belief in gun control. For that reason, it is far more helpful to base our discussion on what it is *that* people believe.

Propositions: Meaning and the Way the World Is

When we shift our language from *believing in* to *believing that*, beliefs become the kinds of things that are true or false. (We will say much more on this in chapter 4.) For that reason, philosophers tend to define beliefs in terms of what we call *propositions*. I do not wish to overcomplicate this discussion unnecessarily—a charge frequently levied against philosophers—but this one small point is crucial, so I will do my best to keep this discussion brief and to the point. To see what a proposition is, note that different people could share the same belief—could believe that the same thing is true—in different languages. A French speaker, a German speaker, and an English speaker could walk out the same door into the same courtyard and each conclude that it is raining. The first might say to herself, "Il pleut!" The second, "Es regnet!" The third, "It is raining!" In doing so, they would not be uttering the same sentence. Sentences are constructed out of words; they are language-specific entities. (More plainly stated, these sentences neither look nor sound the same!) Still, the sentences uttered by all three speakers do share one thing in common: they express the same meaning. They all say the same thing about how the world is. This meaning—this shared claim about the world that is expressed by each of these three sentences—philosophers call a proposition.

Introducing propositions into the discussion allows us to be clear about the way that the same beliefs about the world can be shared across diverse languages. It also allows us to articulate the fact that the same words can be used to make genuinely different claims about the world. As we saw in my fictitious example involving the propagation of Christian philosophers, "We need more Christian philosophers" could mean that university philosophy departments need more Christian faculty members, or it could mean that the church at large needs more careful thinkers. These are very different claims about the world, but they can be expressed using the very same sentence. The biscuit example works just as well. When I say, "There are biscuits on the table," I am reporting the presence of American biscuits—fluffy, savory, best served with butter. When my British friend says, "There are biscuits on the table," she is reporting the presence of a crispy, sweet treat that Americans call cookies. Same words, different meanings; same sentence, different propositions expressed.

For the purposes of this book I will mostly avoid using the term *proposition*, choosing instead the more colloquial term *meaning* whenever possible. Still, it is important that you keep this basic idea in mind: the truth or falsity of a belief cannot be assessed until we are clear about what the belief says about the world. Ambiguous concepts result in sentences with ambiguous meanings—that is, sentences that can be used to express very different propositions. We cannot resolve this ambiguity until we learn to recognize it. The only way to find and resolve ambiguity of this sort is to push beyond vague claims about belief to the deeper question: What do you believe? Or more specifically, what does that belief say about the world? This will be of particular importance in chapter 4 when we turn to the questions of truth, provability, and relativism. When we disagree with one another, we should work to understand the meaning being expressed by the words in use; when we seem to agree, we would benefit from doing the same. As a general rule, we should aim for clarity—about concepts, words, meanings, and, of course, beliefs.

Reasonable Beliefs: Rational Justification

Once you have established what you believe about a subject, the next question ought to ask why you believe it. Ideally, your beliefs will all be true, but in this section our concern will be with whether they are reasonable. A reasonable belief is one that is rationally justified; that is, it is held on the basis of good reasons. Rationally justified beliefs tend to be true beliefs; that is one of the reasons why they are to be valued. When your beliefs are based on good evidence, you are far more likely to establish true beliefs than false ones. Still, truth and justification can come apart, and it is important that we understand the distinction.

It will be helpful to consider a series of four examples. In the rational pursuit of wisdom, one of the primary goals is the development of justified true beliefs—like the following:[5]

1. Marcellus Thomas believes that he was accepted into the Honors College of the University of South Florida (USF). He believes this

---

5. On many accounts, this is what it means to have knowledge. When you hold a belief on the basis of good evidence, and that belief is true, then you may be said to *know* it.

for the following reasons: He received a letter in the mail in an official USF Honor's College envelope. The letter was printed on USF Honor's College letterhead and appears to have been signed by the Dean of Admissions. The letter clearly stated that Marcellus Thomas has been accepted to the Honor's College. Further, Marcellus remembers applying for the Honor's College at USF, and he knows that both his transcript and his standardized test scores ought to have given him a good shot at admission. On the basis of these facts, Marcellus believes that he was accepted into this program.

Marcellus is correct. The letter he received was authentic and he has been accepted into the program.

In this example, Marcellus has a justified true belief. It is justified because he came to believe it on the basis of good reasons. The reasons are good reasons because they are the kinds of evidence that tend to support the truth of his belief. As a general rule, if a person comes to believe that he was admitted into an academic program on the basis of having applied and received an official letter of acceptance, his belief typically will be true. It is very uncommon for a person to apply to a program and receive an official letter of acceptance without actually having been accepted into the program. Marcellus's belief is therefore justified. Because he was in fact accepted into the program, it is also true. He has a justified true belief.

He might, however, have suffered the following misfortune: Suppose that Marcellus had all of the evidence referenced in the first example, that he likewise believed he had been accepted, and that he formed that belief on the basis of that same evidence. That is, suppose that the entirety of the first paragraph in example (1) is true. Nevertheless, the following is also true:

(2) Marcellus is incorrect. The letter he received was a convincing forgery, crafted as a prank by a friend with a very poor sense of humor. The application class was unusually competitive this year, and Marcellus's strong application was not strong enough. His rejection letter is already in the mail and will arrive tomorrow.

In this case, Marcellus has a false belief—but it is a rationally justified false belief. It is justified because he came to this belief on the basis of good reasons. Indeed, he holds this belief on the basis of the very same reasons which justified his true belief in the first example. It is a false belief because it does not accurately reflect reality: he was rejected from the program. This reality does not in any way alter the fact that Marcellus formed his belief on the basis of good evidence. It remains the case that official-looking acceptance letters are a very reliable indication of having been accepted into a program. For that reason, the falseness of this belief cannot undermine its status as reasonable. This is a justified false belief.

In each of these two examples, Marcellus had a justified belief—one true, one false. Now consider two examples in which a person comes to hold a belief on the basis of bad reasons.

(3) Madeline Davis believes that she will be a multimillionaire by the end of the week. She is confident in this belief and has been telling everyone who will listen that she is but a few days away from great wealth. Madeline came to this belief after opening her first-ever fortune cookie. The fortune inside the cookie stated, "You will soon achieve great wealth!" Madeline read the fortune and assumed that *soon* meant "within the month" and *great wealth* meant "at least a few million dollars." Now that the month is coming to an end, she feels certain that she will have several million dollars by the end of the week.

Madeline is incorrect. The week will be uneventful, and she will not receive any money.

Like most beliefs held on the basis of poor reasons, Madeline's belief here is both unjustified and false. Why it is unjustified should be clear. Fortune cookies are not reliable sources of information. They do not tend to predict the future, and beliefs formed on the basis of their contents tend to be false. It is a false belief because is not true; she will not be a multimillionaire by the end of the week.

Although unjustified beliefs tend to be false, they are not always false. It is possible for a person to form a belief on the basis of bad reasons and yet, by something like sheer luck, for that belief to turn out to be true. Suppose that Madeline had all of the evidence referenced in the last example, that she likewise believed she was about to become a multimillionaire, and that she formed that belief on the basis of that same evidence. That is, suppose that the entirety of the first paragraph in example (3) is true. Nevertheless, the following is also true:

(4) Madeline is correct. Unbeknownst to her, she has a third cousin once removed with vast fortunes and a generous heart. This cousin has left Madeline an inheritance of three million dollars, which she will receive before the end of the week.

The first thing to notice about this example is that Madeline's belief is still unjustified. Although, through luck or coincidence, Madeline's belief turned out to be true, it remains the case that she ought not to have believed it. She was not being rationally responsible in forming this belief; she was following bad evidence. Her reasons for this belief are just as bad in this second case as they were in the first—which should be unsurprising, for they are precisely the same reasons! In this example, she holds an unjustified true belief.

Thus, truth and justification come apart; they are not the same thing. Justified beliefs tend to be true, for the fact that you hold a belief on the basis of good reasons requires that you have good evidence in support of that belief. That is what it means to believe on the basis of good reasons: you believe on the basis of the best available evidence, and the evidence really does support the truth of what you believe. However, even good reasons can lead a person astray. It is possible to get it wrong despite following the best available evidence. Sometimes this is due to deception, as was the case involving Marcellus's prankster friend. At other times, however, through no fault of anyone at all, the best evidence simply isn't enough to get you to the truth. This was true for members of the ancient world who believed the earth to be flat, and it has been true throughout history whenever the dominant view or consensus on a subject has gotten it wrong. Justified beliefs are more likely to be true than unjustified ones, but they are not guaranteed to be true. Likewise, unjustified beliefs tend to be false, but they can be true as well. If you form a belief on the basis of unreliable evidence, it will ordinarily turn out to be false. Nevertheless, you might occasionally luck into a true belief. Should you do so, the justification of your original belief is unchanged. Bad reasons are bad reasons, and a belief formed on the basis of these reasons is unjustified—and so, unreasonable—whether true or false.

Becoming a philosophically minded Christian involves getting clear about what you believe, why you believe it, and whether those reasons are good reasons. This leaves an awful lot of questions unanswered. What does it mean to say that a belief is true? If I believe my belief is true and you disagree, how should we resolve this? What if no decisive proof is available? Could my belief be true for me but not true for you? Who gets to decide what counts as good evidence? Each of these questions is important, and each will be addressed in this book. Most immediately, chapter 4 will examine the various difficulties that arise in evaluating the truth of beliefs, particularly in the face of substantial disagreement.

Comments on Faith

Earlier in this chapter I made the following claim: "The truth or falsity of a belief cannot be assessed until we are clear about what the belief says about the world." At face value, this claim is straightforward and unproblematic. We cannot determine the truth or falsity of the belief that biscuits are on the kitchen table until we know what the believer means by *biscuits*! Still, the content of a belief is not always wholly accessible to us, yet we very much want to affirm the truth of that belief. For example, most Christians are committed to a Trinitarian view of God. We believe that there is one God, yet we believe that God is three persons. I have a PhD in philosophy, I have been carefully reflecting on my Christian faith for the entirety of my adult life, and I cannot tell you exactly what this belief affirms or denies about the world. I can cite the creeds, but if I am being honest, I find it difficult to reconcile the three persons of God as one undivided, unified Deity. Does that mean that my belief in the Trinity is irrational? Ought I instead to be agnostic about it, unable to claim that it is true until I fully understand what it requires?

There are two crucial responses here. First, it can absolutely be rational to defer to a trusted authority on matters that you have reason to believe may be beyond your comprehension. Second, this deference to authority is not unique to religious believers, despite frequent claims to the contrary. With respect to the first claim, note that I do have some sense of what the truth of the doctrine of the Trinity requires: it must be the case that there is only one God, and yet it must be the case that the Father, the Son, and the Holy Spirit are three persons in that one God. Beyond that, things get a bit murkier.[6] Fortunately, I have quite a lot of evidence in favor of the reliability of Scripture and of the teachings of the church fathers. I also have good reason to believe that some aspects of the divine reality may be beyond my cognitive reach. Indeed, given my other beliefs about God, it would be odd if I were perfectly able to understand everything pertaining to God. As a finite, temporal, embodied being in a fallen world, I should expect some degree of confusion and error when I try to conceive of an eternal, all-powerful Creator. Thus, although I do not have perfect clarity about the conceptual content of this belief, my belief is nevertheless reasonable.

With respect to the second claim, note that we defer to authorities on matters beyond our comprehension *all the time*. We do not ordinarily believe that a person has to fully understand a mathematical principle in order to affirm it as true. Neither do we believe that the laws of physics must be comprehensible to us if we are to endorse them. Sometimes, these principles are as difficult to grasp as the doctrine of the Trinity! As I sit here at work, I have the overwhelming, undeniable sense of the solidity of both my laptop and the desk on which it sits. This is technically true, for mine are, like all desks and computers, in a solid state. But here is where things get murky: if I am to believe the physicists, the true fundamental makeup of my desk is largely empty space. Indeed, matter itself is almost entirely empty space, for matter is composed of atoms and atoms are more than 99 percent empty space. In *Particle Physics: A Very Short Introduction*, Frank Close offers this explanation:

> Between the compact central nucleus and the remote whirling electrons, atoms are mostly empty space. That is what many books assert, and it is true as concerns the particles that make up an atom, but that is only half the story. That space is filled with electric and magnetic force fields, so powerful that they would stop you in an instant if you tried to enter the atom. It is these forces that give solidity to matter, even while its atoms are

---

6. Basic though it may be, it is crucial that I have at least this much understanding. No amount of faith could enable me to believe that "Grabled musskips are tennlific." I just have no idea what that would mean, so I cannot possibly assert it as true. If you have absolutely no idea what something means, then you cannot believe that it is true. It might *be* true, if it has a meaning that you do not understand and that meaning is accurate. You cannot *believe* it to be true if you don't have any idea at all about what it means.

supposedly "empty." As you read this, you are suspended an atom's breadth above the atoms in your chair due to these forces.[7]

Note Close's final claim: you are not, strictly speaking, actually touching your chair. Well, you *are* touching it, in the way that we ordinarily use the word *touch*, but you are not making direct contact. Not between you and your chair, not between my fingers and this keyboard, not between any two things—not ever. What feels like contact is, in reality, the pressure of opposing forces.

What I find the most striking about Close's introduction is this: it is clear that his goal is both explanatory and deflationary. His clearly sets out to explain this phenomenon, but he also recognizes that it all sounds a bit crazy to the layman, and his aim is to demonstrate that, really, it's not so crazy after all. Yes, matter is mostly empty space, but there is a scientifically grounded, plausible explanation for why and how that empty space generates solidity. And now to my point: most of us can't quite get our heads around this fact.[8] I believe that matter is mostly empty space, but I can't really conceive of how that could be. That is, I accept that my desk is, in reality, largely a bundle of powerful forces, but reconciling that fact with my experience is extraordinarily difficult. So I accept it on the basis of reliable testimony. I suspect that most of you do as well. This is not because we are Christians; it is because we are cognitively limited creatures. We cannot understand everything, but we can use our minds responsibly by doing our best to understand what we can and deferring to trusted authorities when we deem such deference to be wise.

Philosophically minded Christians should work to understand what they believe and why they believe it. This quest for understanding does not mean that Christians must replace their faith with reason. On the contrary, a well-reasoned faith pursues wisdom with the confidence that comes from knowing that God himself is the source of wisdom. Reasonable faith seeks understanding whenever possible. In cases where perfect—or even very good—understanding is beyond our reach, the faithful philosopher defers

---

7. F. E. Close, *Particle Physics: A Very Short Introduction* (Oxford: Oxford University Press, 2004), 2–3.

8. For a fascinating, clear account of the oddness of present day Physics, see Barbara Montero, "Post-Physicalism," *Journal of Consciousness Studies* 8, no. 2 (2001): 61–80. This paper can also be found in my favorite anthology for "philosophy of mind": Brie Gertler and Lawrence A. Shapiro, *Arguing about the Mind*, Arguing about Philosophy (New York: Routledge, 2007).

to reliable testimonial sources. These include the Bible, the church fathers, Christian philosophers and theologians, and other thoughtful followers of Christ who have earned your trust. In deferring to authority, in believing on faith, the Christian is not being philosophically irresponsible but believing responsibly. Just as the layman—theistic or atheistic—may defer to the physicist on matters of fundamental physics, we may defer to authorities on matters of theological complexity.

True Beliefs

4

"What is truth?"

—*Pontius Pilate*

In chapter 3, we considered how the study of philosophy can help foster beliefs that are both clear and reasonable. Of course, the ultimate goal is that our beliefs be true—but what does that mean? In this chapter, we will clarify our concepts of truth in general and of true beliefs in particular. As we will see, truth can be a controversial concept. In a situation with tangible benefit or harm at stake, nearly everybody would agree that establishing the truth is vital. For example, the truth is necessary for punishing or rewarding the right person, diagnosing and treating the right illness, prescribing the right medication, or hiring the person with the right experience and credentials. In cases like these, the value of the truth is uniformly acknowledged. However, understanding truth in the face of uncertainty, disagreement, and competing narratives is and always has been a challenge. When consensus is hard to come by, there is a tendency not only to devalue the truth but also to deny that there even *is* any such thing. This is not a recent development. Perhaps one of the most striking and timeless moments in the Bible is the point at which Pilate wonders aloud to Jesus, "What is truth?" (John 18:38). Truth is important, but it has long been controversial.

True Beliefs

We should begin by clarifying the concept of truth. What exactly are we saying when we say that a belief is true? For the purposes of this book, we will adopt what philosophers call a "correspondence theory" of truth.[1] We might just as well call this the "common-sense" position for it captures most everyday intuitions about what it means for some claim or other to be true. According to this view, truth is correspondence to reality. Thus, the claim "There are elephants in that zoo" is true only if there are, in fact, elephants in that zoo. Likewise, "It is raining in my backyard" is true if it is raining in my backyard and false if it is not raining in my backyard. This is all very straightforward. If a report accurately reflects reality, then it is true; if it does not, then it is false. The correspondence theory of truth has the benefit of being intuitively plausible, capturing our ordinary use of language, and being accepted widely among academic philosophers; it is a common way of understanding what we mean when we say that something is true.

As we saw in chapter 3, the first step in evaluating the truth or falsity of a belief should be establishing what the belief says about the world. If we return to the language of propositions, we can say that when you form a belief you either affirm or deny some proposition about the world. For example, "I believe that God exists" affirms the proposition "God exists," and "I believe that there is no God" denies that same proposition. By combining these concepts, we can easily articulate the sense in which a belief can be either true or false: a true belief is a belief that affirms a proposition that corresponds to reality or denies a proposition that does not correspond to reality. A true belief gets it right about reality; a false belief gets reality wrong, either by accepting a proposition that does not correspond to reality or by denying a proposition that does. To return to our previous examples, the belief that Santa Claus exists is false because this belief affirms a claim that does not accurately reflect the real world. It says yes to the existence of a nonexistent person. A belief that says no to the existence of an existing person or thing would likewise be false. Beliefs are false when they misrepresent the world; they are true when they accurately represent the world. True beliefs correspond to reality; false beliefs do not.

---

1. What's the alternative? Some philosophers have advanced a "coherence" theory of truth. On this view, a claim is true if it fits neatly and consistently within the general web of beliefs held by the believer. Others have been skeptical of the idea of objective truth. For those who are interested in the role of truth in science in particular, I strongly recommend T. S. Kuhn, *The Structure of Scientific Revolutions*, 50th anniv. ed. (Chicago: University of Chicago Press, 2012). For a very detailed account of a wide range of philosophical conceptions of truth, see this entry in the online *Stanford Encyclopedia of Philosophy*: https://plato.stanford.edu/entries/truth/.

Of course, not all beliefs describe the world right now. The belief that dinosaurs once roamed the earth does not say that dinosaurs now roam the earth, only that there was a time at which they did. For that reason, we cannot consult reality as it is in order to evaluate the truth of this belief. Instead, as you have surely anticipated, this belief is true if it corresponds to how the world was and false if it does not. Thus any evidence that supports the existence of dinosaurs in the past also supports the truth of the belief that dinosaurs existed in the past. A belief about some time in the past is true if it accurately describes reality at that time and false if it does not. Again, if this sounds like common sense that is because this is, and is intended to be, a common-sense account. The process of conceptual clarification always begins with ordinary usage of the concept to be clarified, so our conception of the truth ought to sound a lot like what you already believe the truth to be.

Beliefs about the future are a bit trickier, and here we find some disagreement among philosophers. Beliefs about the future are true or false depending upon their correspondence to future reality; on that much, philosophers agree. The disagreement arises about whether we can say that there are now true beliefs about the future or if we should instead say only that some beliefs about the future will be true. For our purposes, it will not be necessary to choose a side here. What matters to this discussion is simply this: in all cases, the truth or falsity of a belief depends upon reality itself. The truth or falsity of a belief about the world right now is determined by the state of the world right now. The truth or falsity of a belief about the past is determined by the state of the world at that time in the past. The truth or falsity of a belief about the future is determined by the state of the world at that time in the future. If truth is correspondence to reality, then reality itself is and must be the deciding factor.

This is important, for out of this straightforward and widely endorsed account of the truth comes a number of more controversial implications. If reality itself is the deciding factor, then the truth of a belief does not depend upon how strongly a person believes it to be true. Neither does it depend upon how many people believe it to be true, how badly a person would like for it to be true, or whether it can be proven true. (It should go without saying that it has nothing whatsoever to do with how the belief makes the believer feel.) Indeed, if truth is a question of correspondence to reality, then it is entirely possible for there to be a belief that is commonly held to be false—even on the basis of excellent evidence—that is nevertheless actually true.

It is not difficult to find an example of exactly this phenomenon. For instance, the Lord Howe Island stick insect—colorfully known as the "tree lobster"—was mistakenly believed to be extinct for decades.[2] These enormous insects lived in abundance on Lord Howe Island in the Tasman Sea until a shipwreck in 1916 introduced black rats to the island. Within four years, the rats seemed to have eaten every last stick insect on the island; all evidence pointed to extinction. It was almost fifty years later when doubts about this species' extinction began to arise, and a full eighty years before a living Lord Howe Island stick insect population was discovered. The details of their survival, while very interesting, are not important here. What matters is that they did exist when the world at large was entirely convinced that they did not exist. The reasonable, scientifically grounded, widely held belief that the Lord Howe Island stick insect was extinct was, despite all that, a false belief. If the truth of a belief is determined by its correspondence to reality, then the popularity, provability, and even the reasonability of that belief are entirely beside the point; these factors do not in any way affect truth.

There is a persistent and pervasive tendency to confuse each of these three factors with the truth. That is, there is a tendency to confuse the truth of a belief with its popularity, its provability, and its rational justification (or reasonability). This is particularly true for beliefs about God and beliefs about morality, but it often extends beyond those domains. As a result, it is increasingly common for people to adopt a position of relativism, especially about the truth of religious beliefs. Broadly stated, to say that truth is relative is to say that the truth of a claim varies with and is in some sense dependent upon whomever espouses the claim. If truth is correspondence to reality, then relativism is false; relativism is wholly incompatible with the correspondence theory of truth.

Truth as Popularity: Cultural Relativism

There are two common forms of relativism: cultural and subjective. Cultural relativism defines the truth of a claim in relation to the culture in which it is espoused. For example, we believe that the earth is spherical, but many members of the ancient world believed it to be flat. Indeed, if we go back far

---

2. I first learned this remarkable story while watching a documentary with my children, but I am afraid I cannot find that original source. Instead, see https://en.wikipedia.org/wiki/Dryococelus_australis.

enough we find whole communities of people raised to believe in the flatness of the earth.[3] According to the correspondence theory of truth, those people were wrong; those cultures held a shared and popular but false belief about the earth. And yet here we find the root of cultural relativism: Who are we to say that they were wrong? In all sincerity, when I raise this example in my college classrooms, I typically find at least a few students who genuinely are offended by my willingness to declare the beliefs of these ancient people to be false. Their reasoning seems to be as follows: If the best evidence available to them indicated a flat earth, and if they all agreed to the flatness of the earth, shouldn't we instead say that their belief was true for them, even if it is now false for us? This is the core of cultural relativism: the claim that the truth or falsity of a belief is determined by agreement among believers—and, in particular, the beliefs affirmed by the majority of a culture. On this picture, truth is a matter of consensus.

Cultural relativism is entirely incompatible with a correspondence theory of truth. In cases where communities hold beliefs that do not correspond to reality, relativism and the correspondence theory will disagree about the truth or falsity of that belief. To see why, consider again the flat-earth example. Note that we do not merely believe that the earth is spherical; we believe that it has always been spherical. We believe that it was spherical even when ancient communities believed it to be flat. We believe that it is spherical now as well, even for those who now believe it to be flat. We can state the tension more clearly: reality does not depend upon what we believe, either individually or communally. The correspondence theory of truth holds that truth is determined by reality itself. Because no amount of believing the earth to be flat can actually render the earth flat, the relativist conception of truth and correspondence theory of truth are wholly and irreconcilably incompatible.

Perhaps you have the following concern: Isn't it cheating to use my own conception of truth in order to show that a rival conception fails? After all, when cultural relativists say that "The earth is flat" was true for ancient peoples, what they mean is that it was widely endorsed by ancient people. The actual earth does not have to have been flat for that to be the case.

---

3. Not as many as were previously thought. It seems that most of the educated world discovered the spherical nature of the earth, despite claims to the contrary. Still, there were certainly some cultures in the past that espoused flat-earth science. For this example to work, we only need one!

Correspondence theory and cultural relativism give different answers about the truth of that claim because they are using the word *truth* in two different ways! Who is to say that my way is better?

Fair enough, as long as we keep the following three things in mind: First, in this book, when we ask whether your beliefs are true, we will be asking about their correspondence to reality. Our question will always be whether God exists, and will never be about whether belief in God is culturally popular. Second, anyone who chooses to define truth in terms of cultural popularity must be careful to do so consistently. It is a logical fallacy to use one word in two different ways without being clear about your shift in meaning; that kind of equivocation is cheating. Consequently (and third), consistently using *truth* to mean "culturally popular" will introduce a whole host of uncomfortable consequences, all of which run counter to our common-sense use of the word *true*.

To offer just one example, if the community at large believes a suspect to be guilty of a horrific crime, it will be true that she is guilty. If actual reality does not support this claim—if, for instance, she didn't actually do it—that will not be relevant to the truth of the claim that she is guilty. As long as she is widely believed to be guilty, the truth of her guilt is secure.

This isn't what we mean by *guilty*, for it isn't what we mean by *true*— not ordinarily, at least. For that reason, note that a turn to relativism cannot actually provide an answer to questions that were constructed with the correspondence theory of truth. If I ask, "Is the belief that God exists true?" and you answer, "Yes, it is widely endorsed by our culture," then you have not answered my question. You simply changed the subject.

Truth and Popularity: Subjective Relativism

Subjective relativism fares no better. Subjective relativism is similar to cultural relativism, but instead of defining truth as consensus among a community of believers, it defines truth in terms of the convictions of an individual person (or "subject"). Thus, on subjective relativism, the belief that the earth is flat is true for anyone who genuinely believes it to be flat. Truth, on this view, is a matter of personal preference. For reasons that should be clear, cultural relativism is more widely espoused than subjective relativism. (It is very difficult to see how merely believing something to be true could make it true, particularly on a person-by-person basis.) The one domain about which subjective relativism very clearly persists is beliefs about the existence of God. There, I regularly encounter students who seem genuinely to believe that it could be "true for" one person that God exists and "false for" another, all depending upon the beliefs of the individual. Subjective relativism about belief in God is alive and well.

One reason for this stems from a confusion about what it means to believe that God exists. A wise friend and fellow philosopher Claire Brown Peterson has suggested that this confusion arises out of a misguided pedagogical movement in our country's elementary schools to teach the distinction between facts and opinions.[4] I believe that she is correct. In my articulation of the correspondence theory, I have used the following beliefs as examples: it is raining, there are elephants in that zoo, and the earth is flat. Reared on the fact/opinion distinction, it is not difficult to see why my students—and perhaps my readers—would classify these claims as facts. After all, they are clearly not opinions. But "I believe that God exists" counts as an opinion in the elementary classroom. After all, it is a report of one person's belief—one person's opinion about the existence of God. And so the trouble begins. These lessons may be well intended, and the distinction between personal preference and factual matters is certainly real. Unfortunately, these lessons have contributed to two troubling tendencies: a tendency to classify belief in God as an opinion, and a subsequent tendency to conflate all opinions with preferences. As a result, I regularly encounter students who have come to the conclusion that all beliefs about God are mere preferences. Thus, as with all preferences, two people can genuinely disagree about them and still both be right.

This is confused. It is true that the belief that God exists is an opinion, but this does not in any way preclude it from being a fact as well. Opinions can be facts; there is no real distinction here. Consider the Merriam-Webster definition of opinion:

Opinion: A view, judgment, or appraisal formed in the mind about a particular matter.[5]

---

4. Claire Brown Peterson first suggested this source of confusion to me. My concerns here are the direct result of her insight.
5. *Merriam-Webster*, s.v. "opinion (n.)," accessed January 21, 2021, https://www.merriam-webster.com/dictionary/opinion.

On this definition, an opinion is merely a view about something, about anything at all. Because a belief is a view about what the world is like, all beliefs are opinions in this sense. Thus, I can truly be said to be of the opinion that the earth is spherical; I am of that opinion because I take that claim to be true. Further, it is true, so it is a fact. Clearly, then, opinions can be facts; the distinction between facts and opinions is both dubious and dangerous.

The corollary claim is still more noteworthy: because a factual belief about what the world is like can be classified as an opinion, we cannot take seriously the claim that all opinions are preferences. "I believe that mint chocolate chip is the best ice cream flavor" is clearly an opinion and a statement of preference; "I believe that God exists" may be an opinion, but it is certainly not a statement of preference. Neither is the opinion that the earth is flat. Indeed, I have many opinions that run counter to my personal preference. I am of the opinion that pediatric cancer is devastating; I would prefer that pediatric cancer not exist. Not all opinions are preferences.

Consider the case of an opinion that does turn out to be a personal preference: the belief that mint chocolate chip ice cream is the best ice cream flavor. What is really being said here? A brief dialogue may be of some use in answering that question:

Me: I believe that mint chocolate chip ice cream is the best ice cream flavor.
You: Uh oh! I thought cookies and cream was better than mint chocolate chip. Are you saying I'm wrong about that? How do you know? What makes it better than the rest? I really like ice cream, and I'd hate to think I was eating an inferior flavor!

I think that most of us can see how silly this is. Presumably, what I meant to say was that mint chocolate chip ice cream is my favorite flavor. I prefer to eat it. It tastes better to me than the rest. If there is an actual belief here, it is only the belief that "given a variety of flavors, I am most likely to enjoy mint chocolate chip ice cream." That is what I really believe, for that is a claim that I actually take to be true; this is the proposition that I would affirm. This belief really is an expression of personal preference. Something else must be noted about this belief: it isn't really a belief about ice cream at all. Instead, it is a belief about me! For that reason, you and I do not have a genuine disagreement. There is, after all, no contradiction whatsoever in holding that mint chocolate chip ice cream is my favorite ice cream but not your favorite ice cream. If it seemed like we were disagreeing, that's because we were talking about two different people and their distinct preferences; we were, once again, talking past one another.

To further demonstrate this fact, suppose instead that I really did believe that mint chocolate chip ice cream is the best flavor—that the superiority of mint chocolate chip is a fact about the world. In that case, I might reply as follows:

> **Me:** I'm sorry to have to say this, but yes, you are wrong. You have
> been eating an inferior flavor. If you want to eat the best flavor,
> you have to switch to mint chocolate chip. Look, it's okay if you
> prefer an inferior flavor. Not everybody has a refined palate.
> Your impoverished preference can't change reality, though.
> Mint chocolate chip is the best flavor, and that's just a fact.

In this scenario, it seems I really meant to express the proposition *mint chocolate chip ice cream is the best ice cream flavor.* I don't merely prefer it; I genuinely take it to be true that this flavor of ice cream is objectively superior. I think this would be a difficult belief to *justify,* and it is unlikely that this belief will turn out to be *true,* but it could nevertheless be a belief. (Not all beliefs are true beliefs.) This belief, unjustified though it may be, would not be a mere expression of preference. This is not a belief about me; it is a belief about ice cream. If I am correct about it, then you are wrong. We cannot both be right here.

To reiterate, there is no contradiction when two people hold opposing preferences. There is a contradiction when two people believe opposite things about the world. In the former case, the beliefs in question are beliefs about the believer; in the latter case, the beliefs in question are beliefs about reality. Beliefs about reality can be true or false. When they are true, they are factual—even if they are also properly described as "opinions." Thus, the purported distinction between facts and opinions must be rejected. Instead, we ought to distinguish beliefs that are about the believer from beliefs that are about the world.

Belief in God

With this distinction in mind, consider the belief that God exists. In particular, consider whether this belief is an expression of the believer's preference or a claim about reality. I hope it is now clear that the belief that God exists is not in any way a belief about the believer; it is a belief about what the world is like.

Twenty years ago, in a book that was tremendously significant for my own undergraduate foray into philosophy, Michael J. Murray wrote the following:

> The claim that God exists is either true or it is not. Its truth does not depend upon the person asserting it in the way the claim "Vanilla tastes better than chocolate" does. My undergraduate students are almost without exception utterly confused about this point. They will often say, "You think that God exists, I don't. It all just depends on what you believe."[6]

Twenty years later, as I teach my own undergraduate students, I wish I could say that we had progressed. Instead, I find myself facing the very same degree of utter confusion. When faced with a claim about the existence of God, it is not at all uncommon for me to encounter students who reply along the following lines:

> Yes, but that's just your opinion. You believe that God exists, and I believe God doesn't exist, but that's okay because these are just our opinions! We can't be wrong about our own opinions.

Let me be very clear about this: We can indeed be wrong about our own opinions. But when our opinions express preferences, we are not likely to be wrong about them. After all, preferences are beliefs about ourselves. When our opinions express a belief about the world, however, then it is entirely possible for us to be wrong about them, for it is entirely possible to hold false beliefs about the world.

Let's look at what it would mean for you or me to hold contrary opinions about the existence of God. Suppose that I am of the opinion that God exists,

---

6. M. J. Murray, *Reason for the Hope Within* (Grand Rapids: Eerdmans, 1999), 16.

and you are of the opinion that no God exists. What is the content of my opinion? That is to say, what do I believe? What proposition am I affirming? Something like the following:

> The world in which we live was created by an all-powerful, all-knowing, perfectly good, eternal being, and that being continues to uphold and interact with its creation—including the earth on which we live, and the lives of those who live here.

And in holding the contrary opinion, what proposition are you affirming? Something like the following:

> There is no such thing as an all-powerful, all-knowing, perfectly good, eternal being. Therefore, no such being upholds or interacts with the earth on which we live or the lives of those of us who live here.

If we must use the word *opinion* to describe these beliefs, then it follows that we can be wrong about our opinions. The alternative is to endorse a straightforward contradiction, for it cannot possibly be the case that we are both right. If we could both be right about this, then the following would be the case:

> There is and there is not an eternal, omnipotent, omnibenevolent being. This divine being created the earth, and this same earth was not created by any kind of divine being. Reality itself is sustained by this being, and reality is in no way whatsoever effected by this being. God is both the true source of all reality and, simultaneously, utter fiction.

This is nonsense in the truest sense of the word. There is simply no way to make sense of these claims. It is not possible for the very same thing to exist and simultaneously fail to exist; it is equally impossible for the same world to have been created by a divine mind and also not to have been created by a divine mind. These claims are contradictory; these beliefs about God are logically incompatible. The belief that God exists is not about the believer; it is about God. For that reason, disagreements over the existence of God are genuine disagreements. It is not possible for both sides of this debate to be correct.

Feel-Good Faith in God

One final hurdle must be addressed here: namely, some people conceive of the claim "I believe in God" as something other than the straightforward view that such a being actually exists. This claim is rarely stated, but it is implicitly held by many people who see belief in God as a matter of mere preference. It is yet another indication of our tendency toward feel-good faith. In my own view, "I believe in God" means "I believe that God exists." Suppose that, instead, we reconceived this belief as "I enjoy believing that God exists" or "I find the belief in God to be valuable and meaningful." Anybody who finds the personal value of religious belief more important than the doctrines affirmed by that religion would likely embrace such a conception of belief in God—certainly when given the choice between it and a conception that requires the believer to believe that God actually exists in the real world.

When this is what is meant by belief in God, then belief in God is more like a preference than a belief that some fact about the world is true. On this view, disagreement about the existence of God turns out not to be a disagreement at all! When I say, "God exists," and you say, "God does not exist," we are disagreeing about the world. When I say, "I find belief in God valuable and meaningful in my life," and you say, "I do not find belief in God valuable or meaningful in my life," we can both be right! There is no contradiction in supposing that I enjoy believing in God and you do not. Logically speaking, this is akin to you preferring vanilla where I prefer chocolate.

Crucially, this is not a belief about God; it is a belief about your belief about God. Its truth or falsity is independent of the truth or falsity of the belief that he exists. For instance, when I was a child, I derived great enjoyment from believing—falsely—that Santa Claus exists. My belief that he exists was false; my belief that I enjoyed having that (false) belief is true. Likewise, God's actual existence makes no difference at all to the truth or falsity of the claim that you enjoy believing in him; that claim is true or false based only on how you feel. False beliefs can be quite enjoyable, though it is admittedly easier to enjoy them if you do not know them to be false. True beliefs can be tremendously uncomfortable and not at all enjoyable. I suspect that it was the discomfort of believing in God that led Judas to end his life (Matt 27:3–5). I think Judas's belief was a true belief, and his awareness of its veracity made it all the more troubling. In short, the enjoyment or personal value of a belief is independent of the actual truth of that belief.

For that reason, Christians (and all sincere religious believers) ought to reject any push to reconceive belief in God in this manner—and they should reject feel-good faith with it. If the actual existence of God is irrelevant to the truth or falsity of your conception of belief in God, then something has gone seriously awry with your conception. Furthermore, there is real and significant disagreement about whether God exists. Reconceiving belief in God as a personal preference does not resolve this question; it merely changes the subject. The primary question remains unresolved: Does God exist? For this question, the truth of the answer cannot be relative.

Truth and Provability

As we have seen, it is possible for a belief to be popular—either because it is culturally affirmed or because it is personally preferred—and false. The truth of a belief is independent of that belief's popularity, for truth is a matter of correspondence to reality, not to popular opinion. There is a second major contributing factor in the push toward relativism: the tendency to confuse truth with provability. This objection, like the first, often takes the form of an accusation of arrogance: Who are you to say that God exists when you cannot prove that God exists? More broadly stated, in cases where the truth cannot be decisively demonstrated one way or the other, isn't it better to admit that there is no true answer?

If truth is correspondence to reality, then it is possible for the truth of a matter to be entirely beyond our grasp—for some parts of reality are beyond our grasp. Once again, an example will help here. Suppose I asked you the following question: Between precisely 11:59 a.m. and 12:01 p.m. on January 29, 1849, how many adult penguins were living in Antarctica? We might have to be a bit more specific about the precise geographical range and age of these penguins, and we ought to require that the penguin have stayed alive for the entirety of that two-second window, but these are manageable requirements. Having fixed them, this much seems clear: this question has an answer, and that answer will be a determinate whole number greater than zero. Something else seems equally clear: we are unlikely ever to know the answer to that question. We are more than one hundred and fifty years too late to tackle the challenge of counting these penguins. Further, we don't even have the technological capability to count the adult penguins in Antarctica right now. There are far too many obstacles preventing us from finding the answer to this question, and as a result, an answer is permanently out of our reach. We will never know how many penguins were in Antarctica at this date and time. Nevertheless, there is a true answer to this question; we can know that there is an answer without knowing what the answer is.

It is very tempting to reject this conclusion. In my classroom I have encountered a strong tendency to insist that, on the contrary, when we can't know an answer to a question, there is no answer. Note the absurd consequence of that position for this particular scenario: What would it mean for there not to have been any true number of penguins living in Antarctica at this specified time? It cannot mean that there were no adult penguins, for then the answer would simply be zero. It cannot mean that there was a wholly ambiguous or undefined number of penguins. For a living penguin is a whole penguin, and a whole penguin is numbered as one penguin, and any sum of whole numbers adds up to yet another whole number! The suggestion that there is no answer to this question is absurd, for it is impossible to conceive of it as being true.

Perhaps what is meant is we can't give an answer to the question. This is surely true, but it is vastly different from the claim that there is no answer. The previous example is intended to show that our inability to find an answer to a question is just not enough to show that no such answer exists. Sometimes truth is beyond our reach. For this reason, it is entirely possible—common, even—for a person to have a true belief without being certain that their belief is true. This can be understood both internally and externally—that is, as the inability to *know* the belief's truth and as the inability to *prove to others* that the belief is true. Both cases share the following two features: the belief in question does accurately reflect reality and thus is true, and the believer does not have enough evidence to evince certainty about its truth.

If this sounds complicated or implausible, note that this is actually a very common occurrence. Consider the case of a crime that receives a great deal of media attention. If a particular murder suspect, for example, is widely discussed, then people far removed from the crime itself are going to form beliefs about her guilt or innocence. These beliefs will be incompatible with one another—some will believe her guilty, others innocent. Which beliefs are true depends not on the believers themselves but on the murderous event in question. If she committed the murder, then the belief that she did so is true. If she did not, then it is false and the rival view is true. Most important for our purposes is the following: if this investigation is never resolved and the suspect never proven to be guilty or innocent, this fact about what we can know cannot change what happened. We cannot retroactively make it such that she neither killed nor didn't kill the victim in question. She did or she didn't, and our ability to know which is frankly beside the point.

In our day-to-day lives, we all know this to be true. Imagine that your apartment was burglarized, and the investigation yielded several suspects but no conclusive evidence. Now suppose having the following conversation:

You: I am so frustrated.

Friend: Why?

You: It's been a full year now and the police still haven't arrested anybody for breaking into my apartment and stealing my stuff!

Friend: But I thought they concluded that nobody did it!

You: What?

Friend: I thought they couldn't prove that any of the suspects were guilty.

You: That's right . . .

Friend: So none of the suspects were guilty!

You: No, they just haven't been able to prove it. One of them did it, and I wish I knew who it was!

Friend: But you're asking for the impossible! Don't you see? If they can't prove that anybody did it, it must be that nobody did it.

You: You mean they haven't found the right suspect? None of the suspects did it, and the real criminal is still out there?

Friend: No, I mean nobody did it. There is no answer to the question "Who robbed you?" This is just one of those questions without an answer!

This conversation is absurd because, on matters of practical importance, nobody actually makes this mistake. In everyday circumstances, we all recognize the distinction between provability and reality. Truth is determined by reality, not by provability.

The central distinction that undergirds each of these examples is the distinction between what exists and what we can know. Questions regarding the former fall under metaphysics, the science of fundamental reality; questions regarding the latter fall under epistemology, the science of knowing. The central conclusion here is that reality does not depend upon our knowledge; truth is a question of what *is*, and not a question of what we know to be the case. There are, to be sure, a number of tremendously important questions in both domains, but they are not the same questions. This is true in all areas, not just questions of religious belief. For instance, "Is there life on other planets?" is not the same question as "Are we able to confirm the existence of life on other planets?" Likewise, "Which creatures make their homes in the deepest parts of the ocean?" is distinct from "Which creatures are we able to observe in the deepest parts of the ocean?" The central conclusion is this: the limits of our knowledge are not limits on reality itself. Because truth is a question of reality itself, the limits of our knowledge cannot affect the truth of our beliefs.

Charity in the Face of Disagreement

There is a third major factor which contributes to a tendency toward relativism. Indeed, I suspect that this factor explains and motivates each of the other contributing factors: the conflation of truth with popularity and the conflation of truth with provability. If I am correct, then we should take heart, for what we have is a case of well-intended but poorly executed charity. That is, the source of all of this confusion about truth seems to come from a desire to be charitable.

Increasingly, we are being encouraged to understand the perspective of people whose lives are very different from our own. Because our experiences of the world are different, often dramatically so, we are enjoined not to judge or correct people whose views are different from our own. After all, your views were shaped by your experiences, and their views were shaped by their experiences. It would be inappropriate, unhelpful, and unkind to use your experiences to tell another person how she ought to understand her own experiences. And just like that, we find ourselves embracing relativism.

The good news is that a little conceptual clarity goes a long way here. It is absolutely true that different people experience the very same world in radically different ways. This is true locally as well as globally. A person raised in a Christian home and educated in a Christian school will have a very different body of evidence available in favor of the truth of Christianity than a person raised and educated in a Muslim, Hindu, Jewish, or atheistic society. A person raised in an abusive Christian home or abused by a member of their Christian school will have to contend with evidence of the harms that a Christian community can bring.[7] A person raised by loving and devoted faithful Muslim parents will have that evidence to consider as well, as will the person raised by loving and devoted atheistic parents.[8] It will not do to insist that no such parents exist, for they do exist. Just as churchgoing followers of Christ can also be abusive parents or teachers, staunch atheists can be loving parents and supportive teachers. The world is a complicated place, and the pursuit of wisdom cannot ignore those complications in the hopes that they will disappear.

In chapter 3, I noted that truth and reasonability can come apart. It is entirely possible for a belief to be rationally justified (reasonable) and yet fail to be true. Reasonable beliefs are more likely to be true than unreasonable ones, but the correlation is imperfect. We are now in a position to introduce one more way in which truth and rational justification differ: truth is not relative, neither to a subject nor to a culture. Rational justification is relative both to the subject and to the culture. In recognizing the relativism of rational justification, we can avoid both harmful dogmatism and harmful relativism about truth. This is the key to navigating sincere disagreement.

We can apply this to our ongoing example about belief in God. When two people disagree about whether God exists, they cannot both be right—but they may both be believing rationally.[9] On this point, even the new atheist Daniel Dennett agrees! In *Breaking the Spell: Religion as a Natural Phenomenon*, he writes:

---

7. For some thoughtful reflection on this, see M. Panchuk, "The Shattered Spiritual Self: A Philosophical Exploration of Religious Trauma," *Res Philosophica* 95, no. 3 (2018): 505–30.

8. Nabeel Qureshi's account of his loving and devout family is particularly powerful: N. Qureshi, *Seeking Allah, Finding Jesus: A Devout Muslim Encounters Christianity* (Grand Rapids: Zondervan, 2016). You can read about the diverse personal histories of a host of Christian philosophers in Tom Morris's book: T. V. Morris, *God and the Philosophers: The Reconciliation of Faith and Reason* (Oxford: Oxford University Press, 1994). (No relation, though I have much admiration for the man, and I am pleased to share that he jokingly calls me "cousin.")

9. I say "may" because I am not yet sure about how to reconcile Romans 1:18–20 with rational atheism.

I should emphasize this, to keep well-meaning but misguided multiculturalists at bay: the theoretical entities in which these tribal people frankly believe—the gods and other spirits—don't exist. These people are mistaken, and you know it as well as I do. It is possible for highly intelligent people to have a very useful but mistaken theory, and we don't have to pretend otherwise in order to show respect for these people and their ways.[10]

Dennett believes that we are wrong, though we may be rational. We should believe the same about him. We must respect other people, never minimizing their life experiences and the impact those experiences have had on their beliefs. It is important, always, that we act with kindness, grace, and charity—even in the face of serious, genuine disagreement on matters of the utmost importance to us. What charity does not require, however, is concession about the truth of those beliefs. Instead, by remembering the ways in which reasonableness and truth can come apart, we ought to operate on the assumption that our interlocutor is reasonable, even if we believe she is wrong.

Conclusion

True beliefs are beliefs that accurately depict reality—whether they be beliefs about our present world, about the past, or about the future. When we cannot be certain about what reality is like, the truth or falsity of our beliefs still depends upon that (inaccessible) reality. We might be wrong about which of our beliefs are true and which are false. We might not ever be able to demonstrate the truth of some of our beliefs, though they be true. We might not ever be able to demonstrate the falsity of some of our beliefs, though they be false. Truth and falsity are a question of reality, not of knowability. In cases of genuine disagreement, two contradictory beliefs cannot both be true. It is, however, possible for two contradictory beliefs to both be reasonable. By being sensitive to the different experiences had by other people, we can navigate sincere disagreement without collapsing into either relativism about truth or uncharitable dogmatism about beliefs.

---

10. D. C. Dennett, *Breaking the Spell: Religion as a Natural Phenomenon* (New York: Viking, 2006), 409.

These are just some of the benefits of the rational pursuit of wisdom. By seeking clear and reasonable beliefs, you will increase the likelihood of those beliefs being true. By reflecting carefully on what that means, you will be better able to defend the truth of those beliefs. In becoming a Christian philosopher, you should find yourself becoming a better interlocutor—even with those with whom you deeply and powerfully disagree.

Christian Objections to Philosophy

5

See to it that no one takes you captive through philosophy and empty deception, according to the tradition of men, according to the elementary principles of the world, rather than according to Christ.

—*Colossians 2:8*

For the LORD gives wisdom;
From His mouth come knowledge and understanding.

—*Proverbs 2:6*

In chapters 1–4, I introduced and defended the discipline of philosophy as a Christian endeavor, the rational pursuit of godly wisdom. This is not an uncontroversial position. Indeed, when I first decided to pursue a graduate degree in philosophy, I was surprised to find a great deal of pushback among some members of my community—in particular, some of my Christian friends and associates. My experience as a philosophy major at the undergraduate level had been entirely positive. I came to philosophy at a difficult time in my life, and I took tremendous comfort in working through my spiritual struggles in a careful and rational manner. Still, while my close family and friends were supportive, I encountered a significant number of people who raised something like the following concerns: "Why study philosophy? Isn't the Bible enough? Isn't it dangerous to think about these kinds of questions outside of a church? If you must, wouldn't a seminary be better?" One sweet older woman captured these concerns in the concise report: "A friend of mine majored in philosophy, and now she is an atheist."

These remarks were well-intended, and they were not entirely unfounded. I have witnessed people taking the path of that sweet woman's friend. I have seen people—young people, especially—walk away from their faith while espousing the teachings of atheistic philosophers. Indeed, we need only look to the book of Colossians for a similar, oft-cited injunction against "worldly" philosophy. Colossians 2:8 instructs the reader to "see to it that no one takes you captive through philosophy and empty deception, according to the tradition of men, according to the elementary principles of the world, rather than according to Christ." Why, then, do I persist in claiming that more Christians should actively pursue philosophical study? The goal of this chapter is to address this reasonable concern. Properly understood and applied, philosophy can enhance your understanding of Scripture, strengthen and ground your religious beliefs, and equip you to navigate religious and moral disagreements. Indeed, I have found that a good philosophical grounding can assist a believer in maintaining faith even in the face of personal tragedy and other common sources of doubt. I also know several people for whom philosophy paved the path from atheism to Christianity, people with stories similar to J. D. Vance's personal account. Philosophical reasoning can and should be an aid, not a threat, to the Christian faith.

This is not to say that the goal of philosophy is merely to confirm and enforce whatever beliefs you currently hold. On the contrary, philosophical study may also lead you to reconsider—and perhaps even reject—some of what you believe. This might be an uncomfortable process. It might, at times, lead you to feelings of uncertainty and doubt about topics of great importance to you. Toward the end of this chapter, I will revisit this challenge—how best to seek the truth without collapsing into doubt—and I will provide concrete logistical advice. For now, I wish only to note that the rational evaluation of dearly held beliefs is a difficult but important philosophical endeavor. The goal of this endeavor is the establishment of true beliefs held on the basis of good reasons. An uncomfortable process that brings you closer to the truth is a valuable process. It is, perhaps, something akin to the process of sanctification.

Doesn't Wisdom Come from God?

The first objection to be addressed is this: "Shouldn't a Christian believe that wisdom comes from God alone?" To this I reply, "Yes, of course!" A Christian should certainly be committed to the view that wisdom comes from God. In Proverbs 2:6 we read "For the LORD gives wisdom; From His mouth come knowledge and understanding." At the same time, we must ask ourselves what this means. (Remember, philosophy is all about conceptual clarification.) When we say that wisdom comes from God, do we mean that God simply places wisdom into the mind of the believer directly? This is certainly something God could do. Indeed, in James 1:5 we read: "But if any of you lacks wisdom, let him ask of God, who gives to all generously and without reproach, and it will be given to him." Perhaps, then, the acquisition of wisdom is an entirely passive endeavor for the Christian; wisdom so understood is a gift received, not a treasure to be sought. On such a view, the pursuit of wisdom is unnecessary. One need only ask for wisdom; why work to pursue it?

This does not seem right. Indeed, to see why it is not right we should give closer consideration to the verses just referenced. Note first that James 1:5 is immediately followed by James 1:6–8,

> But he must ask in faith without any doubting, for the one who doubts is like the surf of the sea, driven and tossed by the wind. For that man ought not to expect that he will receive anything from the Lord, being a double-minded man, unstable in all his ways.

God grants wisdom to those who ask for it in faith. Anybody who has ever attempted to pray in faith for that which she most dearly desires knows that praying in faith is no easy matter. There is work to be done here if we wish to avoid "being a double-minded man, unstable in all his ways." Some of that work—not all of it, surely, but some of it—can be aided by the tools and resources of philosophy. Wisdom comes from God, but it seems that we have some role to play in fostering our ability to receive it.

Perhaps you are concerned that philosophy breeds doubt, the very thing we are enjoined to reject. This is an understandable concern. But consider this: by getting clearer about what you believe, why you believe it, and what it means for those beliefs to be true, your work as a philosophically minded Christian can help you to resolve doubts as they arise. (Furthermore, as we saw in chapter 1, life's challenges also breed doubt. Far better to work through your beliefs rationally before your doubts incur the weight of pressing, personal significance.) The natural consequence of increased clarity about your faith ought to be increased confidence in your faith. As I will argue below, the double-minded man, unstable in all his ways, needs more philosophical training, not less.

Our active role in the pursuit of wisdom becomes significantly clearer when we look to Proverbs 2:6: "For the LORD gives wisdom; From His mouth come knowledge and understanding." It is not insignificant that verse 6 begins with the word *for*.[1] This word is being used here as what philosophers sometimes call a "premise indicator." In plain language, a premise indicator lets the reader know that a reason is about to be given, and the reason is intended to support something that has just been stated. Consider the following sentence: "The Beatles are the greatest rock band of all time, for they have sold more albums than any other band in history." Here, the order of explanation is clear—the words that precede *for* form a conclusion, and what follows is a bit of evidence for that conclusion. In this way, *for* functions like the word *because*. For example, "I should get to bed early tonight, *for* I have a race early tomorrow morning," or "That exam wasn't fair, *for* some of the students were given the answers ahead of time." Each of these examples has the same form: a conclusion is stated and is then linked (by a premise indicator) with some bit of evidence in its favor.

The same is true in this passage in Proverbs. Verse 6 is being offered as evidence in favor of a conclusion that has already been stated. Consider the context:

> My son, if you will receive my words
> And treasure my commandments within you,
> Make your ear attentive to wisdom,
> Incline your heart to understanding;
> For if you cry for discernment,
> Lift your voice for understanding;
> If you seek her as silver
> And search for her as for hidden treasures;
> Then you will discern the fear of the LORD
> And discover the knowledge of God.
> For the LORD gives wisdom;
> From His mouth come knowledge and understanding.

---

1. Here, and throughout this text, I use the New American Standard (1995) translation of the Bible. It is worth noting that in *every* mainstream English language translation—KJV, NJKV, NIV, RSV, and CSV—this verse begins with the word *for*.

In verses 1–5, the reader is given a lengthy conditional promise: If you receive my words, treasure my commands, make your ear attentive to wisdom, incline your heart to understanding, cry for discernment, lift your voice for understanding, seek her as silver, search for her as hidden treasures, then "you will discern the fear of the LORD and discover the knowledge of God." One might summarize this as: "If you pursue wisdom, then you will receive the fear and knowledge of God."

This conditional promise comes immediately before verse 6, and verse 6 begins with a premise indicator. Verse 6, then, is the evidence given in support of the promise stated in verses 1–5. The reason why we ought to believe that the pursuit of wisdom will lead to knowledge of God is this: God is the source of that wisdom. In seeking wisdom you will find wisdom's source. We can combine these verses to get something like the following: "The pursuit of wisdom leads to knowledge of God because wisdom comes from God." The author is instructing the reader to seek wisdom because, in doing so, the reader will draw nearer to God, the source of wisdom.

Note also how a careful reading of this passage reveals the active nature of acquiring wisdom. The reader is being enjoined to seek wisdom, to search for it as he would silver or hidden treasures, to make his ear attentive to wisdom, and to incline his heart to understanding. As followers of Scripture, we are clearly called to work to find the wisdom of God. Wisdom comes from God. Nevertheless, we are called to pursue wisdom, and to do so, at least in part, by making our ears attentive to wisdom and inclining our hearts to understanding—that is, by disposing our minds to recognize and receive wisdom and to reject falsehoods.

We have already begun to see the ways that philosophy fosters clear, reasonable, and true beliefs. In the next several chapters we will be introduced to the methods of philosophy for evaluating arguments and recognizing fallacious reasoning. There, we will see that persuasive arguments are not necessarily good arguments; indeed, the worst sorts of arguments are the ones that manage to persuade by deceptive means. The philosophically trained eye will see those arguments for what they are; the untrained eye may just see their persuasive nature. In short, recognizing and receiving wisdom and rejecting falsehoods is, in many ways, the central task of philosophy. For this reason, the study of philosophy ought to be of much use to the Christian who heeds the call to pursue wisdom.

Isn't the Bible Enough? The Challenge of Translation

Still, one might readily and enthusiastically agree that the Christian ought to pursue wisdom and yet remain skeptical that such a pursuit has anything at all to do with the discipline of philosophy. More specifically, perhaps you believe something like the following: God is the source of wisdom, and God has given us the Bible, so we need not look beyond the Bible for wisdom. The Bible is enough and philosophy, if not entirely dangerous, is at least gratuitous.

There is one obvious sense in which this is true. A Christian need not study philosophy in order to follow Christ. One could faithfully devote her life to the glory of God and the service of his people without engaging in any philosophical study whatsoever.[2] Philosophy is not essential to the Christian life. That said, there is a great deal that, while not essential, is nevertheless spiritually beneficial. Note, for instance, that a Christian need not actually read the Bible at all in order to follow Christ! According to a 2006 UNESCO report on literacy, "In the mid-nineteenth century, only 10% of the world's adult population could read or write."[3] Indeed, for the overwhelming majority of the first two millennia after the birth of Jesus, the average Christian was unable to read anything—including the Bible. This is not to say that they lacked access to the Scriptures, only that they had to rely on other people—religious leaders, in particular—to give them the content of those Scriptures. Their access to the Bible was mediated by another person; it was not immediate. Nevertheless, these illiterate followers of Christ were capable of seeking and finding the wisdom of God.

Unmediated, direct access to the Bible is therefore not essential to the Christian faith. This is a good thing—for, in truth, even in our largely literate age, most Christians continue to read the Bible in a way that is at least

---

2. I would be remiss if I did not mention my own experience with someone not unlike this description. When I began graduate school, a young man I knew told me, "All the philosophy or theology I need is this: Jesus loves me this I know, for the Bible tells me so." In my conceit, I concluded that his faith was shallow and untested, not at all like my own. Within a few years, he was diagnosed with brain cancer. He did not live much past thirty. His faith was profound and unwavering, with roots far deeper than I could have known. His life and death were inspirational in the truest sense of the word. I am being completely sincere when I say that Christians do not *need* philosophy. Still, just as most of us need to train if we are to run a race, *most* of us will undoubtedly benefit from the discipline of philosophy.

3. *Education for All: Literacy for Life*, EFA Global Monitoring Report, p. 189, https://unesdoc.unesco.org/ark:/48223/pf0000141639.

partially mediated. To see why, note first that we do not read the text in its original language. When we read the Bible in translation, we must of necessity trust the translator to accurately convey the meaning of the original text. Anyone who has been tasked with the work of translation knows that this is not a simple process. Words, phrases, and semantic images have both literal meanings and connotations. Translating a text in a way that captures both the meaning and the connotation of the original language is a complex and difficult task. Here is a silly but illustrative example: I once saw "lukewarm soup" on an English-language menu in Germany. *Lukewarm* does mean something like "room temperature," and what we call "cold" soups are often served at room temperature. Thus, the translation was not technically incorrect—but this was a bad translation! It was bad because the connotation of *lukewarm* is just not particularly appetizing. To a native English speaker *lukewarm soup* sounds like soup that has been left out too long.

The challenge of translation is likewise evidenced by the variations we see among competing English language translations of the Bible. Consider one of my favorite verses: Jeremiah 29:11. What follows are four versions of that verse, each in a biblical translation that is now or once was commonly used:

For I know the thoughts, that I have thought towards you, saith the LORD, even the thoughts of peace, and not of trouble, to give you an end, and your hope. (GNV)

For I know the thoughts that I think toward you, saith the LORD, thoughts of peace, and not of evil, to give you an expected end. (KJV)

"For I know the plans I have for you," declares the LORD, "plans to prosper you and not to harm you, plans to give you hope and a future." (NIV)

"For I know the plans that I have for you," declares the LORD, "plans for welfare and not for calamity to give you a future and a hope." (NASB 1995)

There is a sense in which each of these verses says the same thing. Still, there are some real differences between them. The choice between translating the Hebrew *machashabah* as the "thoughts" of God and the "plans" of God is not insignificant. The same is true of the difference between an "end" and a "future" (*acharith*). And the Hebrew *shalom* can be translated as "peace," "prosperity," or "welfare."[4] Presumably, some of these translations are better than others; some come closer to accurately depicting the original meaning and connotation. When we read the Bible in our own language, we place our trust in the wisdom of those tasked with the work of translation. We might work to ensure accuracy by comparing multiple translations or, if we are truly ambitious, by attempting to learn Hebrew, Aramaic, and Greek to approach Scripture in its original languages. What we cannot do is read these texts as native speakers of the languages in which they were originally written; some degree of translation is unavoidable in the twenty-first century.

Furthermore, most Christians do not merely study the Bible on their own in their homes. When we receive teaching on Scripture from our pastors, teachers, or professors, we also receive at least some degree of interpretation and application. We must similarly trust that these interpretations and applications are faithful to the original intention of the text. Again, we might work further to confirm or disconfirm these interpretations by comparing them with biblical commentaries, writings of the church fathers, the sermons and teachings of a variety of pastors, or our own experience with biblical exegesis. In each of these cases, though—concerning the translation and the teaching of Scripture—we recognize that the perfectly accurate, true meaning of Scripture is neither transparent nor obvious to all readers. Instead, there is room for disagreement, and sometimes that disagreement goes beyond the trivial to matters of great significance.

Let me be clear: the purpose of these reflections is not to undermine your faith in the reliability or inerrancy of Scripture. The inspirational work of the Holy Spirit did not stop with the initial textual revelations, and God can use even the least scholastically acclaimed translation of his Word to transform the hearts of his people. Instead, my point is this: We do not "just read the Bible." Instead, we employ a number of conceptual resources—tools—in order to read Scripture in a way that is fruitful. We read it in the translations that are available to us; we read it with the teachings of our childhood in mind, gleaned from parents, pastors, teachers, and friends. It would be foolish to reject an English language translation of the Bible on the grounds

---

4. I am relying on *Strong's Concordance* for these translations. See https://biblehub.com/hebrew/4284.htm.

that "The original Bible ought to be enough." Translation is a tool on which we may rely and on which most of us must rely. Likewise, those who reject or neglect the teachings of church fathers, pastors, scholars, and friends on the grounds that "all they need is the Bible" do themselves a great disservice. The wisdom that can be found in other members of the body of Christ is a tremendous resource. It is yet another tool that the Christian can and should use in the pursuit of godliness. In the same way, the skills cultivated by philosophical reasoning provide further tools that, if not strictly necessary, can nonetheless be of great benefit to the Christian.

To see how the tools and resources of philosophy help with biblical exegesis, consider once more the NIV translation of Jeremiah 29:11.

> "For I know the plans I have for you," declares the LORD, "plans to prosper you and not to harm you, plans to give you hope and a future."

This verse has been invoked more than once to advance the "prosperity gospel" or the feel-good approach to faith. The former says that God promises great earthly wealth and prosperity to the faithful; the latter is less extreme but still maintains that the faithful should expect earthly comfort and protection. When faced with the claim that God promises his children earthly prosperity or comfort, the philosophically minded Christian will stop and ask herself: What does this mean? Why should I believe it? Are the reasons being given in its favor good reasons? In seeking answers to these questions, she will find herself in the rational pursuit of wisdom—that is, the practice of philosophy.

More specifically, the philosophically minded Christian can use these questions to help adjudicate between translations and interpretations of Scripture. First, note that only one of the four translations above uses the word *prosper*. This is not a special feature of my selection of translations; it is an accurate representation of the scarcity of translations of this verse that reference prosperity. The general consensus trends toward *peace* as the proper translation. Thus, the NIV version of Jeremiah 29:11 seems not to be very strong evidence for the claim that God promises to prosper us. Further philosophical questioning will reveal that Scripture as a whole seems to include quite a few stories of Christian martyrs, calls to cast off earthly wealth, and promises that we will suffer as Christ himself suffered on our behalf.

By asking the right questions—the kinds of questions introduced in the first four chapters—the philosophically minded Christian will be in a better position to evaluate competing translations and interpretations of the Bible.

Isn't the Bible Enough? The Challenge of Contextualization

The benefits of philosophical thinking are even clearer with respect to the challenge of understanding Scripture in its historical context. The discipline of philosophy requires us to evaluate what we believe and why we believe it. For the Christian, the answer to the latter question is often "Because the Bible says so." This is a fine answer—belief on the basis of testimony can be both reasonable and reliable—but it is only a good answer if it is true. The challenge posed by contextualization is that we sometimes take the Bible to be saying something that it was not, in fact, intended to say. In these cases, the practice of asking philosophical questions in the pursuit of wisdom is especially beneficial.

When we read the Bible, we read it in our own contemporary societal and historical context—for good and for bad. We do not, and cannot, read the text in its original historical context. As a result, we face two common sorts of difficulty: We miss certain implications that a contemporary reader would have seen, and we see "implications" that early readers would not have seen, for they come largely from our own context rather than that of the original text. The first challenge is relatively straightforward. Consider, for example, the widely read book by W. Phillip Keller entitled *A Shepherd Looks at Psalm 23*. In this text, Keller attempts to contextualize the claim that God is our shepherd. Because most of us don't know many (or any) shepherds, and because we have spent little-to-no time with actual sheep, this book aims to provide the context that most readers lack when approaching Psalm 23. Christians, like all people, are inevitably shaped by the time and place in which they were born and raised. That time and place can restrict our ability to understand some of what is in Scripture. When that happens, supplementary tools and resources that help to fill our gaps in understanding are uniquely beneficial.

The second challenge we face is that historical and societal contexts sometimes encourage us to import meaning from our own culture into these sacred texts, distorting or augmenting the meaning of verses in ways that reflect our contemporary values. To see this, one need only note the vast number of t-shirts, coffee mugs, and motivational posters emblazoned with Philippians 4:13: "I can do all things through Him who strengthens me." In our modern context, this verse is sometimes used to provide a Christian spin on the very modern sentiment that you too can do whatever you set your mind to. Training to run a marathon? Remember: you can do it through Christ who strengthens you! Applying for law school and worried about the LSAT? Remember: you can do it through Christ who strengthens you! Despite my levity, I do not mean to mock those who put their faith in Christ—not at all. I do, however, wish to note that the biblical context for that verse carries with it a meaning quite unlike the one espoused on coffee mugs and T-shirts. Beginning with verse 11, Paul writes:

> Not that I speak from want, for I have learned to be content in whatever circumstances I am. I know how to get along with humble means, and I also know how to live in prosperity; in any and every circumstance I have learned the secret of being filled and going hungry, both of having abundance and suffering need. I can do all things through Him who strengthens me. Nevertheless, you have done well to share with me in my affliction. (Phil 4:1114)

In its proper context, this verse does not seem to be promising the reader success in all areas of life. Instead, Paul is writing from a place of affliction, and he is writing about his contentment in Christ. When he says that he can do "all things," he refers directly to his experience both with "being filled and with going hungry," with "having abundance and suffering need." Thus, to return to your imagined marathon training regimen, you would do well to remember that you can do all things through Christ—just as long as you remember that "all things" might include failing to qualify for or complete the race. The lesson to be learned here is not the affirmation of our Western values of prosperity and success but rather that your peace, your joy, your very identity ought not to depend upon anything other than Christ. He is sufficient, and in him you have all that you need—whether or not you land the dream job, win the race, or ace that exam.

The purpose of these examples is twofold: first, to again illustrate the difficulties with and complexity of biblical interpretation, and second, to reiterate the ways that philosophy can help to adjudicate among these complexities. What does it mean to say that the Lord is our "shepherd"? What did it mean to the Israelites? What did Paul mean by the phrase "all things"? What exactly are we being promised? These are philosophical questions. They are, to be sure, also historical and theological questions, for these categories are not mutually exclusive; there is a great deal of philosophy to be found in history and theology. The philosophical processes of clarifying concepts, clarifying beliefs, justifying beliefs, evaluating the truth of beliefs, and guarding against fallacious reasoning are immensely beneficial to anyone who wants to become a better reader of Scripture. They are important tools in the rational pursuit of wisdom.

We are profoundly privileged to live in a time and place where every believer who wishes to own and read a copy of the Bible may do so. We ought not to take this privilege for granted. We should be thankful for it, and we ought to make the most of the opportunity that it affords. Still, we must recognize the tools we use to glean the wisdom of God from the Bible. If we fail to note our use of these resources, we run the risk of confusing our interpretation of Scripture for Scripture itself. The inerrancy of the Bible is a widely held tenet of the Christian faith. The inerrancy of our own understanding of the Bible is another matter entirely, and not one that is promised in Scripture. Philosophy has the potential to be one more tool in the Christian's toolbelt, one that is significant and oft neglected. Like any tool, it can be misused. A poor translation, a misguided preacher, a deceptive author, a cultural norm inappropriately applied—every resource that we use brings with it some risk. Just as the benefits of a power drill outweigh its minimal risks, so do the benefits to be gained by philosophical study. Neither tool is essential to the task—a screwdriver or a hammer could surely do the job—but both bring value that outweigh their costs.

Christianity, Atheism, and Philosophy

We will now turn to the third and final objection to be addressed in this chapter: Isn't philosophy a particularly atheistic discipline? And if so, wouldn't a Christian be better off not taking the chance of being led astray? My answer here is twofold: First, there is a long history of Christian philosophy dating back to the earliest Christians, and an even longer history of monotheistic philosophy.[5] There is also a rich, ongoing tradition of contemporary Christian philosophy—indeed, there are many such traditions. Historically minded Christian philosophers continue to reap wisdom from Aquinas, Augustine, and other church fathers. Contemporary Christian philosophers in both the continental and analytic tradition are active across a wide variety of philosophical subdisciplines.[6] Many of these areas of Christian philosophy will be addressed in detail in part 2 of this book. For now, we need only note that atheists do not have a monopoly on philosophy. There are, to be sure, quite a lot of atheistic and agnostic professional philosophers. There are also quite a lot of atheistic and agnostic professional biologists, anthropologists, chemists, physicists, attorneys, doctors, musicians, actors, and high school teachers. It would be foolish indeed if the Christian felt compelled only to study those areas of interest in which she could count on avoiding the works of nonbelievers.

Of course, there is a real and significant difference between reading the teachings of an atheistic biologist or anthropologist and an atheistic philosopher—namely, the biologist and anthropologist are not likely to include a lesson on atheism in their textbooks. Philosophers, in contrast, are quite upfront about their atheism. This brings us to my second, more extensive reply to this final objection: it is in many ways better for the Christian to study in a field where the atheistic worldview is on the table for discussion rather than being an unspoken, unaddressed presupposition of discourse. When a particular view about religion is presupposed in a discipline, theists are often required to set aside their belief in God in order to engage with the discipline; when it is explicitly proposed, theists are free to examine the evidence in its favor and to present and defend a contrary position.

Consider the following example: Suppose that Jasmine is a committed Christian believer with an interest in anthropology. Jasmine might be drawn to the study of indigenous communities in Australia and in doing so might encounter something like the following report:

---

5. Christian philosophy cannot, of course, predate Christ. Monotheistic philosophy includes Christian, Jewish, and Muslim philosophy.

6. For more on the distinction between analytic and continental philosophy and the particular ways in which both serve Christian philosophy, I recommend Bruce Ellis Benson, "The Two-Fold Task of Christian Philosophy of Religion," *Faith and Philosophy: Journal of the Society of Christian Philosophers* 32, no. 4 (2015): 371–90. For a longer and more detailed treatment, see J. A. Simmons, *Christian Philosophy: Conceptions, Continuations, and Challenges* (Oxford: Oxford University Press, 2019).

There is no one deity covering all of Australia. Each tribe has its own deities with an overlap of beliefs, just as there is an overlap of words between language groups. Thus, for example, the *Wandjina* spirits in the northern Kimberley of Western Australia belong to the *Ngarinyin*, *Worora*, and *Wunambal* tribes. These *Wandjina* are responsible for bringing the Wet Season rains, as well as laying down many of the laws for the people.[7]

How should Jasmine read and understand the claims in this passage? The author seems to be stating that a variety of divine entities are responsible for the weather and the judicial system of parts of Australia. This is clearly not a set of beliefs that Jasmine can endorse. At the same time, suppose Jasmine were to write a paper for her anthropology class with the following thesis: "Because I believe that there is only one God, not many gods, I conclude that the indigenous people of Australia hold false religious beliefs." I am not an anthropology professor, but if I were—even as a Christian—I would find such a paper problematic. The trouble is not that Jasmine disagrees with the theology of the subject group; the trouble is that that kind of disagreement is not the proper domain of anthropology.

In contrast, suppose that Jasmine's studies also include some philosophy. She might thus encounter something like the following:

1. There exist instances of intense suffering which an omnipotent, omniscient being could have prevented without thereby losing some greater good or permitting some evil equally bad or worse.

2. An omniscient, wholly good being would prevent the occurrence of any intense suffering it could, unless it could not do so without thereby losing some greater good or permitting some evil equally bad or worse.

3. Therefore, there does not exist an omnipotent, omniscient, wholly good being.[8]

---

7. "Aboriginal Religion, Part 1," Aboriginal Culture, http://www.aboriginalculture.com.au /religion.html.

8. This is William L. Rowe's statement of the problem of evil. Rowe, *American Philosophical Quarterly*, 16, no. 4 (1979): 335–41. In E. Stump and M. J. Murray, eds., *Philosophy of Religion: The Big Questions*, Philosophy: The Big Questions (Malden, MA: Blackwell, 1999), 157.

On the one hand, this argument—unlike the above passage about indigenous people in Australia—really is a direct attack on Jasmine's faith. The conclusion of the argument is that the God of Christianity does not exist. In this way, it might be psychologically more difficult for Jasmine to read and evaluate this argument than it was the anthropological text. On the other hand, Jasmine has a great deal more freedom to respond to this disagreement than she did the anthropological one. Here, it would be entirely appropriate for Jasmine to draw on her own beliefs in constructing an objection to the argument.

I do not intend to say that Christians ought to avoid the study of anthropology. Not at all. The point here is that most areas of academic study share a presupposition that the study of religious belief ought to be descriptive rather than normative. In the example above, Jasmine erred in approaching the account of religion as a question of what these indigenous people ought to believe—the normative question—rather than a question of what they do believe—the descriptive question. The same presupposition is shared by sociology, psychology, and history. Anthropology and sociology both involve the descriptive study of people groups, examining how they live, what they believe, what kinds of practices shape their lives. History asks the same questions of people groups from ages past. Similarly, psychology concerns itself with causes of or contributing factors to religious belief and with the impact of belief on the lives of religious practitioners, but the truth or falsity of those beliefs falls outside of the purview of psychology.

Because these disciplines adopt a descriptive attitude toward religious belief, Christians who wish to study or work in these fields must learn to do the same. In the process, it may be tempting to view their own religious beliefs in a similar manner—as the product of their own particular culture and upbringing rather than the real activity of a living God in their own lives. Again, the studies of anthropology, sociology, history, and psychology are deeply important, and I do not wish to be read as encouraging Christians to abandon those disciplines. My point here is that they are no less challenging for the Christian than philosophy. The challenges they raise for the Christian faith are subtler than those found in an argument against the existence of God, but subtle challenges are no less substantial. To that end, I would encourage Christian anthropologists, sociologists, historians, and psychologists to think philosophically about the content of their own beliefs.

Thinking philosophically about religious belief involves adopting a normative attitude toward those beliefs. That is, the philosophical approach to such questions centers not upon what people do believe, but what they should believe. When it comes to questions about religious belief, as with all fundamental questions, philosophers are concerned with the truth (or falsity) of those beliefs. Philosophy thus takes many of the questions that are most central to the Christian faith and incorporates them into the academic conversation. These beliefs need not be set aside. They should not be set aside. In fact, there is a very real sense in which such beliefs may not be set aside in philosophical discourse. A theistic philosopher—a philosopher who believes in the existence of a personal, monotheistic God—is expected to be able to give some degree of rational justification for that belief. An atheistic philosopher faces the same expectation. In this sense, both the theist and the atheist are on equal footing. Neither is free merely to assume God's existence or nonexistence.[9] Further, while the atheistic philosopher believes that a Christian holds false beliefs, she also believes that the truth or falsity of those beliefs matters. In this way, philosophy is a discipline that takes religious belief seriously.

Philosophy is an attractive discipline to atheists, for it brings to the table precisely the kinds of questions that atheists find compelling. For this reason alone, Christians ought not to avoid joining them at the table. Joining the discussion has the potential to benefit their faith in ways that setting those beliefs aside never could. Philosophy takes the claims of religious believers seriously—that is, it takes them to be actual reports about what the world contains. Christians also take their beliefs seriously, and as such they can benefit, and benefit from, the discipline of philosophy.

Evaluating the Risks

If there are so many benefits to studying philosophy, and if Christianity has a long history of philosophical engagement, then what explains the fear,

---

9. As a brief aside, this distinguishes atheistic philosophers from atheistic internet commenters and bloggers. On the internet, merely stating, "There is no evidence of a God, so Christians are irrational," is rather commonplace. In academic philosophy, far more is needed. In my studies, I encountered a number of convinced atheistic philosophy professors who nevertheless had tremendous respect for their theistic colleagues, and the respect went both ways. The reason for this was clear: when you know thoughtful, intelligent people with whom you disagree about the question of God, it is a lot more difficult to dismiss them as "stupid" or "irrational." All the more reason for Christians to study philosophy!

suspicion, and aversion to philosophy that is so common in some Christian circles? I think there are many explanations, some more substantial and justifiable than others. First, it is surely true that there are some staunchly atheistic philosophy professors and popular writers. There seems to be a bit more leeway for atheistic professors to reveal their biases in the philosophy classroom than there is for orthodox religious believers, and perhaps some of my readers have had personal experiences with such a professor. One bad experience ought not to deter a person from a field of study, but it is understandable that it sometimes does. If you find yourself resistant to philosophy and your resistance stems from an experience of this sort, then I hope that I have given you sufficient reason to return to philosophy!

A very different reason for avoiding philosophy (and philosophers) might be this: the fear that Christianity just won't hold up to intellectual scrutiny. This is a worrying concern, for as we noted in chapter 1, it seems to reveal a lack of faith in the truth of Christianity. If your aversion to philosophy stems from a fear of philosophy, then I encourage you to think hard about why you believe that the truth claims of Christianity would be unable to withstand the rigors of philosophical thinking.

Of course, you might be motivated by a third reason: perhaps you believe that Christianity is true, yet you lack confidence in your *own* ability to justify and defend those truth claims in the face of philosophical attack. This is a reasonable worry. After all, as we've seen, professional philosophers have a particular skill set, and that skill set tends to produce persuasive arguments. It is very difficult for an untrained reader to critically evaluate a well-formed argument, even when the argument contains falsehoods. This concern is valid, but it ought nevertheless not to dissuade a Christian from the study of philosophy. Instead, it ought to motivate and shape your studies. Indeed, this very book was written largely in response to this worry!

Furthermore, there is no reason for a new student of philosophy to take on the challenge of atheistic philosophy without the help and guidance of the Christian philosophical community. Instead, there are countless resources available to Christians with an interest in philosophy: popularly accessible books written by Christian philosophers, academic textbooks and journals devoted to Christian philosophy, and conferences organized by Christian philosophers. And if you live near a university, you may even find college courses taught by a Christian philosopher. Believe it or not, there is also an active online community of Christian philosophers! There are experts, and those experts have already done a great deal of work addressing the kinds of concerns that are most likely to arise in your studies. Begin with the experts; there is no need to reinvent the wheel here. If you find the problem of evil challenging, for example, seek out theistic responses to the problem of evil that were written by professional philosophers. You will likely find them rich, thoughtful, biblically grounded, and immensely beneficial.

At the same time, there is increasingly a real cost to not knowing the basic conceptual resources of philosophy; many of the supposed dangers associated with the study of philosophy stem not from too much philosophy but from too little. It is my sincere belief that our growing culture of feel-good faith has been devastating to the church at large. When believers focus more on how their beliefs make them feel than they do on what those beliefs say, we should not be the least bit surprised when that faith is abandoned in exchange for some new source of comfort, identity, or pride. Feelings come and go; preferences change. When faith is a question of feelings or preferences, it is not likely to stand the test of time.

In response, philosophical training equips a person to understand what she believes, to give good reasons for those beliefs, and to construct careful arguments in their favor. Carefully constructed arguments are impressive—particularly when they are compared with only untrained responses on the other side. As we saw in chapter 1, too many Christians have been misled by the clever yet insubstantial arguments of the "new atheist" movement. What these Christians needed was not less philosophy but more and better philosophical training. What the church needs is Christian philosophers, professional and otherwise; what the church needs is philosophically minded Christians.

Reading Philosophy

6

I am aware that I have taken on a difficult task here: attention to the past is a hard sell. I want to argue that you can't understand the place and time you're in by immersion; the opposite's true. You have to step out and away and back and forward, and you have to do it regularly. Then you come back to the here and now, and say: Ah. That's how it is.

—*Alan Jacobs,* Breaking Bread with the Dead[1]

Philosophy interested [Abraham Lincoln] particularly, and . . . he remarked how much he felt the need of reading and what a loss it was to a man not to have grown up among books.

"Men of force," I answered, "can get on pretty well without books. They do their own thinking instead of adopting what other men think." "Yes," said Mr. Lincoln, "but books serve to show a man that those original thoughts of his aren't very new, after all."

—*James E. Gallaher,* Best Lincoln Stories, Tersely Told[2]

Learning to read and reflect upon philosophical texts is a rewarding yet difficult practice. Reading historical texts can be challenging in general, and philosophical subject matter doesn't make things any easier. Additionally, many contemporary philosophers use perplexing graphics and logical variables that strike the average reader as needlessly complicated jargon. Some engage in "thought experiments" in which the author imagines some wildly implausible scenario—often involving a zombie or an evil

---

1. A. Jacobs, *Breaking Bread with the Dead: A Reader's Guide to a More Tranquil Mind* (New York: Penguin, 2020), 23.
2. James E. Gallaher, *Best Lincoln Stories, Tersely Told* (Chicago: Donohue, 1898), 52–54.

neurosurgeon—and then proceeds to draw philosophical conclusions from the outrageous bit of fiction. Others present dry, formally stated arguments with little attempt to engage anyone outside of the narrow community of professional academic philosophers. In light of all this, you might reasonably ask why you should be expected to have anything to do with these texts. The question is reasonable, but as I hope the first five chapters of this book have made clear, there is a ready answer: philosophy is important. Wisdom matters, and we are called to pursue it.

Of course, it is possible to pursue wisdom without ever cracking open a philosophy book. It is even possible to use the general resources of philosophical thinking while remaining quite resistant to actually reading books and articles written by (and often for) academic philosophers. There is, in fact, a surprising amount of good philosophical reasoning available via YouTube and podcasts.[3] Nevertheless, it is my sincere hope that readers of this book will go on to read more philosophy, both in and outside of the classroom. The careful, methodical, slow process of reading encourages a kind of thoughtful engagement that mere listening and watching cannot foster. The collected wisdom of thousands of years of philosophical history cannot be replicated in a YouTube synopsis. For these reasons and more, I want to spend some time defending the importance of reading philosophy.

Context and Consequence

In *Breaking Bread with the Dead: A Reader's Guide to a More Tranquil Mind*, Baylor professor Alan Jacobs makes the case for the sustained study of ancient and historical texts. The first epigraph of this chapter comes from Jacobs's book, in which we find him acknowledging just how hard it can be to read these works:

---

3. Online sources are so frequently changing, but here is a short list of some podcasts and video channels that I do recommend. I will also do my best to continue to share updated information on my website, www.believingphilosophy.com. (Please note, I do not actually know the content of these podcasts or channels very well. I only know that they sometimes interview or feature Christian philosophers I know and admire. Some of their content is quite good, but I obviously cannot attest for all of it.) Michael W. Austin's *Flourish: A Podcast on Cultivating Character*; *The Table Audio* with Evan Rosa; *Pints with Aquinas* with Matt Fradd; the Logia Institute podcast *POGOS*; *Capturing Christianity* with Cameron Bertuzzi (YouTube); *Worldview Design* with Joshua Rasmussen (YouTube); and finally, the website and YouTube channel *Closer to Truth* (Closertotruth.com).

I am aware that I have taken on a difficult task here: attention to the past is a hard sell. I want to argue that you can't understand the place and time you're in by immersion; the opposite's true. You have to step out and away and back and forward, and you have to do it regularly. Then you come back to the here and now, and say: Ah. That's how it is.[4]

If you wish to understand contemporary culture—the political, religious, economic, and social attitudes of the here and now—you must be able to situate the present day in a broader historical context. Where have we come from? Where are we headed? Viewing this present moment in the context of the past and the likely future provides the distance that clarity requires.

The same is true for much of what we believe. If you want to understand your beliefs, then you must sometimes "step out and away and back and forward." I don't mean that you should "question everything"; this trite injunction is, at best, unhelpful and, at worst, impossible. I do mean that you should do what you can to gain a little distance from your beliefs to better understand where they come from and where they lead. Just as the past and future are relevant to how we ought to understand the here and now, so too are your beliefs related to one another in important and inextricable ways.

To continue the analogy, many of your beliefs have a doxastic—that is, belief-related—past and future. So, for example, what you believe about petitionary prayer is largely the result of what you believe about the nature of God, the teachings of Scripture, and other related beliefs. These grounding beliefs are analogous to the historical past which can serve to explain our present moment; they are, in some sense, prior to your specific beliefs about prayer. But those beliefs about prayer, in turn, give rise to further beliefs; these further beliefs are analogous to the future, for they are the result of the beliefs under discussion. Thus, if your beliefs about God and Scripture lead you to believe that God always grants the requests of the faithful, then you will believe that your faithful prayers will be granted in accordance with your desires. This last move is subtle but important. You proceed first from broad beliefs about who God is and what Scripture says to the more specific belief about how God handles petitionary prayer. From there, you likewise move to the even more specific belief about how God will handle some particular

---

4. Jacobs, *Breaking Bread with the Dead*, 23.

prayer or other. In this way, your beliefs about petitionary prayer have what we might call a "doxastic past" in your beliefs about God and Scripture and a "doxastic future" in your beliefs about some particular prayer request.

Now suppose that this particular request is not granted. You do not get the job; the adoption falls through; you learn that it is, in fact, cancer. Whatever it is, your faithfully offered petition is denied. In this moment, you face a choice: revise your view about how God handles the prayers of the faithful or revise your view of your own faithfulness. To be clear, you may not be consciously aware of having to make this choice; the inferential reasoning that we engage in on a daily basis is often unreflective, more habit than deliberation. Still, the tension is there and must be resolved. A person cannot continue to believe that all faithfully offered prayers are granted, and that her own faithfully answered prayer was not granted—at least, not for long. These beliefs are logically inconsistent with one another; it is not possible for them both to be true at the same time. Sooner or later, one or the other will have to give.

When you are the one whose petition is denied, you may feel a high degree of confidence in your own faithfulness. In such a case, you are more likely to resolve the inconsistency by changing your beliefs about God and prayer than you are your beliefs about your own faithfulness—whether that change be consciously or unconsciously made. But what about the prayers of those around you? Suppose it is not you but someone else whose fervent request is denied. In this case, it may be easier to conclude that your friend or family member bears some responsibility for their own suffering. After all, you believe that God always grants the requests of the faithful. If their request was not granted, it is but a small step to see that they must not have been faithful, after all. None of us is truly privy to the contents of another person's heart or mind. It may be—indeed, it often will be—easier to declare someone else faithless than to revise your own long-held beliefs about God.

Beliefs are steeped in context, and beliefs have consequences. When you work to recognize the context and consequences of some belief or other, you get a clearer sense of what it is that you believe. Twenty years ago, R. C. Sproul wrote a book called *The Consequences of Ideas: Understanding the Concepts That Shaped Our World.*[5] Sproul emphasized the shared consequences of the

---

5. R. C. Sproul, *The Consequences of Ideas: Understanding the Concepts That Shaped Our World* (Wheaton, IL: Crossway, 2000).

history of ideas, but we would do well to recognize the specific consequences of our own beliefs as well. In this particular case, I think that a good number of people would revise their beliefs about prayer if they thought through what it meant for their beliefs about their loved ones. (Are we really prepared to say that no faithful Christians die of cancer? Or that if they do, they must not have asked to be spared this death?) More generally, nearly every time that your confidence in some particular belief is shaken, the tension between your belief and your experiences can be resolved by revising some other, related belief. Which belief you revise is significant, for it too has consequences. This is what I mean when I say that in order to understand your beliefs you ought to sometimes "step out and away and back and forward" from those beliefs. You cannot really understand any belief without also understanding the context in which it developed and the consequences it has for your other beliefs.

What does this have to do with reading philosophy? Philosophical texts are substantially devoted to exploring the ways that beliefs are interrelated. If reading ancient and historical texts can help the reader to better situate her present-day experiences in the great web of history, so too can the reading of philosophical texts help the reader to better situate and evaluate what she believes. One powerful example of this exercise can be found in Michael Rea's recent and excellent book *The Hiddenness of God*. There, Rea considers and responds to the philosophical challenge known as the problem of divine hiddenness. This book is, as I have said, truly excellent and well worth reading, but my focus here will not be on the substance of Rea's response to the problem. Instead, I want to look at the way that Rea formulates the problem itself. He writes:

> My first real confrontation with the problem of divine hiddenness as a challenge to faith came from a friend during my first or second year in college. We had gone to church together and afterward, sitting in my parents' kitchen, we got to talking about various kinds of faith struggles. Eventually she broke down in tears, saying "God is supposed to be my heavenly father. So why can't he just whisper 'I love you' once in a while?"[6]

---

6. M. C. Rea, *The Hiddenness of God* (Oxford: Oxford University Press, 2018), vii.

The problem of hiddenness, much like the problem of evil, often begins as a feeling. Hurt leads to doubt, doubt to philosophical struggle.

Fortunately for us, doubt can also lead to philosophical rigor. In reflecting upon the many ways that the absence of desired religious experience effects people, Rea arrives at the following broad statement of the problem:

> The problem of divine hiddenness, like the problem of evil, is fundamentally a problem of violated expectations. We expect certain things of God in light of what we know about God and in light of a wide range of background assumptions about the world—about the nature of love and goodness, various human needs and the ways in which they can normally be met in a world like ours, and so on. But God does not deliver on our expectations; so, we are conflicted: Is something wrong with our expectations? Is God not as we thought? Does God not exist?[7]

Notice how Rea began with a basic human experience shared by a friend and gave us, in turn, a variety of avenues to pursue in order to understand and contextualize that experience. If he is correct that this experience comes from "violated expectations," then we ought to examine those expectations. If he is correct that these expectations come from "what we know about God" and from "a wide range of background assumptions about the world," then we ought to examine our perceived knowledge of God and our assumptions about the world. The experience of divine hiddenness is difficult in part because it hurts; that difficulty is compounded when we do not know how to even begin working to resolve it. In this respect, books like Rea's can help.

This example illustrates two clear benefits of reading philosophy. First, philosophical writing examines and articulates the context and consequences of a whole host of beliefs; this is a core feature of philosophical reasoning. In our ordinary life, when our beliefs are in tension with one another or in tension with our lived experience, we don't always recognize that tension. Even when we do, we often can't identify or articulate which aspects of our beliefs and experiences are in conflict with one another. We may feel the tension and even recognize logical inconsistency, but any hope for resolving it remains out of reach. This is not limited to religious beliefs; our political, ethical, and

---

7. Rea, *The Hiddenness of God*, 26.

social beliefs are equally susceptible. Philosophers are adept at finding and examining the connections between beliefs and ideas. They articulate those findings in writing. Taking the time to read those reflections pays off. This is one important way in which philosophical reading can be of great use.

Second, reading philosophy reminds us that our questions, concerns, and insights are very rarely ours alone. If the anecdote found in the second epigraph of this chapter is accurate, then Lincoln was right: there is very little new under the sun. How many readers, I wonder, were struck by the familiarity of the problem of divine hiddenness? The felt absence of God is a painful experience, but it is hardly a unique one. In this way, reading philosophy often has the result of exposing novelty as old-hat. Sometimes the primary result of this is simply the comfort of the shared human experience, but the potential for benefit goes far beyond that. In 2019, Christian musician and worship leader Marty Sampson went viral with an Instagram post detailing his loss of faith. He wrote:

> How many preachers fall? Many. No one talks about it. How many miracles happen? Not many. No one talks about it. Why is the Bible full of contradictions? No one talks about it. How can God be love yet send four billion people to [Hell] . . . ? No one talks about it.[8]

By now I hope you know what I am going to say about this. With all due charity and respect, it is just false to suggest that "no one" talks about these issues. I suspect that what Sampson meant was that nobody in his community talked about them. If that was true for Sampson, it is deeply unfortunate. If it is true for you, it is unfortunate as well. The remedy is not to enumerate questions and despair; the remedy is to seek answers. I wish that somebody had handed Sampson a copy of Augustine's *Confessions*, C. S. Lewis's *The Great Divorce*, and perhaps William Lane Craig's *Reasonable Faith*. The seemingly revolutionary questions Sampson asks are philosophically well-worn.

Philosophical texts invite the reader to share in the process of asking hard questions—collectively, in community with one another, with the benefit and guidance of philosophically trained authors. Philosophical writing is,

---

8. "Hillsong Songwriter Marty Sampson Says He's Losing His Christian Faith," *Relevant*, August 12, 2019, https://www.relevantmagazine.com/culture/hillsong-songwriter-marty-sampson -says-hes-losing-his-christian-faith/.

at its best, careful thinking put to paper. We would be well-served by taking advantage of the written resources provided by Christian philosophers.

Reading Like a Philosopher

At the same time, you cannot simply open a book like Rea's *Divine Hiddenness* and begin to read it as you would a casual piece of writing. (Well, of course you can, but I wouldn't recommend it.) The passages that I selected from Rea's book are engaging and accessible, but they are only the beginning. As his argument progresses, so does the complexity of his reasoning. This is inevitable, for philosophical reasoning is by its nature complex, but if this is true of a book written by an accessible American professor in the twenty-first century, how much more challenging would it be to delve into the works of Aquinas, Augustine, or Kierkegaard? The challenge is especially keen in a society inundated with technology. As Jacobs notes in *Breaking Bread with the Dead*, "Navigating daily life in the internet age is a lot like doing battlefield triage."[9] Most of the information that we receive each day comes in short bursts, already neatly packaged and designed to elicit a clear response. We can barely keep up with the "breaking news" of the moment, let alone process it in a meaningful fashion. In contrast, philosophical texts take work. It is best to know that ahead of time and prepare accordingly.

No, philosophical reading isn't easy. It requires patience, focus, discipline and charity; it requires a willingness to set aside your own beliefs and attitudes in order to sincerely entertain arguments for views you may oppose. It is sometimes uncomfortable and, to be frank, sometimes boring. It is not at all like reading a novel. For that reason, it is best to be prepared for the process I like to call "reading like a philosopher." What does it mean to read like a philosopher? We can tie together our preceding chapters to construct the following definition: reading like a philosopher requires that you read with the highly general, highly fundamental questions of philosophy in mind; it requires that you read with the goals of conceptual clarity, reasonability, and truth, with an eye toward context and consequence. In plain language, it means that you read carefully with an active and engaged mind.

For most of you, this is something that you already know how to do.

---

9. Jacobs, *Breaking Bread With the Dead*, 12.

By way of analogy, think about the way that you use language. In particular, consider your knowledge of and facility with the rules of grammar for your first native language.[10] If you are like most people, you learned to use the rules of grammar long before you were explicitly introduced to those rules. You learned by watching, hearing, doing, and responding to correction. You learned as you went along. Some of you went on to study the rules of grammar in a classroom; others of you never really learned the rules, though you use them unreflectively. Still others, myself included, only came to learn the rules of grammar when we turned our attention to a second language. In all of these cases, you can use the rules of grammar without thinking about them, but you will do a better job of it if you first spend some time coming to see what those rules say and how they operate. Often, the limitations of your grammatical capabilities only become clear when you are tasked with the challenge of parsing a particularly complex bit of writing.

So it is with careful reading. You may already know how to find the main point in any given passage, and you can probably tell the difference between the position being defended and the reasons given in its defense. You recognize bad reasons, are more impressed by good reasons, and you know how to draw conclusions on the basis of what you have read. Nevertheless, you could do better; we could all do better. Just as with language, the limitations of your natural reasoning skills become most evident in the face of particularly complex reasoning. In order to reason carefully, you must know what it is to reason well. One purpose of this chapter is to unpack, examine, and apply some of the rules that we already tend to follow when we are reading carefully. In learning to recognize these guidelines of careful reading, in devoting your attention to the guidelines themselves, you will be learning to read (and to reason) like a philosopher.

Practical Guidelines for Reading

In the first place, careful reading requires that you go slowly. On this too, Alan Jacobs has much to say. In his 2011 *The Pleasures of Reading in an Age of Distraction*, he writes:

---

10. Credit for this helpful analogy goes to my husband and fellow philosopher, Michael Morris.

A person who had been sedentary for a lifetime would not think that she could rise up from her sofa, head out the door, and run a breezy 10K. Instead she would work up to it slowly, starting with a few strolls around the block perhaps, then longer walks, then a little jogging, and so on. The same applies to the reading of texts written in an unfamiliar idiom or genre, or written in an age whose stylistic preferences differ from our own.[11]

Careful reading is a slow process, and this is not simply a matter of reading at a slow pace and in short increments—though it is that too. In addition, the process of reading philosophy is often less linear than that of casual reading. Jacobs's remarks on reading the philosopher David Hume capture this difference well:

> We don't plan to pause very often, or to thumb back through the pages to earlier sections for clarification or correction—not in the normal course of events. But Hume expects us to be patient, to follow the development of his ideas slowly and methodically, to pause (at the ends of paragraphs perhaps) to make sure that we grasp his chief point before moving on to the next one.[12]

So Jacobs tells us that we must read slowly with a willingness to re-read as needed if we are to understand the arguments of a philosopher like Hume—or, we may add, like Kierkegaard, Aquinas, Eleonore Stump, Alvin Plantinga, or any other philosopher.

Not only must a careful reader be willing to read slowly and to revisit the arguments of each section before proceeding to the next, but the first read-through should be importantly different from subsequent readings. In particular, it is good practice to read or skim the entirety of each article or chapter before beginning to grapple with the details of the arguments contained therein. This is especially true for new readers of philosophy. In my classroom, I often begin my classes with a very short reading by a UNC philosophy professor named Jim Pryor entitled "Guidelines on Reading

---

11. A. Jacobs, *The Pleasures of Reading in an Age of Distraction* (Oxford: Oxford University Press, 2011), 49.

12. Jacobs, *The Pleasures of Reading in an Age of Distraction*, 49.

Philosophy."[13] Pryor's guidelines are written to specifically address the challenge of tackling a difficult article, but they work for longer pieces as well—even books. His advice is simple: aim to read each text at least three times. The first time through you ought only to skim the article (or chapter.) The second time through, you slow down and give the text a good careful read. Finally, only when you have completed these first two readings, you read the text once more with an eye toward evaluation or criticism. Crucially, you do not begin this evaluative process until you are in a good position to understand the arguments being evaluated. Done well, this is a tremendously beneficial way of reading.

When reading a challenging text for the first time, it is also important to keep an eye out for textual clues left by the author. Most philosophical works will have a clearly stated thesis somewhere near the beginning of the article or chapter, and the author will typically make that clear. When you find the thesis, make a note of it. Throughout the text, any time the author writes something like "my point here is . . ." or "I have argued that . . . ," take note and highlight accordingly. This is especially true when careful arguments are being presented. There, you will often find "premise indicators" like the ones discussed in chapter 5. Of equal importance are the "conclusion indicators." We will say more about arguments in the next two chapters, but we can note here that all arguments have premises and a conclusion; the former are the reasons given in support of the latter. Conclusion indicators include words and phrases like "therefore," "in conclusion," "I have shown that," and so on. Finally, take note of any definitions that the author provides. When someone takes the time to give a careful definition, you should note that definition and keep it in mind when considering their subsequent use of that term.

These are just a few practical guidelines for careful reading. Read slowly. Be mindful of the author's points of emphasis. Skim the text for textual markers in advance, and use them to construct a road map of what's to come. This last practice is especially beneficial. When you know where an argument is headed, you will be in a better position to recognize the evidence given in favor of the intended conclusion. As I often say in the classroom, it is far

---

13. "A very short reading" is almost too strong, for this document is but a few pages long and posted for all to see on his website. I highly recommend you read it and keep it in mind as you go. Jim Pryor, "Guidelines for Reading Philosophy," JimPryor.net, updated August 10, 2006, http://www.jimpryor.net/teaching/guidelines/reading.html.

easier to recognize evidence of a crime when you know what the crime is. In the same way, it is far easier to identify the premises of an argument when you know what the conclusion is. Finally, do your best to withhold judgment until you have read the entirety of the text at least twice.

The Attitude of a Careful Reader

This last goal is a tricky one. When I say that you should withhold judgment until you understand a text, I do not mean to say that you should accept and embrace everything that you read. That would be absurd. Indeed, it is just as important that you withhold your immediate assent from any text that you do not yet understand as it is your immediate dissent. As we will discuss in the next two chapters, there are some very bad arguments for true conclusions; the fact that you approve of the basic conclusion of a text should not suffice to tell you that the text itself is persuasive. For example, suppose that you are fully committed to the immorality and illegality of abortion. You might have a tendency to immediately approve of any text that you perceive to be "pro-life." Now suppose that you encountered an article supporting the illegality of abortion on the following grounds: In cases of rape the woman's body shuts down reproduction. Therefore, rape cannot lead to pregnancy, and all pregnancies are the result of voluntary intercourse.[14] Whether you think there ought to be a rape exemption to abortion laws is beside the point. No matter your ethical position, it is empirically false to claim that rape cannot lead to pregnancy. A very basic understanding of female reproduction is enough to demonstrate the untenability of this position. In this case, and in others like it, the fact that you believe the conclusion to be true is simply not enough to show that the arguments given for the conclusion are good. After all, the reasons given in the text might be bad reasons for that conclusion; they might even be terrible![15]

---

14. Politician Todd Akin made a claim of this nature in 2012. He eventually recanted this claim. Unfortunately, he then "regretted" his recantation.

15. There are, of course, bad reasons on the other side of this fence, as well. "The government cannot tell me what to do with my own body" is, for instance, another verifiably false claim. The government does, in fact, tell you an awful lot of things that you may not do with your own body—including drug use, trespassing, and, most relevant here, the use of your body to harm another person. The question of real philosophical interest and import is whether or not the fetus is a person. The simplistic claim that the government cannot govern over bodies is false.

More challenging still is the task of working to understand a text when you know in advance that you oppose its conclusion. Here, again, I do not mean to suggest that you must suspend judgment on the truth of an author's conclusion until you fully understand her argument. Sometimes the evidence that you have for or against the truth of a conclusion is quite strong. A theist does not have to suspend her judgment on the existence of God just because she is working through an argument for atheism; neither must an atheist suspend her judgment when working through theistic arguments. Instead, careful and charitable reading requires only that you not allow your own view to cloud your ability to understand the author's position. No matter how strong your commitment to theism, some theistic arguments are a great deal stronger than others. The same is true for atheistic arguments. A careful reader should be able to tell the difference.

When you jump to the evaluative stage of reading before you have really worked to understand the position being evaluated, your evaluation is not likely to be charitable, reliable, or beneficial. In the book *Generous Thinking*, Kathleen Fitzpatrick recounts the following classroom experience:

> Some years ago, I gave my graduate seminar a recent article to read. I do not now remember what the article was, or even what it was about, but I do remember clearly that upon opening the discussion by asking for first impressions, several students in a row offered fairly merciless takedowns, pointing out the essay's critical failures and ideological blindspots. Some of those readings were justified, but at least a couple of them seemed, frankly, to have missed the point. After the third such response, I interjected: "Okay, okay, I want to dig into all of that, but let's back up a bit first. What's the author's argument? What's her goal in the article? What does she want the reader to come away with?" Silence.[16]

I have had very similar experiences in my own classroom. In their haste to find fault with the assigned readings, students often make no effort whatsoever to understand them. Instead, they come to class ready to disprove René Descartes, Patricia Churchland, or David Hume. Never mind the fact that

---

16. K. Fitzpatrick, *Generous Thinking: A Radical Approach to Saving the University* (Baltimore: Johns Hopkins University Press, 2019), 9.

they are unable to explain the position they wish to reject, they are certain that it—whatever "it" is—is obviously incorrect.

This attitude is not unique to students. I imagine you are, right now, thinking of someone who criticizes your beliefs without first doing the work of understanding them. (If you weren't, perhaps you are now.) So strong is our cultural tendency to form strong opinions that we rarely do the slow and careful work required to understand a viewpoint that doesn't strike us as immediately and obviously attractive. Triage doesn't lend itself to slow and deliberate work; triage is rough and ready, quick and dirty. "Informational triage" is no different. In the classroom it can be remedied. In recent years I have moved away from assignments that require students to critically evaluate a text, asking instead that they carefully explain and defend our readings. I may prompt them on the final exam to evaluate between competing positions, but until then, I want them to focus on comprehension; I want them to be compelled to give the best defense possible of every text that we read and to do so by taking the text seriously. I want them to read charitably.

Fitzpatrick describes her students' response as playing "the doubting game" while failing to play the "listening game." Jacobs similarly laments the widespread tendency to jump into "Refutation Mode," noting that "in Refutation Mode there is no thinking."[17] Careful thinking must begin with the goal of understanding the material being presented. Every teacher knows that if you cannot explain something, you do not yet fully understand it—and if you do not yet fully understand it, you are not yet in a position to critique it.

Instead, read each work as you would read the work of someone you know and like. Pay attention to the author's thesis, and try to find the evidence given in support of that thesis. When you find something you disagree with or dislike, do your best to set aside your position and focus instead on reconstructing theirs. If you are correct and they are mistaken, then the work that you have done to read with charity will put you in a far better position to articulate and defend your objection to their claims. We will return to this discussion about charity in the next chapter when we turn our attention to philosophical arguments.

---

17. A. Jacobs, *How to Think: A Survival Guide for a World at Odds* (New York: Currency, 2017), 18.

A Closing Example

I want to close with an example of what I take to be an instance of uncharitable reading. In *Jesus Interrupted: Revealing the Hidden Contradictions in the Bible (And Why We Don't Know about Them)*, biblical scholar Bart Ehrman aims to show that the Bible is riddled with contradictions. He introduces the following as one of his "favorite apparent discrepancies":

> In John 13:36, Peter says to Jesus, "Lord, where are you going?" A few verses later Thomas says, "Lord, we do not know where you are going." (John 14:5) And then, a few minutes later, at the same meal, Jesus upbraids his disciples, saying "Now I am going to the One who sent me, yet none of you asks me, 'Where are you going?'" (John 16:5) Either Jesus had a very short attention span or there is something strange going on with the sources for these chapters.[18]

Is there really a contradiction here? Is Ehrman right to claim that this points to two inconsistent, irreconcilable sources? That is certainly one way of reading Jesus's question. Perhaps this gospel really was cobbled together from a variety of imperfect, inconsistent, thoroughly human authors.

There are other ways of understanding this passage, however. In fact, this quick insistence on contradiction brings to mind a charge raised by the humanist Jewish scholar Robert Alter against some of his peers. He writes, of some criticism of a passage in Genesis: "Such readings, however, reflect an unfortunate tendency to construe any sign of tension in a narrative as an irreconcilable contradiction, and underestimate the resourcefulness of the Priestly writers in making their own version artfully answer the versions of antecedent traditions."[19] So too does Ehrman's reading underestimate the thought and care that has gone into both recording and preserving the Gospels for

---

18. B. D. Ehrman, *Jesus, Interrupted: Revealing the Hidden Contradictions in the Bible (And Why We Don't Know About Them)*, New York Times Best Sellers (HarperCollins, 2009), 9.

19. R. Alter, *The Five Books of Moses: A Translation with Commentary* (New York: Norton, 2008), 227. This is a beautiful and fascinating translation of the Pentateuch, with commentary. I note that he is a humanist Jewish scholar for two reasons: he is a renowned scholar of Jewish texts, and, at least as far as I know, he is not a theist. This is relevant here because Alter does not have the same need to avoid contradiction that many Christians who affirm the inerrancy of the Bible will feel. Even so, he rightfully recognizes the unity, coherence, and complexity of what we call the Old Testament.

the last two millennia. Can it really be that he is the first to find this tension? Or should we instead believe that he is merely the first to be brave enough to call it the contradiction that it is? I don't think either is plausible. It is far more plausible, more epistemically humble, to ask: What might I be missing? What else might be going on here?

Notice, for instance, that Peter poses his question to Jesus in chapter 13, Thomas does so in chapter 14, and Jesus's admonition comes in chapter 16.[20] What happened in between the questioning and the admonition? In what context did Jesus utter this charge? The answer reveals a straightforward way of reconciling these apparently contradictory verses. Here is the verse in context:

> They will make you outcasts from the synagogue, but an hour is coming for everyone who kills you to think that he is offering service to God. These things they will do because they have not known the Father or Me. But these things I have spoken to you, so that when their hour comes, you may remember that I told you of them. These things I did not say to you at the beginning, because I was with you. But now I am going to Him who sent Me; and none of you asks Me, "Where are You going?" But because I have said these things to you, sorrow has filled your heart. (John 16:2–6)

Here, I would argue, it is not at all clear that Jesus's admonition is inconsistent with the fact that Peter and Thomas have already asked this question. Instead, it seems at least as likely that Jesus is remarking upon the fact that his disciples have been so overcome by fear and sadness at their own circumstances that they are no longer inquiring about Jesus's fate. So understood, his claim is not that nobody ever asked, but instead that nobody is now asking; Jesus might simply have been saying, "I see you've stopped asking where I am going."

This is plausible for several reasons. First, when Peter and Thomas did ask Jesus where he was going, his answers were characteristically opaque. Peter asked, "Where are you going?" and Jesus answered, "Where I am going you cannot follow me now, but you will follow afterward."[21] Thomas asked,

---

20. Ehrman claims that this all transpired in a matter of minutes, but the text itself is not so clear. All that we are told is that it took place over the course of a meal.

21. John 13:36.

"Lord, we do not know where you are going. How can we know the way?" Jesus answered, "I am the way, and the truth, and the life. No one comes to the Father except through me."[22] Not having received a clear answer, the disciples might very well have kept asking the question. Further, throughout this passage Jesus is attempting to prepare his disciples for what was to come, explicitly telling them that he does not want them to be surprised by his death nor to believe that it signals defeat. In light of this context, and the broader context of the Gospels as a whole, it is eminently reasonable to conclude that Jesus's admonition is intended to show the disciples that they are no longer focusing on the question of real importance. Faced with warnings about their own upcoming suffering, they have quickly lost interest in matters eternal. (Anyone who reads the Gospels with any regularity will see this as a singular instance of a frequently recurring theme.)

Finally, this kind of rhetorical point is often made—even now. A teacher who asks for volunteers might see a dozen hands raised, right up to the point at which he explains the difficult, time-consuming task that the volunteer would be required to perform. At that point, faced with no volunteers, he might (truthfully) say, "Not one hand? Nobody is willing?" The teacher need not remind the class that they had their hands raised and then lowered them—they were all present; they already know. Likewise, Jesus need not remind his disciples, "You were asking where I was going. I still haven't really answered that question, but you've all stopped asking." They were there; they remember.

I do not mean to say that these contextual factors would be enough to persuade everyone that there is no contradiction here. Instead, I mean only to note that this charitable reading is one reasonable, textually grounded way of understanding Jesus's admonition. A careful reader ought always to aim for a contextualized, clear, and consistent interpretation of a text—even if they do not agree with its overall message. Readers who have prior reasons for trusting the Gospels will, of course, be more inclined to seek a resolution to any apparent tension between verses rather than admitting inconsistencies; readers who have prior reasons for mistrusting the Gospels will be less inclined to give the benefit of the doubt to troubling passages. What they ought not to do, however, is to too quickly dismiss that which could be explained.

---

22. John 14:5–6 NIV.

Ignoring this context and presenting these verses as obviously contradictory is an example of reading without charity.

Conclusion

When you read a philosophical text, do your best to read with the initial goal of understanding the material. Hold off judgment until you are fairly certain you understand what the author believes and why. Do your best to find textual evidence of your interpretation; if you can't find the author saying what you believe she says, that's a good sign you need to go back and revisit the text. Read slowly, and read with an eye toward textual clues like definitions, premise indicators, and conclusion indicators. Map out the overall structure of the text before you proceed to work through the details of each passage. Read the text, then read it again, and then read it once more. Careful reading in general and philosophical reading in particular take practice.

One aspect of reading like a philosopher goes beyond careful reading, and that is reading with an eye toward arguments. Other kinds of texts contain arguments too, of course, but the role that arguments play in philosophical writing is often more central than it is in historical and literary texts. For that reason, the next two chapters will be devoted to understanding and evaluating arguments.

An Introduction to Arguments

In chapter 6, I introduced some guidelines for reading like a philosopher. It is time to consider one last guideline: reading with an eye toward arguments. More specifically, careful philosophical reading often requires that you, the reader, are able to find, reconstruct, revise, and evaluate the arguments presented in a written work. These next two chapters will introduce you to the kinds of arguments you will encounter when you begin to read philosophical texts—including the arguments found in the final six chapters of this book. It would be a mistake, however, to conclude that philosophical texts are the only place where you will find arguments. On the contrary, arguments abound. They can be found in advertising; politics; self-help books; social, religious, and historical analysis; and even in works of literary fiction. All of what you learn about philosophical arguments can be applied to these arguments as well. Philosophical arguments tend to be better than those found elsewhere, but learning whether, how, and why they are better will equip you to navigate the arguments that you encounter on a daily basis.

---

1. R. C. Sproul, *The Consequences of Ideas: Understanding the Concepts That Shaped Our World* (Wheaton, IL: Crossway, 2000), 41.

You are already bombarded with arguments—good and bad. Increased philosophical prowess enables you to see arguments for what they are and better adjudicate between good and bad arguments.

One note about these next two chapters: the material presented here is more technical than what you have read so far. You may also find it less interesting. It is important, but if you are reading this book on your own and find yourself getting bogged down in the logistics of arguments, feel free to skip ahead to chapter 9. I will refer back to the guidelines outlined here for the remainder of this book, and you can always come back should you feel the need. If you are reading this book in a classroom or as a part of a reading group, I encourage you to work through these examples together. An introduction to arguments is an introduction to logic, and as Sproul articulates in the epigraph for this chapter, "logic is essential to intelligible discourse."[2]

What Is an Argument?

In the classroom, I like to begin our discussion of arguments with these simple questions: What is an argument? What do you think of when you hear the word *argument*? The response is pretty consistent: a fight or a disagreement. My students are not wrong, for it really is the way the word *argument* is used in everyday language. But this is not what philosophers mean by *argument*. A philosophical argument, in contrast to the colloquial use of the term, is neither a debate nor a disagreement. Arguments are frequently constructed in order to be of use in a debate or a disagreement, but the argument itself can at most give a defense of one position. Indeed, this is exactly what a philosopher means by the word *argument*: a series of reasons or evidence given in support of some final claim. Arguments offer a systematic response to the general and fundamental questions of philosophy. An argument says, "This is my clearly-stated belief, and these are some good reasons in its favor." We call the former the *conclusion* of an argument, and the latter the *premises*. Taken together, an argument says, "These premises show that this conclusion is true."

Introductory arguments of the kind found in philosophy textbooks wear their structure on their sleeve, so to speak. For example:

2. Sproul, *The Consequences of Ideas*, 41.

1. All humans are mortal.
2. Eliza is a human.
3. Therefore, Eliza is mortal.

The benefit of these kinds of examples is that they are extraordinarily clear. The conclusion comes at the end, neatly preceded by the word *therefore*. The premises are numbered and proceed in a logically transparent fashion. Nothing extraneous appears in the argument—no rhetorical flourish, no personal opinion, only premises and a conclusion. When an argument is presented in such a way as to make its form evident, we say that it has been "formally stated." There is no difficulty in identifying the conclusion or premises of a formally stated argument. This example, for instance, asks you to accept the conclusion that *Eliza is mortal* on the basis of two pieces of evidence: the fact that all humans are mortal, and the fact that Eliza is a human. Because all humans are mortal, and because Eliza is herself a human, it follows that Eliza must be mortal as well. This argument is clear and effective, albeit uninteresting.

For better or for worse, you will rarely encounter arguments written out like this. The world outside of academic philosophy is rife with arguments, and those tend not to be given as a numbered list of premises for a clearly defined conclusion. Indeed, even within the philosophical community, many authors choose not to formally state their arguments, opting instead to present them—as I have done in this book—as extended essays. Consider chapter 3 of this book. There, I argued that truth and rationality come apart: true beliefs are not necessarily those for which you have good reason, and those beliefs for which you have good reasons are not necessarily true. Rationality tends toward truth, but it does not guarantee it. Broadly stated, the conclusion of this argument was that truth and rationality are not the same thing. I gave evidence for this conclusion in the form of examples—unjustified true beliefs and justified false beliefs. I also relied on one piece of evidence—one premise—that I did not explicitly state: namely, the fact that if truth and justification were the same thing, then there could be no cases in which they came apart. (This last premise I took to be so obvious as to not require stating.) By giving reasons for the conclusion, I presented an argument.

Had I formally stated this argument, it would have looked something like this:

1. If truth and rational justification were the same thing, then all true beliefs would be rationally justified beliefs and all rationally justified beliefs would be true beliefs.
2. Not all true beliefs are rationally justified beliefs.
3. Not all rationally justified beliefs are true beliefs.
4. Therefore, truth and rational justification are not the same thing.

Perhaps some of you find this formal statement helpful. The distinction between the premises and the conclusion is clear; the first premise makes explicit the implicit assumption on which the original argument relied; there is nothing beyond that which is essential to the argument. For those reasons, some readers may find that this formal statement clarifies the original argument. Other readers may find the rigid structure a distraction or an unnecessary complication. In either case, this much is true: these are two statements of one argument. Both the informal and the formal statement make the same argument, for they give the same reasons for the same conclusion.

Together the premises and conclusion comprise an argument. Neither will suffice on its own. Not all arguments for the same conclusion are the same argument, for one could give good or bad reasons for the very same conclusion. Not all arguments invoking the same premises are the same argument, for one could attempt to infer two very different conclusions from the same premises.[3] Only when two statements of an argument invoke the same premises for the same conclusion can we judge them to be two statements of the same argument.

If an argument says, "These premises show that this conclusion is true," then we must consider every aspect of this claim in order to understand an argument. In other words, we must consider: the premises, the conclusion, and fittingness of the former for the latter. We can do so by answering each of the following questions:

1. What is the argument an argument for?
2. What is the evidence given in favor of the conclusion?
3. Is that evidence good evidence for that conclusion?

---

3. To be clear, this is not to say that one could reasonably or rationally infer two very different conclusions from the same set of premises—only that one could try.

It is worth noting that these questions closely parallel and deliberately exemplify the questions of philosophy as they were stated in chapter 1:

1. What precisely do I believe about this?
2. Why do I believe it?
3. Are those reasons good reasons for that belief?

This should come as no surprise, for an argument is, or ought to be, a clearly stated defense of a clearly stated position—an attempt to provide an answer to some philosophical question.

Argument Reconstruction: Finding the Conclusion

To that end, the first step in clarifying an argument is finding an answer to the first question: What is the argument an argument for? That is, you should begin by finding and articulating the conclusion. Why not begin with the premises? The conclusion is the main point of the argument; it is the position being defended. The premises are the reasons given in support of that position. It would be difficult to recognize reasons as such without first knowing what they were reasons for. This would, perhaps, be akin to gathering evidence of a crime without first ascertaining what crime had been committed—not impossible, per se, but also not the best way forward.

It is best, then, to begin by finding the conclusion. When an argument has been formally stated, this will be an easy task—the conclusion always comes at the end of a formally stated argument and is often neatly preceded by the word *therefore*. For informally stated arguments, however, it can be a difficult process.

Consider the following fictitious example:

> I think that capital punishment is immoral. There is no justification what-soever for deliberately taking the life of another person, unless that person poses an immediate threat to your own life. That goes for individuals as well as the state. Murder is always wrong!

What is the conclusion of the above argument? When I have introduced arguments of this sort in the classroom, I have found a tendency among students to confuse the conclusion with the end of the argument, such that whatever claim is made last is taken to be the conclusion. In this example, for instance, such students would suspect that the conclusion is "Murder is always wrong." After all, this passage concludes with a strong statement about the wrongness of murder. Shouldn't that mean that this must be the conclusion?

This line of reasoning is mistaken. While it is true that in formally stated arguments the conclusion always comes at the end, this is often not the case in informal arguments. In fact, it is common for an informal argument to begin with the conclusion. In this example, that is exactly where we will find the proper conclusion, "capital punishment is immoral." To see why, remember that the conclusion is the main point of the argument; it is the answer to the question "What is this argument an argument for?" The main point of this argument is not the immorality of murder in general but the immorality of the death penalty in particular. The immorality of murder is given as evidence of the immorality of capital punishment, which the argument's proponent takes to be an instance of murder. The proper conclusion of the informal argument given in this example is "capital punishment is immoral."

Perhaps, like my students, you are not convinced. The following is an objection that I frequently encounter in the classroom:

> Who are you to say what the main point is? What if we disagree? Couldn't I, instead, maintain that "Murder is always wrong!" is the proper conclusion of the argument? If it is not the proper conclusion, couldn't I at least say that it is as likely a conclusion as your suggestion? Why believe that there is one true conclusion anyway?

I am sympathetic to questions of this nature, particularly because I know that it can sometimes feel as if the rules of philosophical reasoning are being made up as we go along, much like an older brother crushing his younger siblings at some new game. Furthermore, it is true that there is some variation in how a conclusion ought to be formulated. Nevertheless, the variation is minor and most arguments do, in fact, have one clear conclusion. In this case, for example, the conclusion proposed in the objection is not an equally justifiable conclusion to draw from this argument.

To see why, remember that premises are the reasons given in support of a conclusion. With that in mind, we can use the following exercise to separate the conclusion from the premises of any argument: Take your proposed conclusion and ask, "Why should I believe that?" Then proceed, line by line, through the text in question. Any piece of information that answers your question is a premise. If you are unable to find premises using this method, then you have not yet found the correct conclusion. If you are unable to find premises for any conclusion using this method, then the text in question is not actually an argument.

Let's try this now with each of the suggested conclusions for our first argument. Suppose that my students are correct, and "Murder is always wrong!" is at least as plausible a conclusion to this argument as my suggestion is. If that is the case, then we should be able to find answers to the question "Why should I believe that murder is always wrong?" in the remainder of the passage. That is, we should find premises matching the proposed conclusion. What are our options? We can proceed line by line through the passage:

> I think that capital punishment is immoral. There is no justification what-soever for deliberately taking the life of another person, unless that person poses an immediate threat to your own life. That goes for individuals as well as the state. Murder is always wrong!

The very first line gives us this: "You should believe that murder is always wrong because capital punishment is immoral." This can't be right! The over-whelming majority of instances of murder are not instances of capital punishment. The wrongness of capital punishment cannot explain the wrongness of murder; the order of explanation goes in the other direction, if at all.

How about the second line? Here we find: "You should believe that murder is always wrong because there is no justification whatsoever for deliberately taking the life of another person, unless that person poses an immediate threat to your own life." This is certainly a step in the right direction, but it feels a bit like saying, "You should believe that murder is always wrong because murder is always wrong." There is not much here by way of explanation. Our last option is: "You should believe that murder is always wrong because that goes for individuals as well as the state." This is at least a partial explanation—murder is always wrong because the wrong-ness of taking a life applies both to individuals and to the state. Still, with only one of the three potential premises actually supporting the truth of this conclusion, we ought to concede that we have been attempting to defend the wrong conclusion. It's not that the premises are wholly irrelevant to the claim that murder is always wrong, but rather that they are not particularly useful in defending or demonstrating the truth of that claim. They are not premises for that conclusion.

Now consider my proposed conclusion that "capital punishment is immoral." If I am correct, we should find answers to the question "Why should I believe that capital punishment is immoral?" in the remainder of the passage. As before, we should proceed line by line, skipping the proposed conclusion. We thus begin with: "You should believe that capital punishment is immoral because there is no justification whatsoever for deliberately taking the life of another person, unless that person poses an immediate threat to your own life." Already we have an answer that is far more promising than any we found in our first pass. To be clear, I do not mean that everyone will agree with the truth of this answer—not at all! I mean only that everyone should agree that this is an answer to the question under consideration. Whether or not you think it is a good answer is separate question.[4] Moving on, we reach the following: "You should believe that capital punishment is immoral because that goes for individuals as well as the state." Taken in isolation, this says very little. Together with the previous premise, we do have a continuation of the explanation—"You should believe that capital punishment is immoral because, for the state as for an individual, there is no justification for deliberately taking the life of another person apart from self-defense." The final line of text gives us the final explanation: "You should believe that capital punishment is immoral because murder is always wrong!" Again, quite a lot of my readers surely disagree with the implicit suggestion that capital punishment is murder. Our question here, however, is not yet about the strength of this argument—it is about the content of

---

4. I anticipate some frustration here, and I will defend this claim in detail toward the end of this chapter. Briefly, remember that both support and entailment take the following form: If this set of propositions were true, would the conclusion be true? If the answer is "probably," then the relationship is support. If the answer is "certainly," then the relationship is entailment. In both cases it is a further question whether or not the propositions in question are, in fact, true. Thus, "Today is Wednesday" entails "Tomorrow is Thursday," and this entailment holds every day of the week. On Monday, it is false that "Today is Wednesday" but it remains true that "Today is Wednesday" entails "Tomorrow is Thursday." The logical structure of an argument is, and must be, distinct from the truth of its content. In asking which conclusion the premises support, we ought only to consider the structure.

the argument. We are asking what the argument says; we are inquiring after its conclusion.

The proper conclusion of an argument is the main claim which the rest of the text supports and defends—whether or not that claim comes at the end of the text. Now for the really challenging part: sometimes, the conclusion of an argument is left out entirely! It is not uncommon for authors of informal arguments to merely imply, rather than explicitly state, their conclusion. For example:

> Capital punishment is endorsed in the Old Testament and is never wholly condemned in the Bible. It sends the message that serious crime will not be tolerated, and it helps to maintain law and order. Of course it is tragic when a life is taken, but that doesn't mean what's being done is immoral.

What is the conclusion of this argument? Well, what is the point of it? What is the author trying to communicate? The answer, I think, is clear: "Capital punishment is morally permissible."[5] Yet nowhere in this text will you find an actual statement of this conclusion.

If we apply our method for testing a proposed conclusion, we get: "You should believe that capital punishment is morally permissible because capital punishment is endorsed in the Old Testament and is never wholly condemned in the Bible." "You should believe that capital punishment is morally permissible because it sends the message that serious crime will not be tolerated, and it helps to maintain law and order." "You should believe that capital punishment is morally permissible because of course it is tragic when a life is taken, but that doesn't mean what's being done is immoral." Each of these results in a clearly stated defense of our conclusion; the entirety of this passage can be used to support the moral permissibility of capital punishment. The conclusion of this argument is quite clear, yet it is also never actually stated. In casual writings and everyday conversations, this is surprisingly common. When it happens, we say that the argument has an implicit conclusion.

By reading for the main point of a passage and seeking a defense of that

---

5. An equally plausible (and logically equivalent) conclusion would be "Capital punishment is not immoral." Both work! By changing "not immoral" to "morally permissible," I merely removed the double-negative and replaced it with the corresponding positive statement.

main point, you should be able to find the conclusion of any informally stated argument—even when the conclusion is placed where you would not expect to find it; even when the conclusion is left unstated. This is the beginning of a process called *argument reconstruction*. When faced with a text that seems to contain an argument, the very first step toward understanding that argument should be this process of determining the conclusion. Once you have done so, the next step is to check the remainder of the passage for evidence of that conclusion—that is, to find the premises.

Argument Reconstruction: Finding the Premises

As you have likely noted, the methodology that I suggest for confirming or disconfirming a proposed conclusion should give you the premises of an argument as well. To draw on our most recent example, the claim "You should believe that capital punishment is morally permissible because it sends the message that serious crime will not be tolerated, and it helps to maintain law and order" actually serves two purposes: it supports the view that the moral permissibility of capital punishment is the conclusion of this argument, and it indicates that the use of capital punishment as a deterrent is one of its premises. This is a helpful start, but it will not always suffice. To see why, we can formalize the above argument using the implicit conclusion and the premises which resulted from our exercise:

1. Capital punishment is endorsed in the Old Testament and is never wholly condemned in the Bible.
2. It sends the message that serious crime will not be tolerated, and it helps to maintain law and order.
3. Of course it is tragic when a life is taken, but that doesn't mean what's being done is immoral.
4. Therefore, capital punishment is morally permissible.

As a first pass, this certainly captures the general idea of the argument above. That said, as formally stated arguments go, this argument is a mess.

The first thing to note is that the premises contain very little linguistic overlap. The language of each premise is unique and not obviously related to the rest of the premises, making it difficult to see how they are intended to work together in support of the conclusion. We can fix that problem by rewording the premises in order to emphasize their coherence:

1. Capital punishment is biblically permissible.
2. Capital punishment is an effective deterrent of crime.
3. It is tragic when a life is taken, but not always immoral.
4. Therefore, capital punishment is morally permissible.

This is a step in the right direction, though my more philosophically experienced readers will surely note that this is still not a very good argument. This is not to say that the informal argument is weak, only that we have not yet succeeded in adequately capturing the premises.

The process of articulating the premises of an argument is challenging for at least two reasons: not everything that is contained in an argument is a premise (or conclusion), and not all premises are explicitly stated. In the process of reconstructing and clarifying an argument, you will often have to eliminate rhetorical fluff and render explicit any implicit premises. We can begin with the first task by reconsidering premise 3 above. Note that the first half of that premise does not help defend the truth of the conclusion; the fact that death is tragic is something of a sidebar in this discussion. Similarly, when people invoke their own feelings, hyperbolic language, or other rhetorical flourishes in arguments, the proper response is to leave those contributions out of the reconstructed argument. At the same time, some arguments rely on claims that are deemed so obvious as to not require stating. Like the implicit conclusions we considered in the last section, implicit premises are very common in informal arguments.

Before returning to the argument currently under discussion, consider the following example:

> Capital punishment is immoral. I hate it so much! It is still legal in more than half of the U.S and I think that's just awful. Killing a person is always wrong! I am determined to fight to end this great evil!

This passage exemplifies both the need to eliminate fluff and the need to find and articulate implicit premises. By now it should be clear what the conclusion of this argument is: "Capital punishment is immoral." But when we seek answers as to why we should conclude that it is immoral, we find a great deal of information that, while loosely related, is not the least bit useful in defending the truth of this conclusion. For instance, "You should believe that capital punishment is immoral because I hate it so much!" This is no defense of immorality—I hate cooked peas and much of pop music, but I would hardly call them immoral. "You should believe that capital punishment is immoral because it is still legal in more than half of the U.S and I think that's just awful" fares no better. The legality of capital punishment can't demonstrate its immorality; neither, it seems, can the speaker's feeling about that legal reality. At last we find at least one real premise: "You should believe that capital punishment is immoral because killing a person is always wrong."

We have, then, the following:

1. Killing a person is always wrong.
2. Therefore, capital punishment is immoral.

This is clearly not sufficient. What is needed is something to link the first premise with the conclusion—what does killing a person have to do with capital punishment? The answer, of course, is obvious—it is so obvious, in fact, that the proponent of this argument felt comfortable leaving it out entirely. If we add this implicit content and render the language of this argument more consistent, we find ourselves with the following:

1. Killing a person is always immoral.
2. (Capital punishment kills a person.)
3. Therefore, capital punishment is immoral.

This, at last, is what we call a well-formed argument. We will examine well-formed arguments in greater detail in chapter 8. For now, note that this argument is stated in a way that is unambiguous, linguistically consistent, devoid of rhetorical fluff, and fully articulated—that is, extra material has been removed and the implicit content rendered explicit.

Can we do the same for our previous argument? How about the following:

1. Capital punishment is biblically permissible.
2. Capital punishment is an effective deterrent of crime.

3. (Any biblically permissible effective deterrent of crime is morally permissible.)
4. Therefore, capital punishment is morally permissible.

Here, as above, I followed the convention of placing implicit premises in parenthesis. I also removed the claim that some deaths, though tragic, are nevertheless permissible. It would be possible to include this material in a well-formed statement of this argument, but I believe that eliminating it results in a stronger argument. To be clear, there remains much to debate here. Not everybody will agree that capital punishment is biblically permissible. Not everybody will agree that capital punishment is an effective deterrent of crime. Finally, not everybody will agree that biblical permissibility suffices for moral permissibility! This is a well-formed argument, but as we will see in chapter 8, the question of whether an argument is well-formed is entirely distinct from the question of whether its premises are true.

The Principle of Charity

It is time to reiterate an objection from chapter 6 that has, I suspect, already occurred to many of my readers: "Why should the reader have to do so much work in order to strengthen someone else's argument? If an argument lacks a written conclusion, why add one? If it is missing crucial inferential steps, why call those "implicit premises" and insert them? Why not let written (or spoken) arguments stand or fall on their own merit?" This objection captures a line of reasoning that is especially compelling with respect to arguments for positions that the reader rejects. It is one thing to clarify and strengthen an argument that you like; to do so for an argument that you want ultimately to reject is another thing entirely. So why do it?

If our only goal was appearing to win an argument in the moment, then this careful process of argument reconstruction would, indeed, be time wasted. It is far easier to defeat a weak argument than a strong one! If, instead, our goal is wisdom—if we are in the pursuit of truth—then we must aim higher. When you do the work of presenting an argument in the strongest light possible, you are rewarded with genuine insight. A carefully formulated argument reveals a person's line of thought; it illustrates the reasoning behind a position, for better or for worse. For that reason, when it is time to evaluate that argument, a critical evaluation of a properly formulated argument is beneficial and instructive.

When an argument is presented in an obviously weak formulation, the result is what we call a "straw man" fallacy. You would not be impressed by my strength and valor if I built a man out of straw only to then knock him down. In the same way, constructing an argument in a way that is weaker than intended cannot lead to real success. When you demonstrate the failure of this argument, nobody will be surprised or impressed—nobody ever thought it was a good argument in the first place. You have defeated an imagined opponent of your own design, a straw man, and your real opponent remains untouched.

Instead, when interacting with others, it is always good to use a principle of charity. Although we addressed the basic idea behind this principle in chapter 6, it is worth noting that this principle is most necessary in the context of argument reconstruction and evaluation. To borrow a definition from the aptly titled *The Philosopher's Toolkit*, "The 'Principle of Charity' states that interpreters should seek to maximize the soundness of others' arguments and truth of their claims by rendering them in the strongest way reasonable."[6] This means that you ought to assume the best of your interlocutor, not the worst, and that you ought to produce the strongest version possible of any argument that they give, not the weakest. Assume that they have reasons for their conclusion. If it seems that something obvious has been left out, assume that they expect you to infer it. In other words, do for them precisely what you already do for the people who give arguments for conclusions you like! If, having done so, you are still able to find fault in their argument, you will have discovered a genuine source of disagreement. This, after all, is what rational dialogue is all about.

Conclusion

The practice of teasing out the proper conclusion and the useful premises from the rhetorically powerful but unstructured writing that we so often encounter is difficult, but it is tremendously important. Fortunately, one

---

6. J. Baggini and P. S. Fosl, *The Philosopher's Toolkit: A Compendium of Philosophical Concepts and Methods* (Malden, MA: Blackwell, 2003), 115.

need not do it perfectly to reap the benefits of clarification. Indeed, every small step in this direction will be useful. Simply learning to find the primary conclusion of a piece of writing will help increase your understanding of the rest of what has been written. As you improve in this practice you will find yourself better able to isolate premises and to eliminate that which is not, properly speaking, a part of the argument. This is not a skill that one must master in order to use; there are degrees of comprehension, and every step toward clarity should likewise increase your comprehension.

Evaluating Arguments

8

"Then you should say what you mean," the March Hare went on. "I do," Alice
hastily replied; "at least—at least I mean what I say—that's the same thing,
you know." "Not the same thing a bit!" said the Hatter. "Why, you might just
as well say that 'I see what I eat' is the same thing as 'I eat what I see'!"
—Alice in Wonderland[1]

I n chapter 7, I suggested that we understand arguments as saying, roughly,
"These premises show that this conclusion is true." A *good* argument does
what it says it is going to do, with premises that really do show the conclusion
is true. As we will see in this chapter, two standards must be met for this to
be the case: the premises must be true, and their truth must support the truth
of the conclusion. Only when both criteria are satisfied can we judge an argument to be a good argument.

Argument Evaluation: Form and Content

The two criteria for a good argument, then, are that the premises are true
and that they support the conclusion. We call the former the content of the
argument and the latter its structure or form. Like truth and rationality, form
and content come apart. An argument can be well-formed even if one or more
of its premises is false. An argument can have all true premises and yet fail
to be well-formed. A good argument must have both features. Consider the
following analogy: In the US legal system, a person who has been accused of
a crime is entitled to a trial. In that trial, the prosecution will present a case
against the defendant, often employing both forensic evidence and witness

---

1. Lewis Carroll, *Alice's Adventures in Wonderland* (Sweden: Wisehouse Classics, 2016).

testimony. It is the burden of the prosecution to show beyond reasonable doubt that

a. the testimonies and forensic evidence are truthful and accurate, and
b. the testimonies and forensic evidence being presented are sufficient to demonstrate the guilt of the accused.

These are not the same task, and it is important that both be done well.

The defense must, in turn, find a way to undermine the case against the accused. There are two general ways of doing this. The defense might

a. undermine the truthfulness or accuracy of the testimonies and forensic evidence being presented, or
b. accept the evidence but show that it fails to demonstrate the guilt of the defendant.

These are two distinct responses. Either will suffice on its own, though there is no reason the defense could not use both.

To take the first approach, the defense might give reason to believe that the witnesses are not telling the truth. Perhaps they are lying; perhaps they are mistaken—either way, the information they have given is false. Alternatively, the defense might give reason to believe that the forensic evidence is inaccurate. Perhaps the samples were corrupted, the fingerprints planted, or the technicians mistaken—no matter what, the information given in the forensic evidence is false. This is the heart of the first approach: to deny the veracity of the evidence in question.

In order to take the second approach, however, the defense need not deny the truth or accuracy of the evidence. Instead, they need only show that the evidence is insufficient. For instance, when defending a client from a charge of burglary, a defense attorney might offer something like the following response:

> Of course she was seen near his apartment, and of course you found a hair from her head. I'm not even surprised that her fingerprints were found in his living room. They were friends! None of this proves that she broke in and stole his valuables. It only proves that they spent time together in his home.

Such a defense does not depend upon showing that the evidence in question is false; it is enough to show that the evidence fails to prove what it was intended to—that is, it fails to demonstrate guilt. Even truthful testimony and reliable evidence can fail to be sufficient evidence of the charge in question.

The same two criteria apply to arguments. Just as the prosecution must succeed in showing that the evidence is both accurate and sufficient to demonstrate guilt, so must the proponent of an argument succeed in showing both that the premises are true and that the premises support the truth of the conclusion. An argument that succeeds on both counts is a good argument. An argument that fails on either count is a bad argument. All bad arguments must be rejected—no matter how appealing the conclusion may be. A bad argument for a good conclusion remains a bad argument.

Form: Support and Entailment

What does it mean to say that the premises of an argument support the conclusion? To continue the analogy, premises support their conclusion when they really are evidence of the truth of that conclusion. This is why, as we learned in chapter 7, you can find the premises for a conclusion in an informally stated argument by seeking answers to the question: "Why should I believe this conclusion to be true?" When we say that premises support their conclusion, we mean that they give reason to believe in the truth of the conclusion.

This is not to say that premises must always prove the truth of their conclusions. Instead, there are two distinct types of argument, each with its own standard of support. Some arguments are intended only to render their conclusion probable; other arguments are designed to show that their conclusion follows necessarily from the truth of their premises. We call arguments of the first sort "inductive" and the second sort "deductive." Recognizing the difference between inductive and deductive arguments is essential to argument evaluation. An argument that sets out to prove its conclusion only succeeds if it actually proves it; an argument that aims only to demonstrate the likelihood of its conclusion must be judged by that standard.

Both inductive and deductive arguments rely on some degree of support, so we ought to say a little bit more about what it means for one claim to support another. Throughout this book we have considered the ways beliefs are related to one another. Some beliefs, for instance, are more fundamental than others. These fundamental beliefs, if true, have as their consequence a whole host of particular beliefs. To return to an example from chapter 1, the belief in the morality of promise keeping in general should lead you to believe that you ought to keep a particular promise today, whether or not you want to. The truth of the general claim—that promise keeping is morally required— has as its consequence the truth of the more specific claim—that keeping this promise is morally required.

The idea that beliefs have consequences was central to our discussion in chapter 6 as well. We are now in a position to state this notion of *consequence* more clearly. When we say that a belief has consequences, we mean that the truth of the proposition affirmed by one belief supports the truth of further propositions. More succinctly stated: some propositions, if true, increase the likelihood of others. Again, this may sound complex, but it is actually something that you already know and recognize in ordinary everyday life. For instance, if it is true that Xavier is the tallest boy in his school, then it is likely to be true that Xavier is tall for his age. It is certainly possible for this to fail to be the case. Xavier might attend a school where the student body is of unusually small stature—perhaps they are elite gymnasts or jockeys. In most cases, however, a person who is the tallest student at a school will be a taller than average individual in general. The truth of the first claim provides some evidence for the truth of the second; the former supports the latter.

In the same way, sometimes a set of claims, taken together, will support some further claim. Suppose that you have learned that your neighbor's daughter was running for class president, the elections were yesterday, and your neighbor's family had a celebration honoring that same daughter yesterday. Even without being told that your neighbor's daughter won the election, you would be justified in making such an inference. The truths that you do know—that she was running for office, that the decision came yesterday, that she was celebrated yesterday—increase the likelihood of it being true that she was elected. This is a clear instance of support: when the truth of one or more propositions increases the likelihood of the truth of another, we will say that the former supports the latter.

In cases of mere support, it remains possible that the supported claim will fail to be true. (Perhaps your neighbor's family chose to celebrate their daughter's efforts, even in the face of loss!) Crucially, not all support is mere support. Sometimes support rises to the level of necessitation. Sometimes the likelihood increases to the point of certainty. In these cases, the truth of the supporting claims really does guarantee the truth of the claim they support. For instance, if it is true that "Wilbur is a Goldendoodle," then it is true that "Wilbur is a dog." I do not mean that it is probably true or very likely to be true—it must be true. If Wilbur is a Goldendoodle, then Wilbur is a dog. Being a dog is part of what it means to be a Goldendoodle.[2] Like other forms of support, this stronger version can also hold between sets of claims: if it is true that all turtles are mortal, and it is true that Snappy is a turtle, it must be true that Snappy is mortal. We call this stronger form of support "entailment." When the truth of one or more propositions logically guarantees the truth of another, we say that the former entails the latter.[3]

What is a "logical guarantee"? Think of it as a consequence that must follow on pain of contradiction. Thus, in cases of genuine entailment, any attempt to hold the supporting claims true and the supported false will generate a contradiction: "Wilbur is a Goldendoodle, and Wilbur is not a dog" is a contradiction, as is "All turtles are mortal, and Snappy is a turtle who is not mortal." These claims are contradictory because it is impossible for them to be true. If you attempt to affirm a supporting claim while denying the supported consequence and no such contradiction results, then the degree of support between propositions was not, in fact, entailment. For instance, there is no contradiction involved in supposing "My friend Susan accepted a job in California and is looking at real estate in California, but my friend Susan is not relocating to California." Neither is it contradictory to suppose that "Xavier is the tallest student in his school but Xavier is not tall." Each of these would be surprising—Why accept a job and look for real estate if you do not intend to relocate? What kind of a school has a tallest student who is not tall?—but neither is impossible.

This is the distinguishing feature between support and entailment:

2. "But wait!" you say. "What if I use the word *goldendoodle* to mean something different?" This is another reason why philosophers speak of the truth or falsity of propositions rather than sentences. Of course, if you want to use *goldendoodle* to mean "an angry dolphin," then your usage of *goldendoodle* will not carry the same entailments—but whatever words you do use to express the proposition "Wilbur is a goldendoodle" will still entail the proposition expressed by whatever words you use to express the proposition "Wilbur is a dog." Throughout this chapter, for reasons that should be clear, I will assume that words mean what they mean according to ordinary usage.

3. It is worth noting that entailment includes support. If *P* entails *Q*, then *P* also supports *Q*.

support merely increases the probability of a claim's being true, whereas entailment deals in logical necessity. If you know that some claim (call it P) provides some degree of support for some further claim (call it Q), and you do not know whether or not P entails Q, you can test for entailment. Simply assume that P is true and Q is false. If the result of this assumption is an unlikely but possible scenario, then P does not entail Q. If the result is an impossibility, if supposing that Q is false unavoidably commits you to the supposition that P is false as well, then P entails Q. For instance, in supposing that Snappy is an immortal turtle, you are already committed to the falsity of either "Snappy is a turtle" or "all turtles are mortal." There is no way that the world could be, no way that any world could be, such that all turtles are mortal, Snappy is a turtle, and yet Snappy is not mortal. This is entailment; entailment is logical necessitation.

Well-Formed Inductive Arguments

When the premises of an argument are intended only to merely support the conclusion, we say that the argument employs inductive reasoning and is an inductive argument. It will be helpful to consider a series of inductive arguments, each representative of a common form of reasoning. We can begin by returning to the burglary example. There, the evidence of burglary included eyewitness testimony of the suspect near the victim's apartment, the suspect's fingerprints inside the victim's living room, and a hair matching the suspect's DNA found inside the apartment. In order to use this evidence to demonstrate the suspect's guilt, the prosecution might advance something like the following argument:

1. Someone burglarized the victim's apartment.
2. The suspect was seen near the victim's apartment on the day of the burglary.
3. The suspect's fingerprints were found inside the victim's apartment.
4. A hair from the suspect's head was found inside the victim's apartment.
5. The best explanation for the evidence offered in premises 1–4 is that the suspect committed the burglary in question.
6. Therefore, the suspect committed the burglary in question.

This argument takes the form of an *inference to the best explanation*.[4] This is an example of an inductive argument because the premises, taken together, increase the likelihood of the conclusion; they do not prove with logical necessity that the conclusion must be true.

Similarly, consider the following inductive argument:

1. The universe is like a watch in that both are intricately designed to perform highly specific and complex functions.
2. It is not possible for a watch to come into existence without having been designed by an intelligent mind.
3. Therefore, it is also not possible for the universe to have come into existence without having been designed by an intelligent mind.

This "design argument" is an *argument by analogy*. It claims that the universe is analogous to a watch in certain important ways and is therefore probably also analogous to the watch in a third way. Again, these premises are intended to demonstrate the likely truth of the conclusion; the proponent of this argument need not, and would not, claim that the conclusion must necessarily follow from the premises.

Finally, consider one more inductive argument. Arguments of this sort are typically called *inductive generalizations*:

1. Every flower that I have ever observed has had a sweet smell.
2. That plant has flowers.
3. Therefore, the flowers on that plant will also have a sweet smell.

Inductive generalizations, sometimes simply called induction, draw a general conclusion from an accumulation of particular experiences. There is a sense in which arguments of this variety merely formalize a method of reasoning on which we all regularly rely. In any case, the evidence presented by these accumulated experiences increases the likelihood of the next relevant case following suit; they do not, nor do they claim to, make it impossible for the generalization to fail.

---

4. This form of reasoning is sometimes called *abduction*. We will consider and defend an abductive argument in chapters 12–14.

All inductive arguments—whether they invoke inferences to the best explanation, analogies, inductive generalizations, or some other method of inductive reasoning—share this one feature in common: they do not claim logically to guarantee their conclusions, only to render them probable. This is the core feature of an inductive argument. The best explanation may not be the correct explanation, but it often will be; a good analogy may fail on some key point, but it will often succeed; an accumulation of evidence may miss some outlying cases, but it will capture most cases. When the premises of an inductive argument really do support the conclusion, we say that it is well-formed. That is, a well-formed inductive argument is one in which the premises, if true, really do increase the likelihood of the truth of the conclusion.

When an inductive argument is well-formed and has only true premises, it is a good argument; this is the standard to which inductive arguments can and should be held. In order to undermine an inductive argument, it will not suffice merely to show that the conclusion could be false; it is, always and admittedly, possible for the conclusion of an inductive argument to be false, even when the premises are true. Instead, to raise an objection to an inductive argument you must be able to show either that one of the premises is likely to be false or that the premises do not really support the truth of the conclusion.[5] Showing that the premises do not entail the conclusion amounts only to showing that the argument is not a deductive argument. Even the best inductive arguments offer only probabilistic support for their conclusions. They are nevertheless good arguments.

Well-Formed Deductive Arguments

In contrast to inductive arguments, deductive arguments set out to guarantee their conclusions logically. For that reason, a well-formed deductive argument must be an argument in which the premises really do entail the conclusion; mere support is not enough here. There are several common types

---

5. There is a one-third possibility here, though it rarely will be exercised. If you have really excellent reasons for believing the conclusion to be false but no good reasons for believing any of the premises to be false or for believing that the premises fail to support the conclusion, then you may claim that this is the outlying case. That is, you may claim that the premises increase the probability of the conclusion's being true, but that in this case the conclusion turns out (surprisingly) to be false. This is only an option for inductive arguments, for reasons which will become clear as this chapter proceeds.

of well-formed deductive arguments, but all of them have one feature in common: if you attempt to affirm the premises while denying the conclusion, the result will be a contradiction. This is, of course, just another way of saying that the premises entail the conclusion.

It is not difficult to construct simple, well-formed deductive arguments. The formula is simple: find a case of entailment and spell it out. For instance:

1. All squares have four sides.
2. This shape is a square.
3. Therefore, this shape has four sides.

Because a square is one kind of quadrangle, being a square entails being a shape with four sides. Thus, if it is true—as it is—that all squares have four sides, and also true that some particular shape is a square, then it must be true that the shape in question has four sides. It is logically impossible for both of these premises to be true while the conclusion is false. These premises entail this conclusion; this is a well-formed deductive argument. The following is as well:

1. If today is Tuesday, then tomorrow is Wednesday.
2. Today is Tuesday.
3. Therefore, tomorrow is Wednesday.

Again, because Wednesday is the day after Tuesday, today being Tuesday entails tomorrow being Wednesday. For both arguments, it is logically impossible to affirm the truth of the premises while denying the truth of the conclusion. Denying the conclusion requires that you deny at least one premise as well. These arguments may be boring and woefully uninformative, but they are well-formed deductive arguments.

At first glance, it can sometimes be difficult to tell a well-formed deductive argument from a poorly formed one. Once again, a series of examples will be helpful here. The following is a well-formed deductive argument:

1. All humans are mammals.
2. Josie is a human.
3. Therefore, Josie is a mammal.

In contrast, this argument is not:

1. All humans are mammals.
2. Josie is a mammal.
3. Therefore, Josie is a human.

This is not well-formed because there is no contradiction in supposing: "All humans are mammals and Josie is a mammal who is not a human." She might, after all, be a cow. If Josie were a cow, it would remain true that all humans are mammals. It would also remain true that Josie is a mammal. Thus, the possibility on which Josie is a cow is a possibility on which all of the premises are true and the conclusion is false. Because this is possible, we know that the premises do not entail the conclusion. This deductive argument is not well-formed.

For the very same reasons, this is a well-formed deductive argument:

1. If Hector is a dermatologist, then Hector is a doctor.
2. Hector is a dermatologist.
3. Therefore, Hector is a doctor.

But this is not:

1. If Hector is a dermatologist, then Hector is a doctor.
2. Hector is a doctor.
3. Therefore, Hector is a dermatologist.

Hector may be a doctor who is not a dermatologist. Hector may not be a dermatologist who is not a doctor. Hector's being a dermatologist entails his being a doctor, but his being a doctor does not entail his being a dermatologist. (He might, after all, be a pediatrician.)

These last two arguments began with what we call a "conditional statement." A conditional statement says, "If (this antecedent condition is met), then (this consequent must follow)." Philosophers formalize this as "If P, then Q" with P representing the antecedent, and Q the consequent. The clearest way of understanding a conditional is as an entailment claim:

"If P, then Q" says that P entails Q. Thus, "If Hector is a dermatologist, then Hector is a doctor" says that Hector's being a dermatologist entails Hector's being a doctor. In the same way, the previous arguments began with what we call a universal generalization of the form "All A's are B's." For instance, "All squares are four-sided shapes," and "All humans are mammals." Here, again, we find entailment claims: if it is true that all squares are four-sided shapes, then being a square entails being a four-sided shape; if all humans are mammals, then being human entails being a mammal.

Conditional statements and universal generalizations are two ways of clearly stating an entailment claim. It should come as no surprise, then, that most deductive arguments begin with either a conditional claim or a universal generalization. More often than not, they involve a series of conditional statements or generalizations, each building upon the last. And these statements build to create a well-formed deductive argument in which the premises entail the conclusion.

Evaluating the Content: True Premises

To summarize, a well-formed argument is one with premises that really do support the conclusion—either via mere support or entailment, depending upon whether the argument is inductive or deductive. This alone is not enough to render an argument good. To be a good argument, all of the premises also must be true. Remember: an argument can be well-formed and fail to have all true premises. Form and content are two distinct features of an argument, and they can come apart. In fact, it is entirely possible for a well-formed argument to have only false premises. For instance:

1. All human beings are made of chocolate.
2. All things that are made of chocolate can fly.
3. Therefore, all human beings can fly.

This is a profoundly bad argument. In reality, no human beings are made of chocolate, and—at least in my experience—nothing made of chocolate can fly. Nevertheless, this argument is well-formed; these premises entail this conclusion.[6] For this reason, in order to judge whether an argument is a good argument, we must also evaluate the truth of the premises.

This brings us to a question that I frequently encounter in the classroom. How exactly are you supposed to evaluate the truth of the premises of an argument? In one sense, the answer is straightforward: in the same way you evaluate the truth or falsity of any claim. You draw on what you know—from experience, education, what you have learned on the basis of authority, what you can infer. Premises that seem to correspond to reality should be judged true; those that do not should be judged false. The actual truth or falsity of a premise, like the truth or falsity of any claim, is ultimately determined by reality itself.

While the answer to this question is straightforward, the actual process of evaluating the truth of premises is often not. Students and others who are new to philosophical reading often find it difficult to evaluate the truth of an entailment claim. This is especially true when the claim in question is a conditional statement. In addition, the content of the premises found in philosophical arguments often covers aspects of reality that are difficult or impossible to observe. We can see both of these difficulties in the following argument:

1. If objective moral values exist, then God exists.
2. Objective moral values exist.
3. Therefore, God exists.

This is a simplified statement of the "moral argument" for the existence of God, an argument which we will discuss in detail in chapters 11–14 of this book. The first thing to note about this argument is that it is well-formed. Even the most ardent defenders of atheism will have to concede that this argument is structurally sound, for the premises entail the conclusion.

The truth of the premises, in contrast, will not garner the same level of support and agreement. Instead, we should expect significant disagreement about the truth of both premises. Consider the first premise: "If objective

---

6. If you are still not sure why, try to affirm both premises while denying the conclusion. The result is a contradiction! The impossibility of even *conceiving* of the premises as true while conceiving of the conclusion as false is the hallmark of a well-formed deductive argument.

moral values exist, then God exists." There are three things to note about this premise. First, it does not say that objective moral values exist. Second, it does not say that God exists. Finally, it does say that the existence of objective moral values entails the existence of God. That is all it says. If the existence of objective moral values does entail the existence of God, if it is logically impossible for objective moral values to exist in a world in which God does not exist, then this premise is true. Otherwise, it is false.

The tricky thing about evaluating the truth of a conditional claim is that is easy to become confused about what kinds of scenarios would make it false. Fortunately, there is an easy rule to follow here. If P entails Q, then it is not possible for P to be true while Q is false. If, therefore, it *does* seem possible for P to be true while Q is false, then you have reason to believe that the conditional in question is false. Returning to the argument under discussion, the atheist who wishes to reject the truth of this premise must give some reason to believe that there could be objective moral values in an atheistic world. (As we will see in chapter 13, this is precisely what many atheists aim to show.) The crucial thing to remember is that the truth of a conditional as a whole is largely independent of the truth of its parts. To return to a simpler example, "Today is Tuesday" entails "Tomorrow is Wednesday"—and it does so seven days a week. On a Thursday, both "Today is Tuesday" and "Tomorrow is Wednesday" are false. Nevertheless, it remains true—even on a Thursday—that "Today is Tuesday" entails "Tomorrow is Wednesday." The conditional "If today is Tuesday then tomorrow is Wednesday" is true all week long![7]

In the same way, even if it were true that the existence of objective moral values would entail the existence of God, this would not suffice to show that God exists. After all, this entailment claim could be true even if objective moral values did not exist! For that reason, premise 2 explicitly claims that objective moral values do exist. In the classroom, new students often find this step redundant. It is not redundant, it is essential. From the fact that "Today is Tuesday" entails "Tomorrow is Wednesday," you cannot reasonably infer that tomorrow is Wednesday. You must also know that today is, in fact, Tuesday. For these same reasons, this argument absolutely requires the second premise. Together they yield the conclusion. If it is true that the existence of

---

7. At the risk of being redundant, this entailment is true every day of the week because it remains impossible, every day of the week, for it to be true that today is Tuesday and false that tomorrow is Wednesday.

objective moral values entails the existence of God, and true that objective moral values exist, then it must be true that God exists.

There is an obvious difficulty here. Each of these premises is controversial; each of these premises is difficult, if not impossible, to prove or disprove. How could a person ever set about proving that objective moral values are impossible without God? What could constitute decisive proof that objective moral values exist? Here we find a crucial misunderstanding: the proponent of a good argument must be able to provide reasons to believe that the premises are true; she need not prove their veracity. Neither is it the case that a person must disprove a premise in order to reject it as false. As we learned in chapter 3, truth and provability come apart. Truth is a question of how the world is, whereas provability is a question of what we can know about the world. For that reason, our guiding standard must be reasonability. If it is reasonable to believe that the premises of a well-formed argument are true, then you may reasonably conclude that the argument is a good argument; if you have good reasons for believing one of the premises to be false, then you may reject the argument as false. Truth is the goal, as it ought always to be, but reasonability will often be the best available means of attaining that goal.

For that reason, you could be wrong about the strength or weakness of an argument. Like provability, reasonability is distinct from truth; they are not the same thing. If you are incorrect about the truth of the premises, you will be incorrect about the goodness of the argument. If you are correct about the truth of the premises (and if the argument is well-formed), then you are correct that this is a good argument—whether or not you can prove it. The strength of your evidence for believing the premises to be true becomes, in turn, the strength of your evidence for believing the argument to be a good argument. In all of this, reasonability, not provability, is the standard. The truth of a premise and our ability to be certain of that truth are, as always, two distinct questions.

We should, therefore, expect to disagree about the truth of some premises—even premises containing truths we hold dear. When we do, we would be wise to remember what we learned in chapters 2 and 3: truth is not relative, neither to the individual nor to a culture at large; reasonability is relative, both to the individual and to the culture at large. For that reason, we ought always to treat one another with respect and humility, understanding that reasonable people can disagree. At the same time, we ought to resist calls to dismiss those disagreements or reduce them to mere preferences. When two people disagree about the truth of a premise, they may both be reasonable, but they may not both be right.

Some Common Arguments, Good and Bad

Although any argument that is well formed and has only true premises is a good argument, there are some very common argument forms that are standardly used, and it is helpful to recognize them. Likewise, it is important to be able to distinguish them from their poorly formed lookalikes. In this section I will focus on deductive arguments. As I wrote, the core of any deductive argument is an entailment claim. Often this claim is stated in the form of a conditional, which is itself an expression of entailment: "If P, then Q" means that P entails Q; it means that it is logically impossible for P to be true while Q is false. The two most common deductive argument forms are mere extensions of the truth conditions of this conditional claim.

Consider the following argument form, known by its Latin name *modus ponens* or, in English, "affirming the antecedent":

1. If P, then Q.
2. P.
3. Therefore, Q.

We can plug any sentence we wish into this argument form and the result will always be a well-formed argument. It won't always be a *good* argument, for we may end up with false premises, but the structure of this argument is impeccable. For example, if we let P stand for "Susan teaches at USF" and Q for "Susan has a PhD," we get:

1. If {Susan teaches at USF}, then {Susan has a PhD}.
   $\quad\quad\quad\quad P \quad\quad\quad\quad\quad\quad\quad\quad Q$
2. {Susan teaches at USF}.
   $\quad\quad P$
3. Therefore, {Susan has a PhD}.
   $\quad\quad\quad\quad\quad Q$

This argument, like all arguments that follow this form, is deductively well-formed; these premises entail this conclusion.

To see why, remember that the first premise says the following: "It is not possible for it to be true that Susan teaches at USF without it being true that Susan has a PhD." Now, once again, this entailment claim may not be a true one—in fact, some of those who teach at USF may have a master's degrees, not a doctorate. The crucial thing to see is that this *does not matter*. It does not affect the structure of the argument. Instead, for this argument to be well-formed, it must be the case that the premises cannot all be true while the conclusion is false. If we suppose that the first premise is true, we thereby suppose that Susan's teaching at USF does, in fact, entail her holding of the PhD. If we further assume that the second premise is true and Susan does teach at USF, we are committed to the truth of the conclusion. To deny the conclusion would be to either deny the entailment claim of the first premise or deny the truth of the second premise. It is logically impossible to affirm the truth of both premises while denying the truth of the conclusion. This is logically impossible even if the entailment claim in the first premise is false.

The same is true of the following argument, and for precisely the same reasons:

1. If Susan teaches at USF, then Susan has a PhD.
2. Susan does not have a PhD.
3. Therefore, Susan does not teach at USF.

This argument is known as *modus tollens*, or "denying the consequent." The general form is stated:

1. If P, then Q.
2. Not Q.
3. Therefore, not P.

The strength of this argument structure is less intuitively obvious than its counterpart, but it is no less structurally sound.

To see why, assume once again that the entailment in the first premise is true. In doing so, you have assumed that it is not possible for Susan to teach at USF without holding a PhD. On that assumption, if, as the second premise claims, Susan does not have a PhD, it must follow that she does not teach at USF. Suppose that I am wrong and this argument form is invalid. That is, suppose that it is, in fact, possible to assume the truth of these premises while denying the conclusion. What would this involve? In doing so, you would have to believe all of the following: "It is impossible for Susan to teach at USF without having a PhD, yet Susan teaches at USF without having a PhD." This is a straightforward contradiction. These premises, like all premises that follow this form, entail this conclusion.

We can summarize the core of these argument structures by noting the following: If P entails Q, then the only thing we know absolutely for certain is that P cannot be true while Q is false. Armed with this knowledge, we can deduce two things: from the truth of P we can deduce Q, and from the falsity of Q we can deduce the falsity of P. In both cases, we are merely reaffirming the claim that P cannot be true while Q is false. That is, we are reaffirming the claim that P entails Q.

It is equally important to know what you may *not* deduce from an entailment claim. For instance, entailment is not a symmetrical relation. More accurately, while it is sometimes true that the entailment relation works in both directions, this is not a feature of entailment. It is, instead, an additional claim. "This shape is a square" entails "this shape has four sides," but "this shape has four sides" does not entail "this shape is a square." (It could be a rectangle or some other quadrilateral.) In contrast, "Today is Tuesday" entails "Tomorrow is Wednesday" and "Tomorrow is Wednesday" also entails "Today is Tuesday." In this case, we have *two* entailment relations. In fact, for any P and Q, when P entails Q and Q entails P, we call the resulting claim a "biconditional"—because there are not one but two conditional claims being made. A single entailment claim only ever moves in one direction.

From the fact that P entails Q, we may not assume that Q entails P. Here, at last, we see the reason for this chapter's epigraph. The Mad Hatter, for all his madness, was right: "I say what I mean" is not logically equivalent to "I mean what I say." We could understand "I say what I mean" as the claim "Everything that I say is something that I mean." This, in turn, can be understood as the entailment claim: "If I say it, then I mean it." But this is quite different from the same claim in reverse: "If I mean it, then I say it." (Advocates of so-called radical honesty often do the latter when those around them would prefer the former.) It is a very good thing, in most cases, to mean everything that you say. It is often neither appropriate nor kind to say everything that you mean.

For this reason, arguments of the following form are never good arguments. Under no circumstances are they well-formed, so no amount of true premises can render them good:

1. If P, then Q.
2. Q.
3. Therefore, P.

We can continue our previous example to illustrate the problem here:

1. If Susan teaches at USF, then Susan has a PhD.
2. Susan has a PhD.
3. Therefore, Susan teaches at USF.

Even if it is true that Susan cannot teach at USF without a PhD, it hardly follows that Susan cannot have a PhD unless she teaches at USF! Entailment moves in one direction only. For the same reason, arguments like this one fail, as well:

1. If P, then Q.
2. Not P.
3. Therefore, not Q.

1. If Susan teaches at USF, then Susan has a PhD.
2. Susan does not teach at USF.
3. Therefore, Susan does not have a PhD.

Here, again, we are being asked to infer the fact that Susan does not have a PhD from the fact that she does not teach at USF. This inference is not justified by the entailment in the first premise. This argument is not well-formed.

Not all well-formed deductive arguments begin with a conditional, but all involve entailment claims. For that reason, precisely the same kinds of errors can be made with or without conditionals. Consider again the examples from earlier in the chapter. As I noted, this argument is well-formed:

1. All humans are mammals.
2. Josie is a human.
3. Therefore, Josie is a mammal.

But this one is not:

1. All humans are mammals.
2. Josie is a mammal.
3. Therefore, Josie is a human.

We are now in a position to articulate exactly what the second argument gets wrong. From the fact that being human entails being a mammal, it simply does not follow that being a mammal entails being a human. Entailment is not a symmetrical relation.

So far we have considered only deductive arguments. Inductive arguments do not, of course, involve entailment claims, but they do invoke claims of support. Here is the crucial point for inductive arguments: mere support is no more symmetrical than entailment. Support, like entailment, moves in one direction only.

Conclusion

To summarize the work that we have done in chapters 6–8, reading like a philosopher requires that you read with the end goals of conceptual clarity, reasonability, and truth in mind. This requires slow, deliberate, careful reading. It requires that you ask: What is the main position advanced in this text? What reasons are given in support of that position? Are those reasons good reasons for that position? We can now say that these questions often take the form of argument reconstruction and argument evaluation. When you have charitably reconstructed the central arguments of any text, you will be able to ask: Do those premises really support that conclusion in the way that is intended? If it is an inductive argument, do they support the conclusion? If it is a deductive argument, do they entail the conclusion? And finally, are those premises true? When, and only when, you can answer these questions in the affirmative, you will have found a good argument.

Further Readings for
Part 1

Autobiographical Accounts of Christian Philosophers

Augustine. *Confessions*. Translated and notes by Thomas Williams. Indianapolis: Hackett, 2019.

Clark, K. J. *Philosophers Who Believe: The Spiritual Journeys of 11 Leading Thinkers*. Downers Grove, IL: InterVarsity Press, 1997.

Gutting, G. *Talking God: Philosophers on Belief.* New York: Norton, 2016.

Morris, T. V. *God and the Philosophers: The Reconciliation of Faith and Reason.* Oxford: Oxford University Press, 1994.

Philosophically Grounded Christian Apologetics

Copan, P. *True for You, but Not for Me: Overcoming Objections to Christian Faith.* Grand Rapids: Baker, 2009

———. *Loving Wisdom: A Guide to Philosophy and Christian Faith.* Grand Rapids: Eerdmans, 2020.

Craig, W. L. *On Guard: Defending Your Faith with Reason and Precision.* Colorado Springs: Cook, 2010.

———. *Reasonable Faith: Christian Truth and Apologetics.* Wheaton, IL: Crossway, 2008.

Lewis, C. S. *Mere Christianity.* New York: Macmillan, 1960.

Introductions to Philosophy and Logic

Baggini, J., and P. S. Fosl. *The Philosopher's Toolkit: A Compendium of Philosophical Concepts and Methods.* Malden, MA: Blackwell, 2003.

Copi, I. M., C. Cohen, and K. McMahon. *Introduction to Logic.* New York: Routledge, 2016.

Harrell, M. *What Is the Argument? An Introduction to Philosophical Argument and Analysis.* Cambridge, MA: MIT Press, 2016.

Morris, T. *Philosophy for Dummies*. New York: Wiley, 2011.

Papineau, D. *Philosophical Devices: Proofs, Probabilities, Possibilities, and Sets.* Oxford: Oxford University Press, 2012.

Williamson, T. *Tetralogue: I'm Right, You're Wrong.* Oxford: Oxford University Press, 2015.

Introductions to Christian Academic Philosophy

Bartholomew, C. G., and M. W. Goheen. *Christian Philosophy: A Systematic and Narrative Introduction.* Grand Rapids: Baker, 2013.

Morris, T. V. *Our Idea of God: An Introduction to Philosophical Theology.* Vancouver: Regent College Publishing, 2002.

Murray, M. J. *Reason for the Hope Within.* Grand Rapids: Eerdmans, 1999.

Simmons, J. A. *Christian Philosophy: Conceptions, Continuations, and Challenges.* Oxford: Oxford University Press, 2019.

Stump, E. *The God of the Bible and the God of the Philosophers.* Milwaukee: Marquette University Press, 2016.

Stump, E., and M. J. Murray. *Philosophy of Religion: The Big Questions.* Philosophy: The Big Questions. Malden, MA: Wiley, 1999.

Taylor, C. *A Secular Age.* Cambridge, MA: Belknap, 2007.

Vallier, K., and J. Rasmussen, eds. *A New Theist Response to the New Atheists.* Routledge New Critical Thinking in Religion, Theology and Biblical Studies. New York: Routledge, 2019.

Recommended Readings from Other Disciplines

Alter, R. *The Five Books of Moses: A Translation with Commentary.* New York: Norton, 2008.

Jacobs, A. *Breaking Bread with the Dead: A Reader's Guide to a More Tranquil Mind.* New York: Penguin, 2020.

Jacobs, A. *How to Think: A Survival Guide for a World at Odds.* New York: Currency, 2017.

Noll, M. A. *The Scandal of the Evangelical Mind.* Grand Rapids: Eerdmans, 1994.

Pearcey, N. *Total Truth: Liberating Christianity from Its Cultural Captivity.* Wheaton, IL: Crossway, 2008.

Qureshi, N. *Seeking Allah, Finding Jesus: A Devout Muslim Encounters Christianity.* Grand Rapids: Zondervan, 2016.

Sproul, R. C. *The Consequences of Ideas: Understanding the Concepts That Shaped Our World.* Wheaton, IL: Crossway, 2000.

Also See the Online Resources Available Here

Journal of the Society of Christian Philosophers, https://place.asburyseminary.edu
/faithandphilosophy/

www.believingphilosophy.com

PART 2

Philosophy in Action

———

Suffering, Evil, and the Goodness of God

Epicurus's old questions are yet unanswered. Is he willing to prevent evil, but not able? Then is he impotent. Is he able, but not willing? Then is he malevolent. Is he both able and willing? Whence then is evil?

—*David Hume*[1]

We are all sufferers, or we will be.

—*Timothy Keller*[2]

A rguments about whether Wilbur is a Goldendoodle or whether Susan can teach at USF without a PhD are simplistic, straightforward, and trivial—silly, even. The arguments we will consider in part 2 are not. In this chapter, we will consider one of the most persistent and pervasive arguments against the existence of God: the problem of evil.

What Is the Problem of Evil?

Most people's first encounter with what philosophers call the "problem of evil" does not come in the form of a carefully constructed argument with a neat list of numbered premises and a conclusion. Indeed, if you find that this chapter introduces you to a problem that you had not heretofore considered, count yourself blessed! Broadly speaking, the problem of evil is just the reality of evil in a world created, sustained, and governed by a loving God. If I had to pinpoint my own first encounter with this problem, it would probably be the day that I learned that my beloved cousin had drowned. I loved this

1. D. Hume, *Dialogues Concerning Natural Religion by David Hume, Esq* (London, 1779), 106. Eighteenth Century Collections Online.
2. T. Keller, *Walking with God Through Pain and Suffering* (New York: Penguin, 2015), 7.

boy; we all loved him fiercely. One day he was regaling us with the kinds of hilarious comments that only a precocious three-year-old can make, and the next he was gone. I was fifteen, devout, and shattered. My questions were not particularly intellectual; my thoughts certainly didn't comprise well-formed arguments. It just seemed impossible to me that I should go on living in a world where this sort of thing happened—worse still, where God allowed this sort of thing to happen. I remember thinking, in anguish, that it would be emotionally easier not to believe, easier to accept a meaningless world than to make sense of a world in which a sovereign God let children suffer and die.

In response to the reality of evil and suffering, many find it easier to reject belief in God than to reconcile the ubiquity of suffering with his existence. For some this may be a purely emotional response, similar to my initial impulse, but for others it stems from something more substantive—it arises out of the cognitive tension of attempting to believe both that a loving God is in control and that many terrible things happen. Sam Harris succinctly captured this view while reflecting on the lives lost to Hurricane Katrina:

> But what was God doing while a hurricane laid waste to their city? Surely He heard the prayers of those elderly men and women who fled the rising waters for the safety of their attics, only to be slowly drowned there. These were people of faith. These were good men and women who had prayed throughout their lives. Only the atheist has the courage to admit the obvious: these poor people spent their lives in the company of an imaginary friend.[3]

Terrible things happen to innocent people.[4] Terrible things happen to innocent people who love God. In fact, we could go further—terrible things happen to people while they are serving the God they love.[5] If God is who these

---

3. S. Harris, "There Is No God (and You Know It)," SamHarris.org, October 6, 2005, https://samharris.org/there-is-no-god-and-you-know-it/.

4. I am using the word *innocent* here to mean innocent with respect to the evil suffered, not wholly blameless before God. On most, or all, orthodox conceptions of Christianity, there are no wholly innocent people apart from Christ (and perhaps Mary). The point here is that there is no correlation between degree of guilt and degree of suffering. Instead, many of those who suffer great horrors are also those who strive to live righteous and godly lives. Indeed, as Matthew Estel astutely reminded me, Christ himself exemplifies this reality. Christ *was* wholly innocent, and he suffered mightily under the weight of our sin.

5. In addition to the high-profile cases of martyred missionaries, there are doubtlessly many more cases of ordinary people serving God in ordinary ways and suffering violence or death in the process. My church community lost a vibrant young woman two years ago—Tori Bennett—after

people believe him to be, then he could have prevented those terrible things from happening—and he didn't.

This is the heart of the problem of evil: How can it be that an all-powerful, all-knowing, perfectly good God exists when there is so much suffering? Wouldn't such a God protect us from these kinds of evils? We find one statement of the problem in Hume's *Dialogue Concerning Natural Religion*, where his character Philo poses the question featured in the above epigraph: "Is he willing to prevent evil, but not able? Then is he impotent. Is he able, but not willing? Then is he malevolent. Is he both able and willing? Whence then is evil?"[6] If God exists, then he is omnipotent and omnibenevolent—all-powerful and perfectly good. But wouldn't a perfectly good God want to prevent evil? And wouldn't an all-powerful God succeed in preventing it? If, therefore, we find that the world does contain evil, and no small amount of it, shouldn't we conclude that no such God exists? The problem of evil is also sometimes called the "argument from evil," for it moves from the premise "Evil exists" to the conclusion "God does not exist." Whatever the name, the unifying theme of these arguments is that evil is the evidence given in defense of atheism.

Evil and Suffering

But we must be careful, for the word *evil* has a very broad usage. In fact, there is a sense in which the problem of evil has far more to do with suffering than with evil. When used as an adjective, *evil* typically denotes something immoral or wrong: an evil genius or an evil plan, for instance. As a noun, however, the moral connotation is frequently absent: an earthquake or hurricane may be an instance of natural evil, but it hardly seems right to call it

---

she reached out to the troubled teenaged son of a neighbor. He is awaiting trial for first degree premeditated murder, having (allegedly) assaulted her on her thirty-third birthday. Beyond the awful tragedy of her suffering and death, many of us were also struck by the fact that Tori herself was likely devastated to see this young man choose violence and destruction. What a sad end for both of them. It would be easier to believe that nobody ever died as a result of pursuing the call to be the body of Christ, but stories like these—not to mention the martyrdom of the early disciples and of Christ himself—remind us that it is simply not the case.

For a really powerful depiction of suffering in service to God, I recommend Maria Dora Russell's *The Sparrow* and its sequel *Children of God*. M. D. Russell, *The Sparrow*, The Sparrow Series (New York: Random House, 2008); Russell, *Children of God*, The Sparrow Series (New York: Random House, 2007).

6. Hume, *Dialogues Concerning Natural Religion*, 106.

an immoral event. In fact, the *Cambridge Dictionary* offers two definitions of *evil* in noun form: (1) "Something that is very bad and harmful," and (2) "The condition of being immoral, cruel, or bad, or an act of this type."[7] We can tweak these a bit to get a clearer distinction between the two ways that a person might use the word *evil* to refer to an act or an event:

Evil₁: Something that is bad, harmful, painful, or otherwise unpleasant.

Evil₂: Something that is malicious, cruel, or otherwise immoral.

The kind of evil that undergirds philosophical treatments of the problem of evil tends to be the first variety. The problem of evil is, in large part, the problem of harm, pain, or suffering; it is not primarily the problem of immorality. To be clear, quite a lot of the harm, pain, and suffering in this world is the result of immorality, but it is those results and not their cause that most often show up in arguments for atheism. As Eleonore Stump wrote in her seminal work *Wandering in Darkness: Narrative and the Problem of Suffering*, "Suffering, not evil, seems to me to be the salient thing."[8]

This distinction is more significant than it may initially appear. In the first place, many of those who advance the problem of evil don't actually believe in the reality of Evil₂. Although they certainly believe in the kinds of things we like to call cruelty, they do not believe in the objective reality of good and bad, of morality and immorality. In the second place, theists who do believe in the objective reality of morality often use that belief to advance their own argument in defense of the existence of God. That is, they offer what we might call a theistic argument from evil. In other words, while Evil₁ is invoked as evidence against the existence of God, Evil₂ is cited as evidence of his existence. How can this be?[9]

In answer to this question, we can turn to a discussion from Richard Dawkins's book *River Out of Eden: A Darwinian View of Life*. In it, Dawkins raises the case of a local news story about a school bus from a Catholic school that "crashed for no obvious reason." Everybody on board, mostly children,

---

7. *Cambridge Dictionary*, s.v. "evil (n.)," accessed January 25, 2021, https://dictionary.cambridge.org/us/dictionary/english/evil.

8. E. Stump, *Wandering in Darkness: Narrative and the Problem of Suffering* (Oxford: Clarendon, 2010), 4.

9. We will consider this argument in detail in chapters 12–14.

died. In response to this horrific and inexplicable accident, a local journalist posed the question "How can you believe in a loving, all-powerful God who allows such a tragedy?" That is, the journalist confronted local clergy with the problem of evil. Dawkins shares the following reply, which had been offered by a priest: "The simple answer is that we do not know why there should be a God who lets these awful things happen. But the horror of the crash, to a Christian, confirms the fact that we live in a world of real values: positive and negative. If the universe was just electrons, there would be no problem of evil or suffering."[10] Without denying the horror of the accident, this priest turned the evidential question on its head. Rather than seeing the awful death of these children as evidence against God's existence, he held that the opposite was true: that the objective badness of what had transpired was, in a very real way, evidence of objective values—and with it, evidence of God.

The accident, he believed, was not just unfortunate; it was wrong. It was not how the world ought to be. But in order for this to be the case, there must be some way that the world ought to be. In his own words, if there are such things as "real values," then reality itself must not be comprised of "just electrons." You would never blame a falling rock for landing on a car; neither would you praise the rock for making a nice clear path down the hill. In the same way, a universe that is ultimately nothing more than moving electrons is just not the kind of thing that can truly be called good or bad; it just *is*. If, therefore, these values are objectively real, then there must be a value-giver, God, to ground and explain that reality. There is obviously a lot to unpack here, and we will return to this line of reasoning in chapter 12. There we will consider the relationship between Evil$_2$, objective moral evil, and the existence of God. For now, it is Dawkins's position that must take center stage.

Dawkins, of course, disagrees with the priest's overall response to the accident, but there is a kernel of agreement in the midst of his rebuttal. He writes:

On the contrary, if the universe were just electrons and selfish genes, mean-ingless tragedies like the crashing of this bus are exactly what we should expect, along with equally meaningless good fortune. Such a universe

---

10. R. Dawkins, *River Out of Eden: A Darwinian View of Life*, Science Masters Series (New York: Basic, 1995), 132.

would be neither evil nor good in intention. . . . The universe we observe has precisely the properties we should expect if there is, at bottom, no design, no purpose, no evil and no good, nothing but blind pitiless indifference.[11]

Thus Dawkins agrees that a naturalistic, godless universe would be "neither evil nor good in intention," and that tragedies like the bus accident or an earthquake would be "meaningless" in such a world. Unfortunately for us, Dawkins believes that this is the universe that we are stuck with. Meaning and values may be things that we seek, things that we try to construct, even, but they are not real—not in the sense of being actual parts of the universe in which we live.

What is most striking about this in our present context is that Dawkins makes this point while raising the problem of evil. That is, if we are not careful about conceptual clarity here, we may conclude something like the following: that Dawkins simultaneously invokes evil as evidence against the existence of God while maintaining that evil is nothing more than a useful fiction. Surely this is not what he is saying, nor is it the position of most of the atheists who find the problem of evil compelling. Instead, a charitable reading reveals that the word *evil* must be doing double duty. According to Dawkins, the existence and prevalence of $\underline{Evil}_1$ is evidence against the existence of God—which is, in turn, evidence against the existence of $\underline{Evil}_2$. If Dawkins is correct, then the reality of suffering reveals to us both that there is no God and that there is—at the level of ultimate reality—no good or bad, no right nor wrong, no objective values whatsoever.[12]

This is why it is suffering that seems to be "the salient thing." Dawkins and the priest—and theists and atheists more generally—agree that suffering abounds. Suffering, with or without ultimate meaning, is a pervasive and undeniable part of our universe. The problem of evil is, largely, the problem of suffering. How should we understand suffering? Here, again, I turn to Stump. She writes, "What is bad about suffering, then, is that it undermines or destroys what the sufferer centrally cares about, her own flourishing or the

---

11. Dawkins, *River Out of Eden*, 133.

12. To be clear, Dawkins would not deny that there are things that we collectively have decided to favor and to condemn. Neither would he deny that there are things that bring harm and things that help, and that helping is a better way to contribute to society. The point, rather, is that these values must be constructed or created rather than discovered. They are not real features of the universe.

desires of her heart or both."[13] Suffering goes beyond mere pain, for not all pain is suffering. To illustrate this point, Stump uses the example of a woman who chooses natural childbirth—clearly painful, but often experienced as empowering and meaningful. Similarly, quite a lot of athletic training is painful, but few athletes would suggest that the suffering caused by their regimens serves as evidence against the goodness of God. No, the core of suffering is loss—loss of someone or something that you hold valuable or that you need in order to thrive. Crucially, you need not have actually valued this valuable thing in order for your loss to constitute suffering. As Stump notes, "People can be confused about what constitutes their flourishing."[14] Neither must it be the case that other people value what you lost in order for it to constitute suffering. If the desire of your heart is to be a parent, and you learn that parenthood will not be a possibility for you, then you have suffered—whether or not I think you ought to care about parenthood at all. Whether the loss is temporary or permanent, partial or complete, the loss of something valuable to you is at the core of human suffering. It is, therefore, at the core of the problem of evil.

The Simple Logical Problem of Evil

We come, at last, to the philosophical arguments that fall under the heading "the problem of evil." The hallmark of philosophical reasoning is clarity. General discussions about the horrors of this world are, or should be, spiritually challenging to theistic believers, but they are not particularly useful, philosophically speaking. That suffering is awful is surely true; that it abounds is likewise certain. That those who suffer tend not to deserve suffering any more than the rest of us is true as well. In this chapter, I will assume without argument the truth of each of these claims. That is, I will operate on the assumption that ordinary people sometimes face excruciating suffering. The question we will address here is what these facts tell us about God, not whether they are true. Given that ordinary people face excruciating suffering, what should we conclude about God? Does the existence of evil make God's existence impossible? Or does it merely make it unlikely? Or neither? Can the existence of God be reconciled with the reality of evil? In order to answer

---

13. Stump, *Wandering in Darkness*, 11.
14. Stump, *Wandering in Darkness*, 11.

these questions, we will need to proceed carefully, practicing all that we have learned about conceptual clarity, reasonability, truth, and the skills of rational argument evaluation.

In chapter 7, we learned the difference between inductive and deductive arguments: the former are intended to show that their conclusion is likely to be true, and the latter that their conclusion must be true. The philosophical problem of evil has both inductive and deductive formulations. We will begin with the latter, the logical problem of evil.[15] This version of the argument aims to show that the existence of God and the existence of evil (that is, $\underline{\text{Evil}_1}$) are logically incompatible. To say that they are logically incompatible is to say that it would be contradictory, or logically impossible, to suppose that God exists and evil exists. If the logical problem of evil is correct, then God and evil cannot coexist—on pain of contradiction.

We can succinctly capture the basic structure of the logical problem of evil as follows: The existence of God would entail a world free from evil. Our world is not a world free from evil. Hence, God must not exist. Remember, if you can show that some claim (P) entails another (Q), and you can show that the entailed claim (Q) is false, it follows necessarily that the entailing claim (P) is false as well. (This is the argument structure known as *modus tollens*, or "denying the consequent.") This is just what it means to say that P entails Q: that it is impossible for P to be true while Q is false. For that reason, if it is true that God's existence entails a world without evil and true that our world contains evil, it *must* be true that God does not exist.

But why would anyone suppose that the existence of God entails a world without evil? The answer to this question stems from the standard philosophical conception of God. While religious believers may disagree about the precise nature of God, monotheists of the Abrahamic traditions tend to agree on the basic conception of God as being all-powerful (omnipotent), all-knowing (omniscient), and morally perfect.[16] With this conception of God in mind, consider the following formulation of the logical problem of evil:[17]

---

15. Here, and throughout the remainder of this chapter, it is important that you remember that *evil* will be used to denote the kind of suffering that seems like evil to us but is not necessarily objective moral evil.

16. *Omnibenevolent* is often used to describe God's moral perfection. I have left it off here to maintain consistency with the statement of the argument currently under discussion.

17. This is adapted from the online resource *The Stanford Encyclopedia of Philosophy*. I have chosen to keep the original language as much as possible, but it is of course important to remember that *evil* here refers to suffering, or what we have called Evil$_1$, and not objective moral evil.

1. If God exists, then God is omnipotent, omniscient, and morally perfect.
2. If God is omnipotent, then God has the power to eliminate all evil.
3. If God is omniscient, then God knows when evil exists.
4. If God is morally perfect, then God has the desire to eliminate all evil.
5. Therefore, if God exists, then evil does not exist. (1–4)
6. Evil exists.
7. Therefore, God does not exist. (5, 6)

Premises 1–4 tell us that the God of the Abrahamic traditions would anticipate, desire to prevent, and be able to prevent every evil. Premise 5 concludes on that basis that God's existence would rule out the existence of evil. But the world in which we live contains evil (6). Therefore, the world in which we live must be a world without God (7).

Is this a well-formed argument? Do these premises entail this conclusion? In *God, Freedom, and Evil*, Alvin Plantinga maintains that it is not.[18] As he notes, it is entirely possible for someone to have competing, incompatible desires. In such a case, it may be logically impossible for a being—even a perfect being—to do everything that he wants to do. For that reason, it is not enough merely to say that God has the desire to eliminate evil; he must also lack further, overriding desires which might justify some instances of evil. (We will consider this response in greater detail in chapter 11, when we turn our attention to the free will defense.) Without an additional premise claiming that God does not have any good reasons to permit evil, the conclusion does not follow from these premises.[19]

Further, it is not at all clear that a perfectly good God *would* desire to eliminate evil at all costs. In the words of the philosopher Nelson Pike, "As a general statement, a being who permits (or brings about) an instance of suffering might be perfectly good providing only that there is a morally sufficient reason for his action."[20] Some evils are necessary conditions for a greater good. Flu shots are a trivial example; the necessity of hardship for the

18. A. Plantinga, *God, Freedom, and Evil* (Grand Rapids: Eerdmans, 1977), 18–21.
19. I am very thankful to Michael Rea for his helpful comments here.
20. M. M. Adams, *Horrendous Evils and the Goodness of God*, Cornell Studies in the Philosophy of Religion (Ithaca, NY: Cornell University Press, 2000), 9–10.

virtue of perseverance is a more interesting one. Finally, as we will see in chapter 11, there seem to be substantial goods that could only be had by creatures with morally significant freedom. With such freedom inevitably comes the possibility of suffering. Why then should we believe that a morally perfect being would desire to prevent all evils? Instead, it seems that a morally perfect being could allow for some evil—as long as he did so for some morally sufficient reasons.

The Logical Problem of Gratuitous Evil

The simple version of the logical problem of evil is almost universally rejected by academic philosophers of religion. It still rears its head on new atheist websites and online forums, but I know of no academic philosophers who will defend it today. (Peter van Inwagen wrote of the claim that God and evil are logically incompatible, "So far as I am able to tell, this thesis is no longer defended." And that was thirty years ago!)[21] The simple logical problem of evil is just not much of a problem for theism. At the same time, a more pressing problem of evil has grown out of this rejection—one that is not so easily dismissed. In 1979, William Rowe introduced his now-canonical example of the evidential argument from evil. (Precisely 100 years prior, Fyodor Dostoevsky did the same in his powerful novel *The Brothers Karamazov*.[22]) Instead of focusing on the abstract concepts of God and evil, evidential arguments take as their starting point concrete instances of actual suffering—evidence of evil that seems in some important sense to be gratuitous. The evidential argument from evil is typically construed as an inductive argument, but it can also take a deductive form.[23] We will begin with this deductive formulation.

In "The Problem of Evil and Some Varieties of Atheism," Rowe asks the reader to consider the following scenario: "Suppose in some distant forest lightning strikes a dead tree, resulting in a forest fire. In the fire a fawn is trapped, horribly burned, and lies in terrible agony for several days before

21. D. Howard-Snyder, ed., *The Evidential Argument from Evil*, Indiana Series in the Philosophy of Religion (Indianapolis, IN: Indiana University Press, 1996), 151.

22. This novel (one of my favorites) is well worth a read in its entirety, but you can also read the chapters "Rebellion" and "The Grand Inquisitor" as standalone texts. Fyodor Dostoevsky, *The Brothers Karamazov* (San Francisco: North Point, 1990).

23. For example, Adams, *Horrendous Evils and the Goodness of God*.

death relieves its suffering. So far as we can see, the fawn's intense suffering is pointless."[24] Rowe further demonstrates the staggering reality of evil and suffering in subsequent discussions of this argument by pointing to "the actual case of a 5-year old girl who was raped, severely beaten over most of her body and strangled by her mother's boyfriend."[25] These two cases, though vastly different in the degree of evil and suffering they evince, share the following two features in common: the suffering in question is extreme, and the victims of suffering blameless. If the shared commitments of Christianity, Islam, and Judaism are true, then they also to share a third feature: God could have prevented the suffering of the five-year-old girl and the trapped fawn, and he didn't. Finally, both examples are such that it is very difficult, if not impossible, to conceive of some greater good that might justify God's permitting these horrors to occur. In the case of the fawn, a greater good seems unlikely given the apparent irrelevance of the fawn's death to the rest of the world; in the case of the child, the sheer magnitude of the horror seems to outweigh any potential justificatory good.

With this evidence in hand, Rowe offers the following argument:

1. There exist instances of intense suffering which an omnipotent, omniscient being could have prevented without thereby losing some greater good or permitting some evil equally bad or worse.

2. An omniscient, wholly good being would prevent the occurrence of any intense suffering it could, unless it could not do so without thereby losing some greater good or permitting some evil equally bad or worse.

3. Therefore, there does not exist an omnipotent, omniscient, wholly good being.

As written, this early formulation of the evidential problem is deductive. We can call it the "logical problem of gratuitous evil," for this argument claims that the existence of God is logically incompatible with the existence of gratuitous evil, where gratuitous evil is the kind of evil characterized in Rowe's first premise. Furthermore, this deductive argument is well-formed; there

---

24. E. Stump and M. J. Murray, eds., *Philosophy of Religion: The Big Questions*, Philosophy: The Big Questions (Malden, MA: Blackwell, 1999), 159.
25. W. Rowe, "Ruminations about Evil," *Philosophical Perspectives* 5 (1991): 69–88.

is no way to affirm the truth of the premises while denying the truth of the conclusion without collapsing into contradiction.[26]

What are the theist's choices here? She can reject the first premise and deny the existence of gratuitous evil, or she can reject the second premise and deny that God would prevent all instances of gratuitous evil. Neither of these options is as straightforward or uncontroversial as the theist's reply to the basic logical problem of evil. The deductive evidential problem of evil is a formidable challenge to theism. In chapters 10 and 11, we will consider a few ways that Christian philosophers have risen to meet this challenge.[27]

The Evidential Argument from Evil

Unlike Rowe's argument, most evidential arguments rely on inductive reasoning.[28] That is, they don't claim that instances of gratuitous evil would make

---

26. If you find the structure of the argument above unclear, the following simplification may help. In essence, Rowe's argument claims:

1. Gratuitous evil exists.
2. If God exists, gratuitous evil does not exist.
3. Therefore, God does not exist.

The central claim of the argument is, once again, an entailment claim: the existence of God entails a world without gratuitous evil (2). But gratuitous evil exists (1). So God must not exist (3). This is "denying the consequent" again, and it does not matter at all that the order of the premises is reversed.

27. I feel compelled to explain my choice of terminology here. Most of you can ignore this note, but readers who go on to read further in philosophy of religion may find it helpful. I have called this argument both an "evidential argument from evil" and a "logical problem of gratuitous evil." I have done so for the following reason: this formulation of Rowe's argument bridges two distinct ways of invoking the existence of evil in an atheistic argument. On the one hand, some arguments maintain that the existence of God is logically impossible given the reality of evil. On the other hand, some arguments claim only that the available evidence supports atheism over theism, that the existence of God is highly *improbable*. Arguments of the first sort tend to be deductive, logical arguments; arguments of the second sort tend to be *inductive, evidential* arguments. This first statement of Rowe's argument spans both, for it is deductive but it appeals to concrete instances of profound suffering as the evidence upon which it rests. Because even Rowe ultimately advances an inductive evidential argument, I have chosen to call this by another name—the logical problem of gratuitous evil.

28. Rowe often describes his own argument as inductive, though it is clearly written in a deductive form. Based upon later versions of his argument, I believe he means the following: we may inductively infer that some awful horrors are gratuitous. If they are gratuitous, we may deductively conclude that God does not exist. (See, for instance, W. L. Rowe, "The Evidential Argument from Evil: A Second Look," in Howard-Snyder, *The Evidential Argument from Evil*, 262–85.) Because he holds the existence of God to be logically incompatible with the existence of gratuitous evil, I think it best to understand his argument deductively.

the existence of God impossible, but they argue that it makes God unlikely. These arguments take something like the following form:[29]

1. There are instances of intense suffering that seem to us to be gratuitous.
2. If God exists, then there are no instances of actually gratuitous suffering.
3. Therefore, either God does not exist or none of these instances of suffering is gratuitous—each is justified by some (hidden) greater good.
4. It is *more likely* that God does not exist than it is that each of these instances of intense suffering is justified by some (hidden) greater good.
5. Therefore, atheism is more likely to be true than theism.

Arguments like this one begin with the uncontroversial claim that some suffering seems to serve no purpose whatsoever (1). Rowe's cases of the fawn and the murdered child are often cited. It is important to note that this premise does not assume that such suffering is gratuitous, only that it seems gratuitous to us. A brief survey of the daily news supports this premise, for cases like that of the murdered five-year-old girl are devastatingly common.

The next step too is relatively uncontroversial—that an omnipotent, omniscient, perfectly good God would not allow needless suffering to occur (2). Again, it is important to note that this premise does not make the mistake of the simple logical argument, claiming that a morally perfect God would not allow any suffering. Instead, it claims only that God would not allow suffering unless it served some morally justificatory purpose—that God would prevent gratuitous suffering. Finally, the argument presents a choice: either God is operating for reasons beyond our ken, and every one of these apparently gratuitous instances of suffering can be justified, or God does not

29. Unfortunately, quite a lot of probabilistic (inductive) arguments from evil invoke mathematical and logical terminology, placeholders, and abbreviations that nonacademic philosophers may find impenetrable. The more they emphasize the probabilistic aspect of their reasoning, the greater their reliance on such terminology. For that reason, I have chosen to write my simplified own characterization here. Those with an interest in probability theory can see, for example, P. Draper, "Pain and Pleasure: An Evidential Problem for Theists," in Howard-Snyder, *The Evidential Argument from Evil*, 12–29.

exist after all (3). The argument concludes by claiming the latter to be more probable than the former (4), and so atheism more likely than theism (5).

Christian philosopher Peter van Inwagen judges arguments like this one to be "the most powerful version of the 'evidential argument from evil.'" He goes on to characterize such arguments as saying: "There is a serious hypothesis *h* that is inconsistent with theism and on which the amounts and kinds of suffering that the world contains are far more easily explained than they are on the hypothesis of theism. This fact constitutes a prima facie case for preferring *h* to theism."[30] This hypothesis (*h*) is atheism. So understood, the inductive evidential argument from evil asks us to consider the following: In light of all of the suffering in the world, is it more likely that God exists and is acting for reasons beyond our ken or that God does not exist? The atheist advancing the argument concludes, of course, that the latter is more likely than the former.

Taking Suffering Seriously

We have, then, three versions of the problem of evil. The simple logical problem of evil tells us that God and evil (or God and suffering) cannot coexist. The logical problem of gratuitous evil does not go that far, but it does claim that unjustified evil or suffering would rule out the existence of God. Finally, the inductive evidential problem makes no attempt at showing the impossibility of God's existence in light of evil or suffering. Instead, it invokes the occurrence of certain horrific cases of suffering as evidence against the likelihood of God's existence. How should a Christian respond to these arguments? In chapters 10 and 11 we finally will turn our attention to that question and consider a variety of theistic responses to the problem of evil.

At this juncture, some of you may be wondering why I have waited so long to give any substantial defense of theism in the face of this barrage of atheistic arguments. Wouldn't it be better to disarm each argument as it arises? Why read argument after argument for atheism without some sort of theistic respite in between? Here is my answer: the evil and suffering so prevalent in this world are serious, weighty matters. As a committed, reflective Christian philosopher, I believe that these emotionally powerful arguments

---

30. P. van Inwagen, "The Problem of Evil, the Problem of Air, and the Problem of Silence," in *The Problem of Evil: Selected Readings*, ed. M. L. Peterson, 2nd ed. (Notre Dame, IN: University of Notre Dame Press, 2016).

can ultimately be met—resolved even—with reasonable, rational responses. I believe that the goodness of God can be reconciled with the state of our world. What I do not believe, and what I wish to avoid inadvertently conveying to my readers, is that these problems can be easily dismissed. Marilyn McCord Adams expresses a similar concern when she writes, "Our philosophical propensity for generic solutions—our search for a single explanation that would cover all evils at once—has permitted us to ignore the worst evils in particular (what I shall call horrendous evils) and so to avoid confronting the problems they pose."[31] Adams responds to this worry by formulating a theistic response to the problem posed by horrendous evils in particular; I have responded to this worry by resisting the urge to rebut each statement of the problem of evil the moment it arises. It is better, as well as beneficial, to feel the full weight of the problem for a while.

It is a fact of human nature that we, every one of us, are at least somewhat inclined to believe that the worst can't really happen to us. Many are forcefully disavowed of this false belief early on, but for others it persists into adulthood. This belief is neither biblical nor rational. Looking back at the second epigraph, Keller was right to note, "We are all sufferers, or we will be."[32] The Bible tells us that the very first human beings, living in community with God himself, suffered the tremendous loss of the garden of Eden and all that it entailed. Their children, firsthand witnesses of the damage incurred by sin, suffered the fates of the murderer and the murdered. Lest we believe that the God of the New Testament promises something different, Christ's disciples and early followers were martyred in great numbers; Christ himself, as we all know, suffered immensely, even unto death. Christ's instructions to us are to take up our crosses and to lay down our lives to follow him; at no point does he say, "Grab your beach chair and prepare for earthly comfort!"

Martyrdom is not all. The beloved children of faithful Christian parents die of cancer, automobile accidents, stray bullets, overdoses, suicides, homicides. Devout Christians lose their jobs, their livelihoods, their marriages, their health, and their lives. Even more troubling, some people—many of them children—suffer physical, emotional, and sexual abuse at the hands of

---

31. Adams, *Horrendous Evils and the Goodness of God*, 3. I was alerted to this quotation in J. G. Hernandez, *Early Modern Women and the Problem of Evil: Atrocity and Theodicy* (New York: Routledge, 2016), 5.

32. Keller, *Walking with God Through Pain and Suffering*, 7.

their religious leaders.[33] It is too easy to believe that these things happen to other people and to put them out of your mind accordingly. Doing so is dangerous. It is dangerous because it involves two falsehoods: one about yourself and one about others. In the first place, this belief falsely tells you that your life as you know it is basically secure and protected from serious threat. In the second place, this belief falsely tells you that the people who have suffered these massive harms are, in some sense, not like you. Sometimes this latter belief is overt—like the prosperity theology advocate who concludes that the cancer victim must not have had enough faith to be healed. More often it is far subtler but no less insidious.

When we allow ourselves to persist in the belief that serious harms could not come to us or our loved ones, we open the door to two grave dangers: first, that our own faith will collapse the moment we learn that we are not so immune, and second, that we will fail to be sufficiently gracious, compassionate, and supportive to those around us who suffer these losses. Scripture tells us both that God is good and that we should expect suffering. We would do well to listen to this difficult message. The sooner we come to see this reality, the more capable we are able to feel the weight of the problem of evil. Then and only then will we be equipped to address the problem.

This is not to say that you ought to wait until you are actually suffering to contemplate the problem of evil. On the contrary, work it out long before you find yourself in the grips of despair and doubt. This is the delicate balance with which the theist is tasked: the problem of evil is not only a conceptual problem but also a spiritual challenge. Minimize the latter and your response to the former is likely to be cheap and inadequate. Ignore the former until you are faced with the latter and you may find yourself incapable of addressing the problem at all. My goal in these chapters is to tackle the conceptual problem while remaining mindful of the reality of the spiritual challenge.

Conclusion

Evil and suffering *hurt*, and they abound. The crucial question for theism, though, is what they tell us about God. The various formulations of the

---

33. Michelle Panchuk has written some helpful and thoughtful material on the unique damage done by religious trauma. For example: M. Panchuk, "The Shattered Spiritual Self: A Philosophical Exploration of Religious Trauma," *Res Philosophica* 95, no. 3 (2018): 505–30.

problem of evil introduced in this chapter tell us that the evil and the suffering of this world make God's existence at best unlikely and at worst impossible. The theistic responses in chapters 10 and 11 reject these arguments. They do so by showing how a loving God could create a world with so much suffering and evil. I encourage you to read these responses not as dismissals of the horrors of this world and not as accounts of why other people suffer but as theologically and philosophically rich methods of reconciling the fact that we will suffer with the sovereignty and goodness of our God.

In "The Problem of Evil," Eleonore Stump cautions: "Any attempt to solve the problem of evil must try to provide some understanding of the suffering of children, but it must not lessen our pain over that suffering if it is not to become something monstrous and inhumane."[34] Christian philosophers are tasked with reconciling the painful reality of evil with the goodness of God. If in doing so we mistake these rational reconciliations with something like a simple panacea for the sufferer, we will do great harm to ourselves and to others.

---

34. Stump, "The Problem of Evil," in Stump and Murray, *Philosophy of Religion*, 234.

Skeptical Theism

10

"For My thoughts are not your thoughts,
  Nor are your ways My ways," declares the LORD.
"For as the heavens are higher than the earth,
  So are My ways higher than your ways
  And My thoughts than your thoughts."

—*Isaiah 55:8–9*

When I was in graduate school, I took a class called the Problem of Horrendous Evils. Every time we talked, my father would jokingly ask me, "So how is the problem of horrendous evils coming along? Any progress?" The joke, of course, is that there's not much you can do about horrendous evils—not in a classroom at least. The evil, suffering, and harm caused by atrocities can't be argued away. Reconciling the goodness of God with the reality of these horrors is no simple task. Still, there is a difference between the felt awfulness of evil, on the one hand, and what that evil ought to tell us about God, on the other. Christian philosophy may not be able to do much about the former, but it has a great deal to say about the latter. (I think it has something to say about the former too.)

In *Horrendous Evils and the Goodness of God*, Christian philosopher Marilyn McCord Adams characterizes the ways theistic philosophers have responded to the problem of evil as falling under three broad categories: total refutations, defenses, and theodicies:

> *Total refutations* boldly deny that evils are even prima facie evidence against God's existence because God's ways are so much higher than ours that we would not expect to be aware of Divine reasons for their permission if there were any. *Defenses* trot out armies of possible reasons why

God might permit such evils, contending that even if we don't know the actual reasons, the greater the number of apparently available reasons, the less obviously pointless are the evils in question. *Theodicies* suggest actual reasons, whether on grounds of revelation or of common sense.[1]

In the present chapter, we will consider an approach best described as a total refutation. That said, these categories overlap. Many of the responses we will consider fall somewhere between two or more of the categories. For instance, the free will defense, featured in chapter 11, is presented as a mere defense by some and a theodicy by others. And skeptical theism, as you will see, is a total refutation, but in practice it is often adopted alongside of a theodicy or defense. It is perfectly reasonable to offer something like the following response: "I don't think evil poses a conceptual problem for the existence of God, but if I am wrong, here is another possible way of making sense of it." Nothing prevents a theist from advancing a response that includes some aspect of more than one of these categories.

Nevertheless, the categories themselves remain useful as the ends of a spectrum upon which we can locate the ways theists, Christians in particular, respond to the problem of evil. On one end of the spectrum, total refutations claim that the problem of evil offers no theoretical challenge whatsoever to rational belief in theism. (This is not to say that it poses no spiritual challenge.) On the other end of the spectrum, theodicies grant the rational challenge but take up the call to find the reasons why God permits the evil that we see. This chapter will be devoted to a position that more closely resembles the first category, total refutation.

Evaluating the Problem of Evil

As we learned in chapter 7, there are two questions to ask when evaluating any argument: (1) Is the argument well-formed? (2) Are the premises true? So it is with the problem of evil in all its forms. You cannot respond to the problem of evil by rejecting the conclusion alone. You cannot respond to the problem of evil by accepting the truth of the premises and then denying without explanation

---

1. M. M. Adams, *Horrendous Evils and the Goodness of God*, Cornell Studies in the Philosophy of Religion (Ithaca, NY: Cornell University Press, 2000), 15.

that those premises support the conclusion. Instead, any theist who wishes to defend theism from the problem of evil must either dispute the truth of a premise or show why the argument is not well-formed; there is no other option. Furthermore, plenty of versions of the problem of evil are well-formed. Should the theist find some poorly formed version of the argument and reject it on that basis, she will have done very little to defend theism from the actual problem of evil. There are surely some very bad versions of the argument out there. Choosing to focus on these obviously weak constructions rather than face the more challenging ones head-on may give the appearance of defending theism, but it will lack substance and leave the real argument untouched.

The only substantive way of responding to the problem of evil is by disputing the truth of one of its premises. As we saw in chapter 9, there are several versions of the problem of evil. The two most challenging versions, however, are the deductive and inductive arguments from gratuitous evil, both of which are evidential arguments. We can characterize the unifying features of the evidential argument for atheism as containing the following two premises:

Theological Premise: God, if he exists, would (or would probably) prevent gratuitous suffering.

Factual Premise: Some actual instances of suffering are (or seem to be) gratuitous.[2]

The parenthetical notations indicate the difference between the inductive and deductive versions of these premises, but the core claims are the same. It seems as if God would prevent gratuitous suffering if he existed, and it seems as if our world contains gratuitous suffering. The tension that arises for theism out of these two claims undergirds both the deductive and inductive versions of the evidential argument from evil.

For that reason, theistic responses to the evidential argument from evil must take as their starting point the rejection of either the theological or the factual premise.[3] Either it is false that God would prevent gratuitous suffering, or it is false that there are instances of gratuitous suffering. Failing that, the

---

2. Adapted from N. Trakakis, "The Evidential Problem of Evil," in *Internet Encyclopedia of Philosophy*, https://iep.utm.edu/evil-evi/.

3. One could reject both, but that would be an odd choice. If it is not true that God would prevent gratuitous evil, then it is odd to maintain that no evil is gratuitous.

atheistic argument succeeds. To suppose otherwise would be contradictory, for it would mean supposing: "God exists, and God would prevent gratuitous suffering if he existed, and there is gratuitous suffering." By way of analogy, consider the following dialogue:

Ezra: I hate lazy dog owners who let their dogs jump all over people. It's the responsibility of a dog owner to train his dog, no matter how much work it involves.

Ellie: Do you see your dog right now?

Ezra: Yes, why?

Ellie: He's jumping on me. Right now. As we speak.

Ezra: I know.

Ellie: And you're not stopping him.

Ezra: What's your point?

Ellie: You are *telling* me that you would never allow your dog to jump on anyone, and you are doing so *while allowing your dog* to jump on someone!

Ezra: Again, what's the problem?

This absurd behavior is just exactly what the theist would be doing should she choose to accept both the theological and the factual premise without thereby granting that God does not exist. It simply cannot be the case that God exists, that God would prevent all gratuitous suffering if he existed, and that gratuitous suffering exists. To be consistent, the theist must deny at least one of these premises.

Skeptical Theism: A Total Refutation

As we read above, Adams characterizes total refutations as responses that "boldly deny that evils are even prima facie evidence against God's existence because God's ways are so much higher than ours that we would not expect to be aware of Divine reasons for their permission if there were any."[4]

At first glance, this response seems unreasonably dismissive—callous, even. Indeed, new atheist Sam Harris glibly captures this response when he

---

4. Adams, *Horrendous Evils and the Goodness of God*, 15.

writes: "Pious readers will now execute the following pirouette: *God cannot be judged by merely human standards of morality*. But, of course, human standards of morality are precisely what the faithful use to establish God's goodness in the first place."[5] According to Harris, Christians who invoke this response to the problem of evil want to have it both ways: they want to appeal to ordinary morality in order to ascribe goodness to God, but then they plead ignorance when asked to explain how that goodness can be reconciled with the evil of this world. If total refutations are such a paltry response to the problem of evil, then why are they even worth mentioning here?

The answer is that they are not, on reflection, as glib as Harris would have us believe. Instead, most recent versions of this response to suffering are to be found in a view known as *skeptical theism*. Skeptical theism is not skepticism about the existence of God—that is, it is not skepticism about theism. Instead, it is theism, commonly Christian theism, combined with a degree of skepticism about what we can know about God. Michael Bergmann characterizes skeptical theists as affirming something like the following theses:[6]

> ST1: We have no good reason for thinking that the possible goods we know of are representative of the possible goods there are.
>
> ST2: We have no good reason for thinking that the possible evils we know of are representative of the possible evils there are.
>
> ST3: We have no good reason for thinking that the entailment relations we know of between possible goods and the permission of possible evils are representative of the entailment relations there are between possible goods and the permission of possible evils.

All three theses begin with the phrase "We have no good reason for thinking that." Note that this is not the same as saying, "We have good reason for thinking that it is not the case that." These theses claim that we have a lack of evidence about some suppositions, not that we have evidence against them. Let's take each of these theses in turn.

---

5. S. Harris, "There Is No God (and You Know It)," SamHarris.org, October 6, 2005, https://samharris.org/there-is-no-god-and-you-know-it/.

6. Michael Bergmann denies that he is offering a definition of skeptical theism, instead specifying that these are just some of the theses which skeptical theists tend to affirm. M. Bergmann, "Skeptical Theism and Rowe's New Argument," *Noûs* 35, no. 2 (June 2001), 278–96.

First, ST1 says that we lack evidence that the possible goods of which we know are all of the possible goods that there are. What does this mean? Here and throughout this chapter, the parent-child relationship will be a helpful analogy. A toddler is familiar with a fairly narrow range of goods: bodily pleasure, entertainment, and the pleasure of emotional closeness. That is, a toddler sees good food, fun toys, and parental snuggles as being, roughly, all that is good in life. Ask a toddler to suffer hardship in order to develop perseverance, and you will likely get ignored or perhaps kicked. Yet we know that perseverance is a good; "grit" is the hot new predictor of human flourishing.[7] Parents encourage their children to join a sports team, take up a musical instrument, or challenge themselves academically because the work required, difficult though it will be, pays off in the end. To be clear, the payoff goes beyond the specific skill developed and the relevant tangible rewards. It is not merely that practice makes for a better athlete, better scholar, or better musician. Neither is it merely that practice leads to scholarships, career opportunities, and financial gain. Rather, all three of these diverse endeavors also cultivate the shared good of perseverance. Perseverance is itself a good. The hard part, as most parents know, is that they often want to encourage their children to pursue this good long before the children view it as a good at all.

Thus, it is conceivable that some population is unaware of a good that another population takes to be indisputable. If this is the case for human beings at varying developmental stages—and let's be honest, teenagers and adults, young adults and older adults, often persist in holding different sets of goods as goods—then how much more should we expect such divergence between human creatures and their divine creator? This is the basic line of reasoning which supports ST1. Supposing God to be omnipotent, omniscient, and perfectly good, and supposing ourselves to be none of those things, we have no reason to believe that the goods we know of are all of the goods that there are.

For precisely the same reasons, we have no reason for believing that the evils we know of are all of the evils that there are (ST2). To return to our analogy, toddlers steal. They also hit. In fact, they often hit in order to steal! Worse yet, when confronted with the wrongness of their behavior, these

---

7. See, for instance, A. Duckworth, *Grit: The Power of Passion and Perseverance* (New York: Scribner, 2018).

children often fail to see it as wrong at all. Instead, they seem to think something like: "He had the toy I wanted. Hitting him and grabbing the toy fixed that situation, so hitting him and grabbing the toy was a great thing to do!" At this point, parents might respond by saying, "How would you feel if he hit you and took your toy?" In my own experience, this does not work as intended with the under-four crowd. Instead, they seem to think that you have changed the subject. "Of course it would be terrible if he hit me and took my toy. I want that toy, and I hate being hit! But we aren't talking about that. He had the toy I wanted, so I hit him in order to get it." Very young children are often pretty bad at empathy. They don't always see the evil done against another as an evil at all, especially if the act of evil results in a benefit to themselves.

Generally speaking, some people fail to see certain evils as evils. In the case of small children we can hardly blame them, for they are genuinely unable to conceptualize evils at this level of abstraction, but this epistemic failure does not only apply to small children. In 2013, a wealthy teenaged boy (sixteen years old, very nearly a man) flouted the law by driving on a restricted license while under the influence of alcohol and illegal drugs. Although four people died as the direct result of his disregard for the law, he was sentenced to rehabilitation and probation rather than prison. His case received a great deal of national attention due in large part to his proffered defense of *affluenza*: "a psychological malaise supposedly affecting wealthy young people, symptoms of which include a lack of motivation, feelings of guilt, and a sense of isolation."[8]

To be clear, just about every adult person recognizes dangerously negligent driving as an evil. I'm sure even Ethan Couch would have granted, prior to getting into that car that night, that it would be bad if he ended up killing four people. What he likely would not have granted, however, was the way in which his affluent, permissive upbringing had harmed him. A person with limitless material goods and very few boundaries will not necessarily see these features of their life as an evil or a potential source of evil. But others will, and

---

8. This definition comes from the website Dictionary.com. *Merriam-Webster* goes further, defining *affluenza* as "the unhealthy and unwelcome psychological and social effects of affluence regarded especially as a widespread societal problem: such as (a) feelings of guilt, lack of motivation, and social isolation experienced by wealthy people . . . [and] (b) extreme materialism and consumerism associated with the pursuit of wealth and success and resulting in a life of chronic dissatisfaction, debt, overwork, stress, and impaired relationships." *Merriam-Webster*, s.v. "affluenza," January 25, 2021, https://www.merriam-webster.com/dictionary/affluenza.

they may be correct. If it is true that a permissive and affluent life is bad for a person, then it is true that many people do not see that the life that they have or the life to which they aspire is bad for them. Further, one need not believe that affluenza is real in order to believe ST2; it is enough simply to believe that we don't know the full range of evils. It might be that some of what we view as good is, in fact, bad; it might be that there are potential evils so great we haven't even managed to conceive of them.

ST1 and ST2 suppose that our moral knowledge and moral imagination have limits. ST3 goes a step further, supposing that we do not know all of the ways goods and evils are related to one another. Again, it is not transparently obvious that wealth should often lead to vices and hardship to virtues, but maturity seems to show that it often does. We know of many goods and many evils. Even if we assume that our ability to parse these goods and evils is perfect, it would not follow that our list of goods and evils is exhaustive. Neither would it follow that we have perfect comprehension of the ways that good can lead to suffering and suffering to good. We might know only a small subset. When you add to this the Christian claim that human beings are limited, fallen creatures whereas God is an infinite and perfect Creator, the skeptical theist sees eminent plausibility in the claim that our moral imagination would fall short of capturing the fullness of the true moral landscape.

The Factual Premise: Noseeum Inferences

Skeptical theism provides the conceptual and theological resources to reject the factual premise of the problem of evil. Consider the argument in its deductive form, the logical problem of gratuitous evil:

1. There exist instances of intense suffering which an omnipotent, omniscient being could have prevented without thereby losing some greater good or permitting some evil equally bad or worse.
2. An omniscient, wholly good being would prevent the occurrence of any intense suffering it could, unless it could not do so without thereby losing some greater good or permitting some evil equally bad or worse.
3. Therefore, there does not exist an omnipotent, omniscient, wholly good being.

In this first response, skeptical theism says that we have no good reason for supposing premise 1 to be true. Yes, there are cases of profound suffering which seem to us not to serve any greater purpose. If skeptical theism is correct, however, then it may be that the justification for these horrors simply eludes us. Because we have no reason to believe that the goods and evils we know of are representative of the moral landscape in its entirety, we have no grounds for inferring that there are no justifications for these awful cases; these horrors seem unjustified, but that doesn't mean that they are actually unjustified. In short, we just don't have any good reason to trust our moral intuitions here.

A small child will see no good reason whatsoever for getting a vaccine; the good of immunity vastly exceeds her limited conceptual grasp on goods. A college student embracing newfound pleasures at the cost of academic success will see no good in being asked by her parents to fund her own education. The good of responsibility may not, in the moment, seem like a good at all when offered at the cost of other hedonistic pleasures. If this is so among our own species, how much more likely is it between God, should he exist, and his creation? For these reasons, while it is doubtlessly true that some evils seem to defy moral justification, it simply does not follow that they do defy it. It remains possible that these evils seem gratuitous without actually being gratuitous.

One prominent articulation of this response to Rowe's argument comes from Stephen Wykstra's "Condition of Reasonable Epistemic Access," or "CORNEA." Wykstra summarizes the basic claims of CORNEA as follows: "In brief, CORNEA says that we can argue from 'we see no X' to 'there is no X' only when X has 'reasonable foreseeability'—that is, is the sort of thing which, if it exists, we *can reasonably expect* to see in the situation."[9] In violating CORNEA, Wykstra says that a person fallaciously commits a "noseeum inference," that is, "I don't see it, so it must not exist!"[10] On CORNEA, a person is only entitled to make such an inference if she has good reason to believe she would have seen the thing in question. Remember, *epistemic*

---

9. Stephen Wykstra, "Rowe's Noseeum Arguments from Evil," in *The Evidential Argument from Evil*, ed. D. Howard-Snyder, Indiana Series in the Philosophy of Religion (Indianapolis, IN: Indiana University Press, 1996), 126.

10. Named after the vicious tiny bugs. If you have never encountered noseeums, count yourself fortunate!

means "pertaining to knowledge," so *epistemic access* means "access suitable for knowledge or access to reliable evidence."

Once again, an illustration will be helpful here. Suppose that I told you that my front yard was home to a three-hundred-year-old oak tree. Now suppose that you wanted to see this epic tree, so you drove to my address. Upon arriving, you found no such tree. Not only were there no likely candidates for a tree of such an impressive age, but there were no oaks at all. You would be justified in concluding that there was no three-hundred-year-old oak tree in my front yard. Of course, this assumes that you actually knew my address, and that my yard was small enough to be visible from the street. In such a case, your epistemic access to the relevant facts would be quite good, and your noseeum inference justified. You would be right to conclude that no such oak tree existed in my yard. Now suppose, instead, that I lived on a two-hundred-acre farm. Further, suppose that I planted dense pine trees all along the border where my farm hit public roads. Even if you knew my address, it would be entirely *unreasonable* in this case to conclude "There is no three-hundred-year-old oak tree in your yard" from "I looked from the street and did not see a three-hundred-year-old oak tree in your yard." In these circumstances, your epistemic access to any potential oaks in my yard would be extremely limited.[11]

If the skeptical theists are correct, then our ability to judge evils as gratuitous is more like the last case than the first. From the fact that we can't see any morally justificatory reasons for certain instances of suffering, it does not follow that there are no such reasons. Wykstra characterizes our epistemic situation as follows: "The disparity between God's vision and ours . . . is comparable to the gap between the vision of a parent and her one-month-old infant. This gives reason to think that our discerning most of God's purposes is about as likely as the infant's discerning most of the parent's purposes."[12] On Wykstra's account, our epistemic access to the full range of goods and evils which God would take into account is very poor indeed. We have, therefore, no reason at all to believe that an inference from "I can't see any good reason why God would permit this evil" to "There is no reason why God would permit this evil" is justified.

---

11. This is a little simplistic. Assuming you had some way of getting onto the farm, or flying a drone over the farm, you could improve your epistemic access pretty quickly. For our purposes here, we are considering only the access you have through the specified road-side observation.

12. Wykstra, "Rowe's Noseeum Arguments from Evil," 129.

Weighing the Probabilities

What about the inductive version of the argument? The skeptical theist can again reject the factual premise, but one important difference is worth noting. The inductive argument runs as follows:

1. There exist instances of intense suffering that seem to us to be gratuitous.
2. If God exists, then there are no instances of actually gratuitous suffering.
3. Therefore, either God does not exist or none of these instances of suffering is gratuitous—each is justified by some (hidden) greater good.
4. It is more likely that God does not exist than it is that each of these instances of intense suffering is justified by some (hidden) greater good.
5. Therefore, atheism is more likely to be true than theism.

The skeptical theist who wishes to reject only the factual premise should reject premise 4 of this argument. After all, premise 1 says only that some suffering seems to us to be gratuitous. This is easy to accept and hard to reject; a lot of really awful things happen without any obvious good resulting. Premise 2, the theological premise, claims that God would not permit gratuitous suffering. Premise 3 is entailed by 1 and 2, so it cannot be rejected without rejecting either 1 or 2 as well. It is premise 4, then, where we find the best candidate for the factual premise. Premise 4 claims that the evidence of gratuitous evil outweighs the evidence for God; that is, it claims that the existence of gratuitous evil is more probable than the existence of God.

So what's the "important difference"? Well, most defenses of an argument like this include a lengthy discussion on why a rational person ought to see the atheistic hypothesis as more probable than the theistic one. Philosophers do not merely state the argument; they defend it. This is true for the deductive argument as well, but the factual premise in the deductive argument is a very strong claim. In claiming that gratuitous evil does, absolutely exist, the proponent of the deductive argument gives the theist a relatively easy way out. "I don't see a reason to believe that is true" is a perfectly reasonable response here. Accepting the factual premise of the deductive argument means accepting the reality of genuinely gratuitous suffering; accepting the factual premise of the inductive argument means accepting only that atheism looks more probable than theism when considered in the light of apparently gratuitous suffering.

This brings us to the crucial difference. The theist who wishes to reject the factual premise of the inductive argument will likely be called upon to answer the following questions: "Why would a loving, all-powerful, all-knowing God allow for so much suffering without revealing to us the goods that make it all worthwhile? Why would such a God leave the evidence so unclear?" In this way, the atheist who defends the inductive argument also challenges the very core of skeptical theism itself: the claim that a loving, perfect God would allow us to be relatively oblivious to his reasons on matters so upsetting and so significant. For this reason, the skeptical theist who rejects the factual premise of the probabilistic evidential argument will have to address a subsequent challenge, the "problem of divine hiddenness."[13]

A Circularity Problem?

Skeptical theism asserts that the nature of God and the nature of his creation are so disparate that creation ought not to expect to be able to see all of the reasons why the Creator might do as he does. But isn't it cheating to assume the existence of God in order to respond to an argument against the existence of God? It certainly would be a problem. Indeed, the fallacy of *begging the question* is a fallacy because it does just that.

Suppose the skeptical theist offered something like the following argument:

1. God is omnipotent, omniscient, and perfectly good, and we are not.
2. If God is omnipotent, omniscient, and perfectly good, and we are not, then we do not have any good reason to believe that our moral knowledge is exhaustive.

---

13. For an in-depth and engaging book on the problem of divine hiddenness, I recommend M. C. Rea, *The Hiddenness of God* (Oxford: Oxford University Press, 2018). For a shorter philosophical treatment of the problem: C. Anderson, "Divine Hiddenness: Defeated Evidence," *Royal Institute of Philosophy Supplement*, no. 81 (2017): 119–32.

3. Therefore, we do not have good reason to believe that our moral knowledge is exhaustive. (1, 2)
4. If we do not have good reason to believe that our moral knowledge is exhaustive, then the problem of evil fails.
5. If the problem of evil fails, then God exists.
6. Therefore, God exists. (3–5)

To be clear, this argument is bad in more than one way. Premise 5 is false, for as we learned in chapter 7, there can be bad arguments for true conclusions. Demonstrating the failure of an argument does not suffice to demonstrate the falsity of its conclusion.

More important for our present purposes, however, is the fact that this argument begs the question: the very first premise assumes the truth of the conclusion. Arguments that beg the question in this way are also called instances of "circular reasoning," and circular reasoning is always fallacious. You cannot use the conclusion as evidence in support of the truth of the conclusion! The argument above can essentially be reduced to the claim: "You should believe that God exists because it is true that God exists." If God does exist, then of course you should believe in him, but the truth of that conditional does not in any way demonstrate or support the truth of his existence. After all, if Santa Claus exists, then you should believe in him too. This isn't very good evidence—or any evidence at all—that Santa actually exists.

Fortunately, this is not the argument advanced by the skeptical theist. Instead, the skeptical theist claims only that it is possible for God to exist and for our moral knowledge or moral imagination to be incomplete. But if this is the case, then we have no good reason to believe that we could judge whether an instance of evil was gratuitous in the sense under discussion. The logical problem of gratuitous evil claims that there are instances of evil that God would have prevented if he existed. Thus the argument begins by asking the theist to consider what the world would be like if God existed. In crafting their response to this problem, the skeptical theist is simply responding to this prompt. Premise 1 claims, "There exist instances of intense suffering which an omnipotent, omniscient being could have prevented without thereby losing some greater good or permitting some evil equally bad or worse." Skeptical theism responds, "We have no good reason for believing this to be true."

Suppose that you and I were friends, and that Jason was a friend of mine about whom you had deep suspicions. Although Jason is my friend, you neither like nor trust him. Now suppose that you and I are waiting for Jason to pick us up at 12:00 p.m. for a planned outing:

> **You:** I told you he wasn't coming.
> **Me:** What do you mean?
> **You:** If he were coming, he would have been here already. It's five minutes past 12:00!
> **Me:** He's probably just stuck in traffic. He'll be here.
> **You:** If he were actually coming, he would have left enough time for traffic. He's obviously not coming, like I expected.
> **Me:** Well, I think he's on his way. Traffic can be unpredictable, and I see no reason at all to suppose he's not coming just because he isn't here yet.
> **You:** There you go, assuming that he's coming to show that he's coming! Nice circular reasoning there!

This is, of course, not circular reasoning. You and I are both answering the same question: What should we conclude about Jason based on our circumstances? You think there is enough evidence to conclude that he is going to leave us stranded. I think it is premature to draw that conclusion, and I trust that he is on his way. Clearly our prior beliefs about Jason have shaped our interpretation of the evidence, but neither of us is engaging in irresponsible or fallacious reasoning. In the same way, both the atheist and the theist are answering the question: What should we conclude about God based on our circumstances? The atheist says we should conclude that he does not exist; the skeptical theist says we do not have anywhere near enough evidence to draw that conclusion. Neither is guilty of begging the question.

This analogy is helpful for another reason as well. In deciding what conclusion we ought to draw from Jason's absence, both you and I appeal to beliefs we already hold about Jason. I believe him to be a good, reliable friend; you believe him to be worthy of suspicion. Both of those prior beliefs obviously influence how we evaluate the current evidence. So it is with theism and atheism. The Christian skeptical theist will, of course, hold beliefs about God that go beyond philosophical theism; their specifically Christian beliefs will influence how they evaluate the evidence. Eleonore Stump addresses this when she writes:

> The problem of evil is generally presented as some sort of inconsistency in theistic beliefs. . . . And yet *mere* theists are relatively rare in the history of religion. Most people who accept [theism] are Jews or Christians or Muslims. If we are going to claim that *their* beliefs are somehow inconsistent, we need to look at a more complete set of Jewish or Muslim or Christian beliefs concerning God's goodness and evil in the world.[14]

The evidential problem of evil asks us to weigh the evidence for and against theism. It asks what we ought to expect from a theistic world. In answering that question, it is entirely fair for the Christian theist to consider specifically Christian beliefs.

In the above dialogue, you asked me to explain how my friend Jason could still be on his way despite his tardiness. It would have been very odd, indeed, had you insisted that I stick to generic evidence about persons in general. If I know Jason, then I can and should appeal to evidence drawn from my knowledge of and experiences with Jason. Perhaps I know his car to be a little unreliable or his job frequently to demand last-minute overtime. Perhaps I remember that he often stops for broken-down motorists because he likes to help those in need. Each of these could be relevant to the question of why Jason is late; each of these should play a role in my consideration of the question. In just exactly the same way, the Christian theist is being asked what she ought to expect from the existence of the God of Christianity. If it is true that Christian Scriptures tell us that we ought to expect suffering, perhaps even to pursue it, and that God himself was incarnated and suffered, then all of this is relevant to the question at hand.

Throughout our treatment of the problem of evil, it is important to remember that the theist does not need to prove the existence of God to reject an atheistic argument. More broadly, nobody needs to prove that a conclusion is false in order to reject the argument defending it. Instead, it is enough to show that you have good reasons for rejecting the argument,

---

14. E. Stump and M. J. Murray, eds., *Philosophy of Religion: The Big Questions*, Philosophy: The Big Questions (Malden, MA: Blackwell, 1999), 230.

reasons for believing that the premises do not demonstrate the truth of the conclusion. The problem of evil says that the kind and degree of suffering that we encounter here on earth is incompatible with what we ought to expect from a good and loving God. The skeptical theist calls this charge into question by undermining our faith in our intuitions. It is perfectly appropriate to do so, and to bolster this response with biblical evidence in support of the claim that God might very well allow (and even redeem) exactly the kind and degree of suffering that we find in our world.

Sam Harris Revisited

One question remains outstanding: What should we say about the charge raised by Sam Harris in section 2? As we read, he accuses skeptical theists of the following equivocation: "God cannot be judged by merely human standards of morality. But, of course, human standards of morality are precisely what the faithful use to establish God's goodness in the first place."[15] If Harris is correct, then the skeptical theist cannot reasonably say both that God is good and that skeptical theism is true. We are now finally in a position to see why his charge is not quite right. Skeptical theists do not say that we have no reliable notions of good and evil; neither do they say that we are wholly unable to judge divine actions as good or evil. Instead, they say only that we don't have all the information. We don't have good reason to believe that we know all of the goods that there are, but that is not because we don't know what good *is*. Skeptical theism does not say that we are radically unclear on what it means for something to be good or bad; it says only that we are not perfectly able to discern the full range of goods and evils.

To return to the parent-child analogy, the child who views the flu shot as an evil is, in some sense, correct. She recognizes the evil of pain as an evil. What she fails to recognize is that there is also a greater good in play; this is not the same as failing to know what good is. She likely recognizes, for instance, the pleasure of the consolation lollipop and hug as a good. Most significantly, the child can persist in believing her mother to be good even when confronted by the inexplicable fact of her mother having held her down while a stranger jabbed her in the arm. She can do so because she knows, at some

---

15. Harris, "There Is No God (and You Know It)."

level, that her understanding of things is imperfect. In the same way, the skeptical theist can recognize the suffering of this world as evil and the love of God as good and yet remain skeptical of her ability to judge every instance of evil as either justified or gratuitous. She can do so because she, like the child, knows that her understanding of things is imperfect.

Conclusion

The evidential argument from evil asks us to take a hard look at the sufferings of this world, and the way that such suffering seems to us to serve no purpose at all. One benefit of skeptical theism is that it does not ask us to deny this uncomfortable fact. Instead, the skeptical theist can agree that much of the world's suffering seems to us to be gratuitous. There is a kind of comfort here. Anyone who has suffered a great loss knows full well the hurt that can be done by a well-intentioned person with a ready-made explanation for why this horror may have happened. If skeptical theism is correct, then there is a reason why these paltry consolations are so paltry—we are simply not in the epistemic position to find these kinds of reasons. We are often, epistemically speaking, well out of reach of the goods in play here. Still, there is a difference between citing the reason for each instance of suffering and suggesting a reason why the world might be as it is. In the next chapter, we will turn our attention to attempts to understand why God, if he exists, might allow not only some evil but exactly the kinds of evil with which we are faced.

The Free Will Defense 11

Try to exclude the possibility of suffering which the order of nature and the existence of free-wills involve, and you find that you have excluded life itself.

—C. S. Lewis[1]

Job has the longest face-to-face conversation with God of any character, anywhere in the Biblical stories ever, ever. That's part of the story, too. If you leave that out, it's harder to understand what's going on in that Biblical book.

—Eleonore Stump[2]

Not all theists are comfortable with the kind of skepticism outlined in chapter 10. Some worry that it will lead to skepticism about God in general; others don't share that worry but still see skeptical theism as less desirable than a good theodicy—that is, a defense or explanation. Eleonore Stump suggests the following:

> We can think of attempted theodicies as thought experiments designed to test the skeptical theist's assessment of human cognitive capacities. If, in fact, all attempted theodicies should turn out to be demonstrable failures, then the skeptical theist may consider that the demonstrated lack of success of theodicies is grist for his mill.[3]

1. C. S. Lewis, *The Problem of Pain* (San Francisco: HarperSanFrancisco, 2001), 24–25.

2. "Wandering in Darkness: Eleonore Stump on Suffering, Evil, and Personal Encounter," *The Table* (podcast), hosted by Evan Rosa, 2019, https://cct.biola.edu/wandering-in-darkness/.

3. E. Stump, *Wandering in Darkness: Narrative and the Problem of Suffering* (Oxford: Clarendon, 2010), 15.

When you construct a theodicy, you do your best to find and articulate some good reason why God might allow the evil and suffering that we see in this world. If skeptical theism is correct, then it will likely be beyond our capabilities to do so, but the converse holds as well. If we are able to conceive of a way of reconciling the goodness of God with the suffering in this world, then we may not need to be so skeptical about our ability to understand the ways of God.

One benefit of this approach is that it encourages theists to seek answers to the questions raised by the problem of evil. In particular, it encourages Christian theists to turn to Scripture. The Bible seems to provide at least some indication as to why God allows suffering. As we discussed in the end of chapter 10, it is perfectly appropriate for a Christian to consult Scripture in search of a solution to the problem of evil. After all, the crucial question that a Christian must answer is not "What does evil tell us about the existence of some generic God?" but instead "What does evil tell us about the existence of the Christian God?"

Suffering in Scripture

When we look to the Bible for inspiration for a theodicy, we find a common theme. In Matthew 23:37, Christ expresses the divine desire for union and relationship with his people—and the people's resistance, much to their own detriment: "Jerusalem, Jerusalem, who kills the prophets and stones those who are sent to her! How often I wanted to gather your children together, the way a hen gathers her chicks under her wings, and you were unwilling." Similarly, 1 Samuel 8:7–9 tells the story of Israel's demand for a king. Again, God warns of the suffering that a human kingship would bring but orders Samuel to heed the people's will.

> The LORD said to Samuel, "Listen to the voice of the people in regard to all that they say to you, for they have not rejected you, but they have rejected Me from being king over them. Like all the deeds which they have done since the day that I brought them up from Egypt even to this day—in that they have forsaken Me and served other gods—so they are doing to you also. Now then, listen to their voice; however, you shall solemnly warn them and tell them of the procedure of the king who will reign over them."

As a final illustration, consider the story of the "rich young ruler" as told in the Gospel of Matthew:

> And someone came to Him and said, "Teacher, what good thing shall I do so that I may obtain eternal life?" And He said to him, "Why are you asking Me about what is good? There is only One who is good; but if you want to enter life, keep the commandments." Then he said to Him, "Which ones?" And Jesus said, "You shall not commit murder; You shall not commit adultery; You shall not steal; You shall not give false testimony; Honor your father and mother; and You shall love your neighbor as yourself." The young man said to Him, "All these I have kept; what am I still lacking?" Jesus said to him, "If you want to be complete, go and sell your possessions and give to the poor, and you will have treasure in heaven; and come, follow Me." But when the young man heard this statement, he went away grieving; for he was one who owned much property. (Matt 19:16–22)

In light of these verses, it seems clear that at least some suffering is permitted in order to honor the free will of human creatures. Rather than force Jerusalem into communion with himself, Christ laments their rejection and reiterates the divine invitation. Rather than withhold the desired but dangerous earthly king from Israel, God gives them what they want. Rather than commandeer the rich young ruler's wealth, Jesus allows him to walk away.

I am reminded of a prayer of confession that I recently encountered at my church. It was written by the Rev. Kaji Douša and drawn from Psalm 1:

> *Happy are those who turn away from the counsel of the wicked.*
> *But oh, that counsel can be so seductive—*
> *it draws us in, holds us fast, distracts our priorities,*
> *obstructs our capacity to love.*
> *But we seek no obstructions, we reject wicked counsel.*
> *We embrace God's embrace.*
> *For whatever ways we don't, we confess.*
> *In whichever ways we sin, we repent.*
> *Hear our prayers, O God, as, before you, we seek wholeness.*[4]

---

4. Many thanks to my worship pastor and friend Rich Van Voorst for introducing me to this prayer. See https://re-worship.blogspot.com/2011/10/confession-assurance-psalm-1.html.

It is good for humanity to be comforted and protected by God, but sometimes we just don't want that. It is good for humanity to be ruled by God, not by human beings, but sometimes we just want a ruler we can see. It is good for humanity to value fellowship with Christ above earthly possessions, but sometimes we just cannot bring ourselves to do that.

In each of these biblical stories, God has a choice: honor the will of the people involved or bring happiness and comfort to those same people. What he cannot do, it seems, is both honor their choice and help them to avoid suffering; neither can he honor their choice without allowing them to harm those around them. When the people of God resist his call to fellowship and communion with him, their children suffer as well. When they prefer the rule of humankind to the rule of God, entire communities, including future generations, pay the price. Even when someone chooses earthly pleasures over a life spent following Christ, those around him suffer the inevitable consequences. Freedom introduces risk to our world, and the result is often widespread suffering. These verses, among others, provide a biblical basis for the free will defense.

Theodicy and Defense

What exactly is a defense? As we read in chapter 10, Marilyn McCord Adams describes theodicies and defenses in the following terms:

> *Defenses* trot out armies of possible reasons why God might permit such evils, contending that even if we don't know the actual reasons, the greater the number of apparently available reasons, the less obviously pointless are the evils in question. *Theodicies* suggest actual reasons, whether on grounds of revelation or of common sense.[5]

In this chapter, the term *defense* refers to both the theodicies and defenses under discussion. Both theodicies and defenses involve constructing a scenario on which God would have good reasons for permitting the scope and magnitude of evils that we encounter in our world. Both involve telling a story with the intent of reconciling what we know of God with what we know of evil. Perhaps theodicies, properly understood, go further, claiming to

---

5. M. M. Adams, *Horrendous Evils and the Goodness of God*, Cornell Studies in the Philosophy of Religion (Ithaca, NY: Cornell University Press, 2000), 15.

have actually found God's true justificatory reasons. For a while, at least, this seems to have been the consensus. Plantinga, for instance, introduced his own defense with the caution: "Quite distinct from a Free Will Theodicy is what I shall call a Free Will Defense. Here the aim is not to say what God's reason is, but at most what God's reason might possibly be."[6]

I am inclined to believe that most theodicies were never so bold as to meet the standard of that stricter definition, that nobody really took herself to be saying "this is what God's reason is." For that reason, I prefer to view defenses and theodicies as falling somewhere along a spectrum, with one side offering only the merest possibility and the other a robust, fully fleshed-out account. More to the point, there is simply no way to even approach the theodicy end of my proposed spectrum in the space of a single chapter. The problem of evil is far-reaching, more a cluster of problems than a single problem, and those who construct theodicies tend to defend them with books, not chapters.[7] For that reason, although some of the defenses I will introduce are crafted as theodicies by their authors, I will simply call them all defenses. So by *defense* I mean any story that goes some distance toward explaining why we might have the evil that we do under the providential guidance of a loving God.

To get a better sense of what this looks like, consider the following dialogue:

Bonnie: I cannot believe that my mom forgot my birthday. My own mother!

Susana: That's so unlike her! What makes you think she forgot?

Bonnie: She hasn't called, hasn't texted, and she always swings by on my birthday morning with some kind of a treat. It's almost noon! She's clearly forgotten.

Susana: Maybe she's planning a surprise party! She probably just wants you to think she's forgotten so that you are really surprised. I'm sure she hasn't forgotten!

---

6. A. Plantinga, *God, Freedom, and Evil* (Grand Rapids: Eerdmans, 1977), 28.

7. The problem of evil includes not only the harm suffered by rational, free adult humans but also the harm suffered by very small children, persons with significant cognitive disabilities, and nonhuman animals. It is entirely possible that an adequate defense for one of these will not suffice for the rest. Likewise, there are both natural and moral sources of evil—earthquakes and tsunamis, but also abusive parents and callous murderers. Again, it is not clear that these diverse *kinds* of evils can be explained in precisely the same way.

Conversations like this are a common plot device in sitcoms and comedic films. What is going on here? Susana is not claiming to know that Bonnie's mom is planning a surprise party. She is not certain that she has figured out the right explanation for Bonnie's mother's atypical behavior. Instead, she is trying to reconcile what she knows of Bonnie's mother—namely, that she is usually loving, kind, and attentive on Bonnie's birthday—with the difficult fact that she is not currently displaying that behavior. Susana is telling a story with the goal of reconciling Bonnie's upsetting experience with the loving nature of Bonnie's mom. On a much larger scale, this is what a defense aims to do for the problem of evil and a loving God.

In keeping with the analogy, note that it would be wholly disingenuous for Susana to make this suggestion if she had reason to believe it to be false. (For instance, if she had overheard Bonnie's mother talking about her plan to ignore Bonnie on her birthday as a punishment for some prior slight.) She doesn't have to know that it is true in order to suggest it, but she should at least believe it could be true. In the same way, a defense must at least be compatible with what we already have reason to believe about God.

A second point is worth noting. Suppose the conversation had continued later in the day, as follows:

Bonnie: So . . . you were totally wrong about my mom.
Susana: Oh no! Did she really forget? I'm so sorry!
Bonnie: No, she didn't forget. She's just super sick at home. Apparently, she's so sick she couldn't even text. She's been throwing up all morning, and she has a fever.
Susana: Oh how awful! So she didn't forget? Well that's good, at least. Right?
Bonnie: Maybe, but you kind of lied to me. I mean, she is not planning a surprise party for me. Even if you didn't mean to lie, you really misled me. You shouldn't have done that.

Putting aside the fact that it's not fun to expect a party that you don't receive, Bonnie's response here is wrong. It is wrong because it misconstrues what Susana had been trying to say. In suggesting that maybe Bonnie's mother was planning a party, Susana was essentially saying, "I am sure there is a reasonable explanation here. Perhaps this is it. If it isn't, there is surely some other explanation." So it is with a defense. The goal of a defense is not to promise or guarantee that you have discovered God's motivations; a defense claims, "I am confident that there is a reasonable explanation here. Perhaps this is it. If it is not, there is surely some other explanation."

The Free Will Defense

So what kind of a story can we tell to explain how the loving God of Christianity might allow the degree of suffering and evil that we see in this world? The details vary, but most Christians who offer a defense agree that human freedom must feature heavily in any such story—that is, most defenses are versions of the free will defense. Alvin Plantinga succinctly captures the core of the free will defense in the following passage:

> A world containing creatures who are significantly free (and freely perform more good than evil actions) is more valuable, all else being equal, than a world containing no free creatures at all. Now God can create free creatures, but He can't *cause* or *determine* them to do only what is right. For if He does so, then they aren't significantly free after all; they do not do what is right *freely*. To create creatures capable of *moral good*, therefore, He must create creatures capable of moral evil; and He can't give these creatures the freedom to perform evil and at the same time prevent them from doing so.[8]

In this brief passage, Plantinga touches upon the two key aspects of any free will defense. First, God judges significant human freedom to be a great good. Second, significant human freedom cannot be had without suffering. When Plantinga writes that God "can't give these creatures the freedom to perform evil and at the same time prevent them from actually doing so," he means that it would be logically impossible for God to do such a thing. The freedom to perform evil entails the ability to perform evil.

Why should that be? Not all freedom entails suffering. After all, God could simply allow us to choose between various flavors of ice cream, types of leisure activities, and perhaps favorite colors. Then we could all be free without ever harming ourselves or others! The kind of freedom at the heart of the

---

8. Plantinga, *God, Freedom, and Evil*, 30.

free will defense, the freedom to perform evil, requires far more than this. Consider the words of Richard Swinburne:

> Of course thrills of pleasure and periods of contentment are good things, and—other things being equal—God would certainly seek to provide plenty of those. But a generous God will seek to give deeper good things than these. He will seek to give us great responsibility for ourselves, each other, and the world, and thus a share in his own creative activity of determining what sort of a world it is to be. And he will seek to make our lives valuable, of great use to ourselves and each other. The problem is that God cannot give us these goods in full measure without allowing much evil on the way.[9]

This kind of freedom is central to the free will defense—namely, *morally significant freedom*. Morally significant freedom is the freedom to choose between good and bad options: between benefitting and harming yourself or someone else; between helping and hindering a friend; between helping and hindering an enemy; between generosity and stinginess, encouragement and destruction, love and hate.

To see why the existence of morally significant freedom entails the possibility of suffering, first suppose that it did not. That is, suppose it were possible for there to be creatures with morally significant freedom and yet no possibility of suffering. What would that require? It seems that there are two options here: either these creatures must believe that they can choose between good and evil but are in fact made in such a way that they always choose the good, or these creatures can choose evil but are immediately thwarted every time they attempt to execute their choice. In the first case it should be clear that these creatures do not actually have morally significant freedom after all; they have the feeling of freedom, but it is an illusion. What about the second case? Well, if every time I choose to hit you my arm muscles refuse to cooperate, or a powerful force-field prevents me from being able to make contact with your body, or you are simply transported to a new location, then was I actually free to hit you? I don't think so. I was free to choose

---

9. R. Swinburne, "Why Does God Allow Evil?," in *Questions about God : Today's Philosophers Ponder the Divine*, ed. S. M. Cahn and D. Shatz (Oxford: Oxford University Press, 2002), 20.

to hit you, but actually hitting you was never really an option. Stranger still, if suffering is to be wholly avoided, then it seems that you must also be protected even from the knowledge that I wanted to harm you, and that I must somehow be made not to mind when my will is thwarted.

In this scenario, I may choose between good and evil, but I may not do evil. When I choose evil, I do not succeed in doing what I aim to do. To prevent my suffering, God prevents me from caring about these failed acts; to prevent your suffering, he prevents you from knowing that I intended to bring you harm. I hope that it is clear that this is not the kind of freedom that can "give us great responsibility for ourselves, each other, and the world." This so-called freedom is not morally significant freedom. There is just no way to give creatures morally significant freedom without thereby allowing them to bring harm to themselves and others. Morally significant freedom really does entail the possibility of evil and suffering.

One final consideration must be noted: morally significant freedom relies on what philosophers call a *libertarian* conception of freedom. On the libertarian account, a person is only free with respect to some action if she is genuinely able to choose between two viable alternatives. For example, I intend to have a salad for lunch this afternoon. I could, instead, have a sandwich. If my lunch decision is to be free on the libertarian conception, then the following must be true: if I have the salad, I could have had the sandwich, and if I instead choose the sandwich, I could have had the salad. The distinguishing feature of libertarian freedom is that it requires the ability to have done otherwise. If it turns out that only one of these choices is actually available to me—that God or nature has ensured that I will choose the salad—then the libertarian conception of freedom says that my choice was not free.

What is the alternative? Isn't all freedom this way? Although libertarian freedom closely mirrors our common sense notion of free will, it is not universally accepted as the right way to understand freedom. For a whole host of reasons—most notably, questions of divine sovereignty and of the apparently deterministic nature of the universe—many philosophers reject the libertarian conception of freedom. Instead, they embrace a compatibilist account, on which freedom is entirely compatible with *determinism*, that is, with having your choice determined either by God or by the laws of physics. (Thus, those who embrace libertarian freedom are called incompatibilists.) To do justice to this distinction would require at least another chapter, but the general idea behind this conception of freedom is this: a person is free with respect to some choice just as long as she is able to do what she wants to do. Provided her will isn't thwarted by some external factor, it is free. On this conception of freedom, even if God or nature has ensured that I will choose salad for lunch today, that is no threat to my freedom. Because God (or nature) can also ensure that I *want* salad for lunch today, my choice of salad accords with my own desires. It is, therefore, a free choice, if freedom means getting to do what you want to do.

One benefit of the compatibilist conception of freedom is that it allows for both total providential control by God and for human freedom: as long as you do what you want to do, you are free—even if God controls both what you want and what you do. For precisely this reason, however, the compatibilist cannot avail herself of the free will defense. If compatibilism is the right way to understand human freedom, then it is simply false to say that "God can create free creatures, but he can't cause or determine them to do only what is right." Compatibilism tells us that God could, in fact, do exactly that. If compatibilism is true, then human freedom does not entail the possibility of suffering. (Whether we want to call such freedom morally significant is a question for another day.)[10] For that reason, the free will defense rests upon a libertarian conception of freedom. This is no great cost, however, for the libertarian conception of freedom is widely held and intuitively plausible; most of us already believe that our future contains genuine options, many of which are genuinely available to us. Correspondingly, the compatibilist account of freedom makes the problem of evil significantly more troubling. If God can give us robust freedom without thereby introducing the possibility of evil and suffering, then it really is difficult to see why there is any suffering at all.

With the libertarian conception of freedom in hand, we are now in a better position to articulate why morally significant free will logically entails at least the possibility of suffering. As we learned in chapter 8, in cases of genuine entailment, any attempt to hold the entailing claim true and the

---

10. Briefly: compatibilists do and incompatibilists don't! Allow me to confess my bias here—I am an incompatibilist about free will. I can't see how a wholly determined "choice" could be a choice at all, let alone a morally significant one, so I will leave the defense of morally significant compatibilistic free will to the compatibilists. For instance, J. C. Wingard Jr., "Confession of a Reformed Philosopher: Why I Am a Compatibilist about Determinism and Moral Responsibility," *Themelios* 42, no. 2 (August 2017), https://www.thegospelcoalition.org/themelios/article/confession-of-a-reformed-philosopher/.

entailed false will generate a contradiction. Let's suppose, then, that there is morally significant human freedom but no human suffering. We can do so by supposing that God creates just one significantly free human being, but he prevents him from causing any harm or introducing any suffering into the world. (Perhaps there are other human beings in his community, but he is the only one endowed with freedom.) We may as well go ahead and call him Adam. Now if Adam has morally significant freedom, then he is able to choose between good and bad, where those words carry their full moral import. Adam may add or detract value from the lives of others; he is free to make a genuine difference in the world—be it positive or negative. But if *free* means that he is genuinely able to do either of those things, then Adam's helping and Adam's harming are both possible. For that reason, if libertarian freedom is the right way of understanding freedom, then it is logically contradictory to suppose that God could create Adam with morally significant free will and prevent him from doing harm. This would be akin to saying, "It is possible for Adam to help and possible for Adam to do harm, but it is not possible for Adam to do harm." This is an outright contradiction, a confirmation of the fact that morally significant libertarian free will entails the possibility of suffering. If Adam's freedom is morally significant, then both help and harm are viable options. If Adam's freedom involves a genuine choice between two available options, then harm is a real possibility. Morally significant libertarian free will logically entails the possibility of harm and therefore suffering.

Thus we have a sketch of the free will defense. God, in his wisdom and moral perfection, values human (libertarian) freedom so highly that he permits the evil and suffering that it requires. Because he is omnipotent, he could have created a world with no suffering, but such a world could not have contained creatures with morally significant freedom. Even an omnipotent being cannot do that which is contradictory: God could not create a four-sided triangle, a round square, a married bachelor, or a creature who has morally significant free will but who cannot choose to do harm.[11]

---

11. To address an objection that frequently arises in the classroom, God could, of course, have created a world in which we called four-sided figures "triangles" and circles "squares." What he could *not* do is create a four-sided figure that is the figure we refer to with the word *triangle*. Whatever proposition is expressed by our sentence "that is a four-sided triangle" is the logically impossible scenario under discussion here.

Why do I call this a "sketch" of a free will defense? Because questions abound, and Christians who advance the free will defense disagree significantly about how best to answer those questions. Is the free will defense sufficient to explain all kinds of suffering? Even the suffering caused by natural disasters? Even the suffering experienced by animals who seem themselves to lack this freedom? If it is sufficient, what makes it so? How is human freedom related to things like natural disasters and the violence of animal predation? If it is not, are there alternative defenses available to explain these other kinds of suffering? In response to these questions and others, advocates of the free will defense propose a variety of diverse answers. For that reason, there is no free will defense; rather, there are free will defenses. (And as I noted earlier, these fully fleshed out defenses often occupy entire books, not mere chapters.) Our focus in this chapter is on what these defenses have in common—namely, the centrality of morally significant human freedom and its implications for human suffering.

The Problem of Evil Revisited

To that end, two questions are equally pressing for any version of the free will defense: How exactly is the free will defense a response to the arguments presented in chapter 9? And what is so great about morally significant freedom? These two questions are closely related, and we will begin with the first. As we saw in chapter 10, the only real options for the theist are either rejecting the factual premise or the theological premise. In other words, anyone who wishes to reject the evidential argument from evil must either deny that gratuitous evil exists (or that it is probable) or deny the claim that a perfectly good God must prevent gratuitous evil. Perhaps unsurprisingly, advocates of the free will defense offer different answers to this question as well.

Most of those who offer the free will defense do as the skeptical theist does and deny the factual premise. If the goodness of morally significant human freedom justifies the harms of human suffering, then no suffering is truly gratuitous, and every instance of suffering is outweighed or justified by the goodness brought by free creatures.[12] But what does this mean? Up to this

---

12. One notable exception here is Peter van Inwagen's free will defense. He accepts the factual premise but denies the theological premise. See, for instance, P. van Inwagen, *The Problem of Evil: The Gifford Lectures Delivered in the University of St Andrews in 2003* (Oxford: Clarendon, 2006).

point, I have explained the justification of suffering in terms of the benefits accrued to the sufferer. For instance, the suffering caused by an inoculation is justified by the good of immunity; the suffering of hardship is justified by the good of perseverance; the suffering of a child being made to take a nap is justified by the resulting health and wellness of that child. In all of these cases, the good that justifies the suffering is a good to the person who suffers. The patient who gets the jab gets the immunity; the victim of hardship gains perseverance; the exhausted child gets the rest and resulting wellness. Must this always be the case? That is, in order for an instance of suffering to be justified and therefore not gratuitous, must the justificatory good be given to the sufferer? Or is it enough that the general goods of the world outweigh or otherwise justify the evils and suffering of the world?

Some proponents of the free will defense maintain the latter position, insisting that the goods of human freedom need only outweigh the suffering of this world in general. For instance, the free will defenses of both Richard Swinburne and Peter van Inwagen largely explain the suffering caused by natural disasters by appealing to the overwhelming good of a universe with lawlike regularity. On these views, although humanity will learn or gain something from a devastating earthquake, those who are most directly impacted by that earthquake may not. For these defenses, an instance of suffering will only be gratuitous if it is not, on balance, good for the world.[13]

One philosopher who is unwilling to accept this position is Eleonore Stump. In correspondence with van Inwagen, she objects to any defense which "represents God as allowing people to suffer misfortunes that do not (even in the long run) benefit them."[14] Instead, Stump, Marilyn McCord Adams, and others believe that the suffering permitted by God must introduce at least the potential for an outweighing good in the life of the sufferer.

---

13. I believe that this largely explains why van Inwagen accepts the factual premise. As he notes, in order for there to not be any gratuitous suffering on this view, there would have to be some precise degree of suffering such that it is just exactly what God needs in order to secure the goods he seeks. Van Inwagen believes this to be mistaken, likening it to the belief that there is some precise minimum number of raindrops that must fall on France in order for the soil to be fertile. Without rain, the soil will surely be barren. Still, for any given fertile period, it surely holds that two raindrops fewer would have made no difference. In the same way, he writes, "There is no minimum number of horrors consistent with God's plan of reconciliation, for the prevention of any one particular horror could not possibly have any effect on God's plan" (van Inwagen, *The Problem of Evil*, 106).

14. E. Stump and M. J. Murray, eds., *Philosophy of Religion: The Big Questions*, Philosophy: The Big Questions (Malden, MA: Blackwell, 1999), 209.

For example, in discussing the particularly awful kinds of suffering Adams rightly dubs "horrors," she writes that God must use the horror to benefit the victim "by giving it positive meaning through organic unity with a great enough good *within the context of his/her life*."[15] In the same way, Stump, after exploring the suffering of Samson, Mary Magdalene, Abraham, and Job, concludes: "I asked how anyone could justify God's allowing such suffering. The answer . . . is that this appalling suffering is the best or only means in the circumstances for the sufferer to have what he himself cares about."[16] This is of crucial importance on both Adams's and Stump's defenses: God is justified in permitting the suffering we see in this world because he uses that suffering as a part of his redemptive work in the lives of the sufferers. In rejecting the factual premises, as they do, both Stump and Adams commit to the claim that God uses every instance of suffering to bring the potential for an overriding good for the sufferer. In this way, there is no gratuitous suffering.

The Benefits of Morally Significant Freedom

But how? Van Inwagen shares the true story of a woman who was violently assaulted by a stranger, raped, mutilated, and left to die. Adams and others invoke similar horrors, including those perpetrated against infants and small children. What could outweigh horrors of this magnitude? Here, again, advocates of the free will defense have offered different replies. In this closing section, I will focus on the reply that I find most promising.

All advocates of the free will defense agree that morally significant human freedom is somehow a part of whatever the overriding good might be—but how, exactly? Very often, in one form or another, the answer offered has something to do with character formation. In a recent (and exceptionally good) podcast discussion of *Wandering in Darkness*, Eleonore Stump offers the following criticism of this trend:

> If you think that the point of suffering is character formation, then here's what you're saying to Job. "Hey, Job. I'll take all your kids and kill them all. Don't worry. I'm going to trade you something for this. Here's what I'm going

---

15. Adams, *Horrendous Evils and the Goodness of God*, 31.
16. Stump, *Wandering in Darkness*, 415.

to trade you for. You'll have a much better character than you otherwise would." Any decent person would say, "Keep your stupid character formation. Let me keep the kids." It is important to understand that suffering has got a lot more human detail, a lot more human complexity to it than something as simple as intrinsic individual valuable characteristics of a person.[17]

If this is true for Job, then surely it holds for the victim of rape and mutilation as well. Can anyone really believe that a person would voluntarily suffer that experience for the paltry reward of character formation?

No. Of course not. Instead, Stump argues, the greater good at stake is far greater than that. Drawing on a theodicy first offered by Thomas Aquinas, Stump maintains that the outweighing good offered to the sufferer must be something that she values. She says, "Think about it this way. In suffering, you lose something that you care about. If God is going to be justified in allowing that suffering, it has to be that somehow, you get more of what you care about than you would if you hadn't suffered."[18] What might that be? Fellowship with God and with other human beings. Suffering brings with it an awareness of our own vulnerability. To be clear, as Stump notes, we were already vulnerable! What suffering does is to open our eyes to that fragility. In doing so, suffering offers us the possibility of nearness with God and with others.

Here we find the source of Stump's epigraph for this chapter. Throughout this chapter, most of what I have used of Stump's words have come from her written work. In truth, there is a more polished statement of the claims central to the epigraph too. In *Wandering in Darkness*, Stump walks the reader through the lives of four great heroes and great sufferers of Scripture. In the passage from which our epigraph is clearly drawn, she writes:

> Job has the most sustained face-to-face conversation between God and a human person recorded in the biblical narratives. Samson fulfills his mission and draws near to God when he does so. Abraham becomes the father of a whole people and also the father of faith. And Mary's act

---

17. "Wandering in Darkness," *The Table* podcast.
18. "Wandering in Darkness," *The Table* podcast. I have edited the punctuation here a bit. Stump is an eloquent writer and speaker. Audio transcripts being what they are, the official transcript contains grammatical errors. I am choosing not to ascribe those errors to Stump herself because she did not write the transcript.

191

of adoration in anointing Jesus is so striking and great-hearted that she becomes emblematic in Christian thought for it.

Still, I love the frankness of Stump's spoken words on this point. In that podcast conversation, while noting the importance of recognizing the unique, individual circumstances surrounding every instance of suffering, Stump concludes: "Job has the longest face-to-face conversation with God of any character, anywhere in the Biblical stories ever, ever. That's part of the story, too. If you leave that out, it's harder to understand what's going on in that Biblical book."[19] In the wake of all their losses, what do Job, Samson, Abraham, and Mary gain? God himself. They gain nearness to the creator, and in Job's case, he has a personal, meaningful conversation with the Lord of the universe. Perhaps most of us are not so fortunate as to receive hours of literal conversation with God, but all who suffer can take comfort in the words of Psalm 34:18: "The LORD is near to the brokenhearted and saves those who are crushed in spirit."

But what if the victims of suffering don't want that? If Stump is right that the goods on offer must be something that we care about, then what is there to say to those who don't care about fellowship with God? On this point, Stump and Aquinas maintain that there are no such people, not really. As we read in chapter 10, Stump writes, "What is bad about suffering, then, is that it undermines or destroys what the sufferer centrally cares about, her own flourishing or the desires of her heart or both."[20] Nothing is more central to human flourishing than a right relationship with our Creator. Though some people believe they don't care about their relationship to God, they are wrong about that. Were they really able to understand their desires, they would see that their deepest desires can only be satisfied by God—what they want, properly understood, is God. Crucially, Stump argues, you do not need to know that you want something in order for it to be true that you want it. It is a well-known truth that children want stability and discipline, even if they believe they want spontaneity and freedom. It is equally true that the human body wants proper nutrition, even if it often craves junk food and empty calories. A quick glance at the celebrity news reveals that, even with

19. "Wandering in Darkness: Eleonore Stump on Suffering, Evil, and Personal Encounter," *The Table* podcast.
20. Stump, *Wandering in Darkness*, 11.

nearly unlimited resources, human beings are overwhelmingly bad at knowing and pursuing our flourishing. What we want is God, regardless of what we believe. Suffering brings with it the increased possibility of seeing this need and of turning toward God to have that need met.

Conclusion

There is so much more I could say here, and too little space in which to say it. Instead, I will conclude by revisiting the passages of Scripture introduced in section 1. We looked at three examples: the people of Israel refusing God's comfort and fellowship, the nation of Israel demanding a king, and the rich young ruler asked to sacrifice his wealth in order to follow Christ. In all three cases, God desires a deeper relationship with his people, and those people refuse it. In all three cases, the suffering involved is the direct result of a free choice to pursue autonomy and independence from God rather than deeper union with him. Can we also understand these cases as ones in which the potential outweighing good is that they are brought nearer to God?

We can and should; they do. In Matthew 23:37, Jesus references the resistance of Jerusalem to God's comforting presence as a means of repeating that invitation. This chastisement is at once a lesson and a call to change. Likewise, the nation of Israel received their king, but throughout their history the failures of those kings brought increased opportunities to honor God above earthly rulers, to seek his fellowship. Finally, the rich young ruler went away sad, as he ought to have done. It is good that he was sad, for sadness is the proper response to choosing earthly riches over union with God. I once heard an optimistic exegetical suggestion that we encounter this same young man a few chapters later in Mark 14:51–52. There we read, "A young man was following Him, wearing nothing but a linen sheet over his naked body; and they seized him. But he pulled free of the linen sheet and escaped naked." I can't say that I find the evidence of this claim to be great, but I can absolutely hope for its truth! That is, it would be good if the sadness of the rich young ruler led him to abandon his riches in pursuit of Christ; fellowship with God would surely outweigh the suffering of lost possessions. Of course, the real suffering of this world comes from the loss of things much dearer than possessions. Even so, if Stump, Aquinas, and others like them are correct, there is no loss so great such that it could not be outweighed by fellowship and union with God.

A World of Real Values

12

The horror of the crash, to a Christian, confirms the fact that we live in a world of real values: positive and negative. If the universe was just electrons, there would be no problem of evil or suffering.

—*A London Priest*[1]

But the most remarkable thing is this. Whenever you find a man who says he does not believe in a real Right and Wrong, you will find the same man going back on this a moment later. He may break his promise to you, but if you try breaking one to him he will be complaining "It's not fair" before you can say Jack Robinson.

—*C. S. Lewis*[2]

A fter devoting the last three chapters to the problem of evil as an argument against theism, it is time we turn our attention to a corollary question: Can evil and suffering serve as evidence *for* the existence of God? Many like the London priest quoted above believe that it can. Their central line of reasoning goes as follows: The world contains instances of evil and suffering that are really and truly bad. They are not merely unpleasant, undesirable, or unfortunate; they are wrong in some fundamental sense. They are contrary to how the world ought to be. But if that is the case, then there must be some way that the world ought to be. A world that is the result of blind forces generated by the rapid expansion of matter and energy does not, at face value, seem to be the kind of world that ought to be one way or another; it seems like the kind of place that just is. A world that was created and designed by a personal

---

1. Quoted in R. Dawkins, *River Out of Eden: A Darwinian View of Life*, Science Masters Series (New York: Basic, 1995), 132.

2. C. S. Lewis, *Mere Christianity* (New York: Macmillan, 1960), 19.

God seems like a far better candidate. In this way, the reality of objective moral values is used to support the likelihood of theism over atheism.

The moral argument can be formulated in a number of ways, but we can begin with the following:

1. There are objective moral values.
2. The best explanation for the existence of objective moral values is the existence of God.
3. Therefore, God (probably) exists.

As brief as it is, this is a well-formed argument. It follows the standard inductive form of "inference to the best explanation," or "abductive reasoning." Remember, inductive arguments are well-formed as long as the truth of the premises makes the truth of the conclusion likely. Abduction clearly meets this criteria; the best explanation for some phenomenon is, more often than not, the correct explanation. Should you arrive at your home to find the window broken, muddy boot prints through your living room, and all of your valuables missing, the best explanation would be a burglar. It is possible that something else occurred—aliens, perhaps, or an oddly selective tornado with muddy boots caught up in its midst—but the most likely explanation is that someone broke your window, tromped through your living room, and stole your valuables. When we say that this is the most likely explanation, we mean it is the most likely to be true. If it is true that God is the best explanation of the existence of objective moral values and true that there are objective moral values, then it is likely to be true that God exists as well. This is a well-formed argument.

Of course, not all well-formed arguments are good arguments. For it to be a good argument, we need reason to believe that all of the premises are true. Why should we think that these premises are true? In the first place, why should we think that morality is objective? People disagree about good and bad, right and wrong. Different cultures have different standards, both across time and across the world. Isn't it better to leave moral judgments to the individual? At the very least, shouldn't we grant that each culture gets to decide its own moral code? When it comes to morality, maybe truth really is relative. This is a pervasive attitude in our culture today, and it is dangerous. It is also nearly untenable. For that reason, we will begin with a discussion of the importance of recognizing the reality and objectivity of morality. Only after having done so will we turn our attention to the second premise, the claim that God is the best explanation of morality so understood.

First, a brief disclaimer is in order: the question under discussion in the moral argument is not about the tendency among atheists to be morally admirable people; it is the question of whether atheism can ground or support the objectivity of moral claims. In the words of the twentieth-century Quaker theologian David Trueblood, "The problem is not that of what will give the moral law power in men's lives, but that of a conception of the universe which will make the very existence of a moral law understandable."[3] The former is a question of human psychology or sociology; the latter is a question about the coherence of a worldview. In my experience, both theists and atheists alike run the full moral spectrum. Some atheists live morally degenerate lives; others live lives of moral virtue. The same is true of theists. (This should not surprise us. After all, as we read in James 2:19, even demons are theists.) I will ultimately conclude that objective morality makes more sense in the context of a theistic worldview, and that the objectivity of moral judgments can be seen as evidence of the existence of God. It would be a mistake, however, to take this as evidence of the immorality of atheists.[4] The coherence of a worldview and the actions of the individuals who espouse that worldview are two very different things.

Objective Moral Values

When we say that moral values are objective, what exactly are we saying? What are moral values? And what does it mean to be objective? We can begin with this last question. In a paper titled "Moral Arguments for Theistic Belief," Robert Adams answers that they would be "objective in the sense

---

3. D. Baggett and J. Walls, *The Moral Argument: A History* (Oxford: Oxford University Press, 2019), 198.

4. It is not only theists who sometimes make this mistake. In *The God Delusion*, Richard Dawkins spends a fair amount of time refuting the claim that "we do not need God in order to be good—or evil" (Dawkins, *The God Delusion* [Boston: Houghton Mifflin, 2006], 258). Although he ultimately concedes that the moral argument is making a different claim, that "without God there would be no standard for *deciding* what is good," he devotes the bulk of his treatment of morality to the behavioral challenge rather than the philosophical one (264). The moral argument does not say that individuals need God, or the belief in God, in order to act well. It says that a world without God would likely be a world without objective morality, and that goodness itself, as an objective moral value, points toward the existence of God.

that whether they obtain or not does not depend on whether any human being thinks they do."[5] Thus, if moral values are objective they are, in some important sense, a part of reality. As a result, statements about moral values are the kinds of things that are rightly called either true or false. This isn't the case for everything that we say. When I say to my children, "Please go clean your room," I have said something neither true nor false. Instead, I've issued a command. When you take a bite of something that has spoiled and say, "Yuck!" you have said something neither true nor false. You have expressed an emotion—namely, disgust. Some philosophers have claimed that moral language is more like one of these two kinds of expressions than it is a language about reality. According to "prescriptive" moral theories, "Murder is wrong" means something like "Do not murder." According to "emotivist" theories, it means something like "Murder—yuck!" In each case, "Murder is wrong" expresses something about murder, but since that something is either the speaker's emotion or a command, it would be a mistake to say that "Murder is wrong" is true. It can't be true; it's not that kind of a claim.

Emotivist moral theories have fallen from favor in recent decades. Still, they remain useful as demonstrations of what the objectivity of morality means. If morality is objective, then the person who says "Murder is wrong" is not talking about her emotional response to murder. Neither is she merely issuing a command not to murder. Instead, she is ascribing a moral feature to murder. She is saying that murder is wrong. If she is correct, she is so because of some feature of reality external to herself. In other words, the wrongness of murder is not a question of how she feels, what she believes, or what she would prefer the world to be like. If morality is objective, then the wrongness of murder comes down to reality itself. Those who affirm the objectivity of morality may not agree about why or how the universe contains real moral values, but they agree that it does. In this way, objective moral claims are analogous to the truths of mathematics: they may not be directly observable features of reality, but their truth or falsity does not in any way depend on how you feel about them.[6]

---

5. R. M Adams, "Moral Arguments for Theistic Belief," in *Rationality and Religious Belief,* ed. C. F. Delaney, University of Notre Dame Studies in the Philosophy of Religion 1 (Notre Dame, IN: University of Notre Dame Press, 1979), 117.

6. I heard Peter Singer reference this analogy in the Future of Life Institute podcast: "On Becoming a Moral Realist with Peter Singer," *AI Alignment Podcast,* hosted by Lucas Perry, October 18, 2018, https://futureoflife.org/2018/10/18/on-becoming-a-moral-realist-peter-singer/.

If this is what makes the objectivity of morality objective, what makes it moral? To answer this question, we can refer back to chapter 9 where I distinguished the following two ways of using the word *evil*:

Evil$_1$: Something that is harmful, painful, or otherwise unpleasant or undesirable.

Evil$_2$: Something that is malicious, cruel, or otherwise immoral.

The problem of evil is largely generated by the prevalence of Evil$_1$. Often, suffering, not immorality, is invoked as evidence against the existence of God.[7] Yet in turning our attention to Evil$_1$ we find what seems to be overwhelming evidence of Evil$_2$. It is not merely that the world contains vast amounts of unpleasantness; it seems also to include a great deal of moral wrongdoing. If all of the suffering in the world were the result of natural disasters or accidents, then it would be easy enough to content ourselves with an understanding of the reality of Evil$_1$. The person who falls victim to a hurricane has clearly been harmed, but it is not at all clear that she has been wronged. In contrast, the victim of theft, assault, murder, and other kinds of deliberate harm does seem to have been both harmed *and* wronged. This latter kind of evil, wrongdoing, involves a moral value. Thus Evil$_2$ generates the moral argument for theism.

Of course, evil is not the only moral category. Goodness is at least as important. Indeed, the richness of the moral universe goes well beyond the categories of good and evil. We can narrow our scope by focusing on two key features of morality. In the first place, morality tells us how we ought to act. If moral values are objective, then there are right actions and wrong actions— not just right for me or wrong for me, but really and truly right. To be more specific, the objectivity of morality renders some actions forbidden, some permitted, and some obligatory. As you might expect, forbidden actions are those that you ought not do: steal, lie, physically assault another person, and the like. In contrast, obligatory actions are those you ought to do. In these cases, we can say that you have a moral obligation to act in a certain way. Finally, permitted

---

7. An important terminological note: the phrase *moral evil* is often used in discussions of the problem of evil to describe the suffering caused by acts of morally free creatures. In this context, *moral evil* is used to distinguish the harms caused by nature from those caused by humanity. Understood in this way, the problem of evil is very much a problem of moral evil. In contrast, our discussion here is not about the effects of human action but about the classification of that action as evil. It is evil itself, as a category, that is at stake here.

actions are those that fall somewhere in the middle: acts which you may either do or refrain from doing. Note that the forbidden and the obligatory are often two sides of the same coin. For instance, if refusing to repay a loan is forbidden, then you have an obligation to repay what I lend you. Of course, this is not to say that you can't shirk your obligations. No, if morality is objective, then it operates more like the laws of the land than the laws of nature. Morality tells us how we should act, and then it is up to us to obey or not.

In the second place, morality tells us what kind of a person we ought to be. If the London priest is correct, and we "live in a world of real values," then there are good and bad ways of living—not just good or bad for me, but truly good or bad. This does not simply mean that some ways of living are more conducive to health, financial success, or pleasure than others; that much is surely true, regardless of morality. Instead, this second consequence of the objectivity of morality has more to do with proper function than it does earthly success. Where the Westminster Catechism asks, "What is the chief end of man?" this second conception answers, at a minimum, that there *is* a chief end of man. Humanity is directed toward some goal, a telos, and the closer you get to achieving that end, the closer you get to having *lived a good life*.

To see what I mean, note that we have no difficulty whatsoever distinguishing a good watch from a bad one. A good watch keeps time. A bad watch does not. Likewise, a good apple tree yields apples. A bad apple tree is barren. If moral values are objective, then one can either succeed or fail at being a person in much the same way that a tree can succeed or fail at thriving as a good tree. Consider the Psalmist's account of the righteous man:

> He will be like a tree firmly planted by streams of water,
> Which yields its fruit in its season
> And its leaf does not wither;
> And in whatever he does, he prospers. (Ps 1:3)

The flourishing tree is firmly planted where it ought to be and draws what it needs from the earth. It yields the fruit that it ought to yield, and it does so when it ought to do so. Its leaf does not wither, but instead is nourished by the earth and sun and nourishes the tree in return. This is the picture of a tree doing precisely what it was designed to do. When we say that moral values are a real and objective part of the world, we are affirming the fact that humans are like trees in this way. They can flourish or wither, succeed or fail at achieving their proper end. Above all, whether they achieve it or not, they do have a proper end. These two categories, the right action and the good life, rise and fall with the objectivity of moral values.

Ought and Is

In these two ways, the reality of objective moral values would do what observable reality cannot do: namely, ground and explain true claims about what we ought to do and how we ought to live. Why do I say that observable reality cannot tell us these things? Because as David Hume famously claimed in his *Treatise of Human Nature*, you cannot derive an *ought* from an *is*.[8] *What is* is a matter of description. It tells us what the world is like. In contrast, *ought* is normative and prescriptive. It tells us what we should do, how we should act, or how the world should be.[9] To briefly illustrate this point, suppose that you had two loaves of bread, and you encountered a person who was hungry and had no bread. What should you do? We could enumerate all of the relevant descriptive facts without ever arriving at an answer to that question. To be clear, I do not mean that you could never figure out what you ought to do, only that you could never reach this conclusion without relying on some kind of normative moral consideration. Mere facts about how the world is can never be enough, all on their own, to tell us how we should act.[10]

We can see this point more clearly by considering it in terms of logical entailment. Suppose I were to try to construct an argument for the conclusion "You should give the hungry man bread." Using the descriptive facts as premises, we get something like the following:

1. You have two loaves of bread.
2. That man is hungry and has no bread.
3. Therefore, you should give the hungry man bread.

---

8. D. Hume, *A Treatise of Human Nature*, ed. D. F. Norton and M. J. Norton, Oxford Philosophical Texts (Oxford, Clarendon Press, 2000).

9. This distinction is discussed in some greater detail in chapter 5.

10. If you are familiar with Sam Harris's *The Moral Landscape*, you may be wondering how I can state this claim so confidently when Harris is so certain to have refuted it. Very briefly, atheistic and theistic philosophers alike agree that Harris is mistaken on this point. I will return to Harris's position in chapter 13.

Although this argument is straightforward, and although it would be persuasive to the average morally sensitive person, it is not a well-formed argument. The premises do not entail the conclusion. In order to be well-formed, it needs something to link the descriptive premises to the normative conclusion. It needs an explicitly moral premise, such as "If you have two loaves of bread, and a hungry man has no bread, then you *should* give him bread." When Hume wrote that you cannot derive an ought from an is, he meant that no amount of descriptive premises could ever entail a normative conclusion. How the world *is* could never entail any claims at all about how we *ought* to act.

If you are not persuaded, perhaps another dialogue will help. Suppose that you were very hungry, and your friend brought two large sandwiches for lunch. You might have something like the following exchange:

You: I'm so hungry. I totally forgot my lunch this morning, and I skipped breakfast. I can barely think straight!

Friend: That's too bad. I have two sandwiches with me today. Just your bad luck, I guess!

You: You have two? Do you usually eat two sandwiches?

Friend: Oh no! I could never eat two for lunch. I just bring two in case something comes up later and I need it.

You: So . . . could I please have your second sandwich? I'm just so hungry!

Friend: No, you can't. It's mine. I'm not really into sharing.

You: But you aren't even going to eat it today, right?

Friend: Right. I don't think I've ever eaten my second sandwich.

You: But I'm hungry . . .

Friend: Yeah, you said that. What's your point?

You: My point is that you have an extra sandwich, I have no sandwich, and I'm hungry!

Friend: Yes . . . and?

You: So you should give me your extra sandwich!

Friend: But why? It's mine, and I just told you I don't like to share!

In this imagined scenario, your friend does not dispute any of the relevant descriptive facts about your situation. She knows that you are hungry and without food. She knows that she has extra food. What she rejects is the moral principle that you have left unspoken in this conversation—that a person should share with those in need.

Most of us add these kinds of premises to informal moral arguments without even noticing that we are doing so. For that reason, it is easy to look at an argument that tries to derive an ought from an is, like the one I gave above, and mistakenly conclude that it is well-formed. The trick is to ask yourself: Will someone who doesn't already believe the conclusion be persuaded? Do the premises alone provide reason to believe the conclusion? This dialogue is intended to show that they do not. If it seems as if they do, that is because you have smuggled in your prior moral beliefs. You have added a premise that is not yet there. The person who does not share those beliefs can affirm the descriptive premises while denying the normative conclusion and can do so without contradiction because the former do not entail the latter. This is what Hume meant when he wrote that you cannot derive an *ought* from an *is*.

Why does this matter? Because the world seems to contain genuine wrongdoing. Some people seem to do what they ought not do and live as they ought not live. It also seems as if moral principles like "You should share when you are able" and "You should not deliberately harm a person for your own entertainment" are true. If this is the case, if there are true moral judgments and actual moral obligations, then the truth of those judgments and the force of these obligations cannot be explained in terms of observable reality alone.

By way of analogy, consider claims about legality. When we say that some type of behavior is legal or illegal, we are saying something that is either true or false. We are not merely expressing preferences or issuing commands; we are making claims about how the world is. Whether our claim is true or false depends upon what the law says. If it is against the law for a woman to drive in some particular country, then it is true to say that it is illegal for women to drive in that country. The law itself is the reality to which that claim corresponds. (In this case, as in all cases, it is entirely possible for legality and morality to come apart.) If a citizen of that country came to the United States and mistakenly claimed that it was illegal in the United States for women to drive, she would be saying something false. In both cases, the truth or falsity of the claim depends upon the content of the law. The law grounds and explains the objective truth or falsity of legal judgments.

In the same way, if our claims about morality are ever true or false, then there must be something in virtue of which they are true or false. Something has to ground and explain their truth or falsity. Whatever this grounding feature of reality is, it must go beyond descriptive facts about the world. As we have seen, you cannot derive an *ought* from an *is*. Real, objective moral values—right and wrong, good and bad—would ground and explain the truth or falsity of claims about the right action and the good life. Objective moral values enable us to bridge the gap between *is* and *ought*.

Moral Relativism

But why should we think that moral values are objective? Even if we agree that moral claims are more than an emotional expression or an issuance of a command, must we really conclude that moral truths are akin to the truths of mathematics? Perhaps there is a middle ground. Maybe our moral language isn't grounded in some ultimate reality but is somehow grounded in human aspiration. After all, in light of the diversity of moral attitudes that we find across space and time, why should we believe that moral values are objective? What are the costs of denying objectivity? We can begin with this last question, for the costs are quite high. I said in the introduction that moral relativism is nearly untenable. In what follows, I hope to show why.

To that end, suppose that morality is not objective. Suppose that all of morality—both the rightness of an act and the goodness of a life—is relative. On this view, moral claims can rightly be said to be either true or false, but their truth or falsity will vary from person to person; instead of one objective standard for a good life or a right act, we find many individual standards of goodness and rightness.[11] In chapter 4 we distinguished two concepts of truth as relative: subjective and cultural relativism. Beginning

---

11. Here and throughout this chapter, I am considering one popular account of moral relativism. It is not the only way of construing morality as relative, but it is the one I encounter most frequently in the classroom. Alternatively, one could go further and insist that relativistic moral claims are never true at all. We will briefly consider two of these positions—emotivism and prescriptivism—in chapter 13. For now, note that they would take us further from objective morality, not closer to it. Finally, there are some philosophically sophisticated views that deny the objectivity of morality. Many fall under the categories of emotivism or prescriptivism, but some do not. To address those accounts would require far more than can be done in this chapter. For those interested, you might begin with R. Rorty, *Philosophy and the Mirror of Nature*, Princeton Classics Series (Princeton, NJ: Princeton University Press, 2009).

with subjective relativism, suppose that moral values are not objective but are instead subjectively relative. That is, suppose that the truth of moral claims depends not on correspondence to reality but on the deeply held beliefs of an individual person, or "subject." On this view, an action is morally permissible just as long as it does not violate the deeply held moral values of the subject, and an action is forbidden when it violates the deeply held moral values of the subject. Likewise, the good life is the life most desired or valued by the individual in question, and failure to thrive is failure to achieve some personal goal. Thus morality is in the eye of the beholder.

What follows from this position? Let's begin with a relatively benign example. Many teachers believe that plagiarism is not merely a violation of an academic code but is also immoral. Some students disagree, especially those who come from a family or community that sees no harm in plagiarism. Now suppose that one such student submits a plagiarized paper and gets caught. They might have something like the following exchange:

> **Teacher:** Your paper was clearly plagiarized. What do you have to say for yourself?
>
> **Student:** You got me! I sure hope you're willing to show me some mercy.
>
> **Teacher:** Is that all? No apology? No explanation?
>
> **Student:** Well, I'm certainly sorry I got *caught*. I didn't see that coming. I would never have submitted a plagiarized paper if I expected to get caught doing so. For that I really am sorry.
>
> **Teacher:** But what about the academic code? You violated it! Have you no remorse?
>
> **Student:** That's true. I did violate the code. I regret it because you seem pretty angry right now, but I wouldn't say I have remorse. I don't think I did anything wrong, just stupid. I never got the big deal about plagiarism anyway.

Note that both the student and the teacher can agree that plagiarism violates the academic code of their school. Where they disagree is on the question of morality: Did the plagiarism violate some deeper moral code? Is there a moral obligation not to plagiarize? Academic codes are explicit written contracts, but moral codes are not nearly so transparent and accessible.

The student believes herself to be innocent of the charge of immorality. If moral truths are relative to the subject, then she is correct; she did not do anything immoral. (After all, she finds plagiarism to be morally permissible.) But what are we to say about the teacher's view? After all, the teacher is equally convinced that plagiarism is immoral. Is the teacher wrong? Or can they both be right? Well, that depends upon what the teacher means by wrong. If the teacher means that it was wrong for the student to plagiarize, then subjective relativism would say that the teacher is incorrect. The student is not morally opposed to plagiarism, so plagiarism is not a moral wrong for her. If instead the teacher remembers to limit the scope of her moral claims to her own behavior, then it would be wrong for the teacher to plagiarize and wrong for any student who opposes plagiarism to do so as well, but for students who have no such qualms, plagiarism is morally permissible. If wrong is relative to the person, then an action is only ever wrong for one person or another.

Now imagine that this were the case for all moral claims. It is one thing to suppose that the unabashed plagiarizer is subject only to her own conscience, but what ought we to say about stealing? Just imagine how this might go. Consider the following dialogue between two fictitious roommates:

Gary: Have you seen my wallet? I left it on the kitchen counter.

Steve: Oh yeah, it's in my room. I took the cash.

Gary: You took my cash!

Steve: Yeah. You left it on the counter, and I wanted to buy something.

Gary: But it was mine . . .

Steve: Legally? I don't know the law around shared property. Pretty sure if there's cash on my kitchen counter, I can use it.

Gary: Not just legally . . . I mean, the cash was mine. You knew that, and you stole it. Are you going to pay me back?

Steve: Pay you back? This wasn't a loan. And anyway, I'm all out of cash. That's why I took it!

Gary: That's just wrong!

Steve: Not for me it isn't! Maybe taking other people's money is wrong for you, but for me it's no problem at all. I don't see anything wrong with using money I find in my kitchen.

Once again, if moral judgments are true or false relative to the individual, then Steve is in the clear here. He may be an undesirable roommate, he may have broken the law, but if he genuinely does not believe that taking money is wrong, then subjective relativism tells us that he is not guilty of any moral wrongdoing.

Perhaps none of this is too alarming. After all, as long as we can define legality and other similarly explicit codes in a way that applies equally to all people, does it really matter if we can say that morality is objective and universal? The plagiarizing student need not be morally guilty in order to be penalized for violating the school's precepts, and Steve can find a new roommate, lock his wallet and valuables in a safe, and follow up with the police. There are legal consequences for theft that are independent of any deeper moral judgment. What is gained by insisting on objective moral wrongdoing in addition to these other kinds of judgments?

Well, one gain is that it accords with our commonsense notion of how the world really is. This is especially clear when we consider the crimes of murder and sexual assault. If the morality of action is really and truly dependent upon the individual, then the person who is not opposed to taking the life of an innocent person can truthfully claim that murder is not wrong for him or her. We can put murderers in jail because legal consequences depend only upon legal culpability, but we cannot infer moral guilt from legal guilt. The sincerely unabashed murderer, according to subjective relativism, is innocent of any moral wrongdoing. Are we really prepared to say that sexual assault and murder are only wrong for those who condemn these acts? If not, if instead we affirm the objectivity of even one moral obligation—the obligation not to wantonly rape or kill for pleasure, for instance—then objective moral values exist. We can disagree about the details, such as how many, what they require, and so on, but if we agree that some acts are wrong for everyone, then we have already agreed that there is objective wrongness.

We can say the same for the goodness of a life. To fully grasp the implications of subjective relativism for morality, consider the following two cases:

> Anika believes that she should treat other people in the way that she would like to be treated. She was born into a financially comfortable family, though not a wealthy one, and she has dedicated her adult life to improving the lives of those around her. She gives to charities, volunteers at a local

food bank, and works as an attorney where she frequently does *pro bono* work for those who cannot afford legal representation.

Mia believes that you only get one life, and it is up to you to make the system work to your advantage. Her guiding code is a combination of *carpe diem* and *look-out for yourself*. Mia works as an attorney as well, but she refuses to work *pro bono*. She charges her clients in billable hours based largely on what she thinks she can get away with rather than how many hours she actually has worked. When Mia finds someone's wallet, she keeps the cash. When she finds a phone, she sells it. She once struck and killed a pedestrian while speeding and drove off before she could get caught. She does not feel guilty about this. Instead, she is proud of her success at escaping unpleasant and disruptive consequences. She really and truly believes that her only moral obligation is to herself.

Both Anika and Mia live by a deeply held moral code. Both live consistently with their own code. Do they both live lives of equal moral value? Must we really say that both are living good lives, that neither life is morally superior to the other?

If subjective relativism is true, then there is no shared standard against which to judge the lives of Mia and Anika—no moral standard, that is. We can say that Anika does a better job of obeying the law. We can say that we find Mia's life appalling. Yet subjective relativism does not allow us to say that Mia's life choices were morally inferior to Anika's. For subjective relativism, the subject decides what, if anything, is the chief end of her own life. When we leave this to the individual, we are left with no ability to evaluate the lives of others against a shared moral standard. If Mia and Anika both succeed at living the life they set out to live, then according to subjective relativism they both lived a good life. This does not fit with our commonsense views about morality.

If subjective relativism is the right way to think about morality, then a moral judgment is just like any other preference claim: I prefer mint cookies and cream ice cream over other flavors; I prefer kalamata olives over green olives; I prefer benevolence over theft, and peacemaking over warmongering. I hope that you can see why most people ultimately find this view to be untenable. Most of us don't merely think that murder is wrong for us; we think that murder is wrong, period. We think that a life lived kindly in pursuit of truth is not merely a good life for us; it is a good life, period. We may disagree over the details of something as minor as speeding on the highway or plagiarizing a short assignment, but we do not disagree on the reality of at least some objective moral values. It isn't that we prefer it if people don't murder and rape. We condemn these actions, and we do so universally, regardless of the beliefs of the murderer or rapist.

Cultural Relativism

In the classroom, this is the point where I typically face the following objection: "Perhaps this is true of Americans and other Westerners, but what about other cultures? Isn't it arrogant of one culture to pass judgment on the morality of a different culture?" The attitude behind this accusation is just one reason why cultural relativism is far more common than subjective relativism. A moral truth is culturally relative if its truth depends upon the deeply held beliefs of a community or culture. On this view, an action is morally permissible as long as it does not violate the deeply held moral values of the culture, and an action is morally forbidden when it violates the deeply held moral values of the culture. Likewise, a life is good (or bad) relative to the culture in which it is lived. Unlike subjective relativism, cultural relativism does allow for the moral judgment of other people in your community. What it does not allow for, however, is cross-cultural comparison.

It is easy to see why cultural relativism is more popular than subjective relativism. Different cultures disagree about all sorts of codes: standards of beauty, varieties of food, ideal family structures. A thirty-year-old American man who still lives with his parents, for instance, may be judged as a case of "failure to launch" in the United States; in Italy or India he may be considered an appropriately devoted son. Similarly, when it comes to how different cultures treat women, children, migrants, the disabled, criminals, or any other people group, there is a strong temptation to defer to cultural differences in place of moral judgment. That is, the reality of cultural differences leads to cultural relativism about the truth of moral claims.

But this is a mistake. To see why, note first that the boundaries of a culture are drawn both in space and in time. American culture today is surely not the same thing as American culture in 1795. For that reason, past versions of our own culture are just as immune to moral comparison as are geographically distinct cultures. If it is unfair to hold one country to the moral norms of another, it is equally unfair to hold past cultures to present moral norms. This leads to a surprising result: cultural relativism makes it impossible to speak of a culture improving in a moral sense. Instead, we can at best note that the culture has changed. Take, for instance, one of the more obvious moral failings of our country's history: the abduction and enslavement of Africans and their descendants. I presume that my readers will agree that the legality of slavery in the United States was wrong and that the abolition of slavery brought about a moral improvement. However, if cultural relativism is true, then we cannot say that abolishing slavery was a moral improvement, not unless early US society largely condemned the slave trade. Let me say that again: if cultural relativism is true, and if it is true that early US culture largely approved of the slave trade, then it was not wrong of the US to engage in the trafficking and enslavement of African men, women, and children and their descendants. Are you beginning to see why cultural relativism is a difficult position to defend?

Now consider early abolitionists. On cultural relativism, those who resisted and opposed their culture's attitudes about slavery were not morally right—in fact, they were advocating for something that was morally wrong.[12] The thing for which they advocated—freeing enslaved people—was widely deemed immoral. (It was also illegal.) Because slaves were seen as property, assisting a person who had escaped slavery was, in the eyes of this culture, akin to aiding and abetting a thief. But if morality is determined by broad cultural consensus, and if the consensus said that it was wrong to help an escaped slave, then it was immoral for the abolitionists to assist anyone fleeing slavery. We can all agree that slavery is wrong now, of course. Our culture now condemns it. But we cannot call this change an improvement without

---

12. Here, again, I am writing about the strain of cultural relativism that is most common in popular discourse. There are some philosophically substantial varieties of cultural relativism on which this might not be true. For example, it is possible to believe that morality is relative to a culture, but not always to the consciously held specific beliefs advocated by the members of that culture. Instead, it is theoretically possible to tie moral truth to consistency with other widely affirmed principles. On this view, the moral reformed might hold the true belief, but only if her position is more consistent with the greater web of beliefs espoused by her culture. This view has problems of its own—for instance, on such a view the moral reformer in a profoundly depraved culture would still count as immoral—but I cannot address these views here. See, for example, R. Rorty, M. Williams, and D. Bromwich, *Philosophy and the Mirror of Nature*, Princeton Classics Series (Princeton, NJ: Princeton University Press, 2009).

condemning a culture different from our own, without applying our moral standard to their moral judgments. This is precisely what cultural relativism about morality prevents us from doing.

Cultural relativism thus removes the possibility of a culture's moral improvement, and this example reveals a second, related problem: if moral truths are culturally relative, then there is no such thing and can be no such thing as a moral reformer inside a community. A reformer always speaks against a current trend, and according to cultural relativism, the current trend is the moral standard. By definition then, the voice that speaks against the common view is always wrong. This goes for early abolitionists in the United States, for people today who speak out against pedophilia, child brides, and genital mutilation in cultures where these practices are accepted, for those who condemn so-called honor killings in cultures that largely accept them, and for those who speak out against genocide in any society that views certain people groups as less than fully human. In fact, on cultural relativism, for any question of the form "Is it morally permissible to . . . ?" the best way to answer it would be a very good, widely distributed national (or cultural) poll. In a real and important sense, cultural relativism about morality means that the majority gets to decide what is and is not morally permissible. If the majority favors infanticide, incest, rape, or any other practice which we find morally abhorrent, then those practices are morally permissible and not at all immoral in those cultures.

Most of us find these consequences untenable and unacceptable. It simply cannot be that the rightness or wrongness of pedophilia depends entirely upon the attitudes of the culture in which it occurs. It cannot be that the job of the slave-catcher was morally superior to that of the abolitionist. It cannot be that it is morally permissible to kill a woman for marrying the wrong man as long as her culture permits it. If this is what morality requires, then morality is an empty and meaningless category, needlessly lofty language for mere popular opinion.

Cultural relativism fares no better with respect to the question of a good life than it does right action. I would ask you to suppose that some culture broadly condoned pedophilia, but you need not suppose it, for it is a part of the history of our world. Khaled Hosseini's best-seller, *The Kite Runner*, includes a particularly painful but powerful depiction of something like this, and Plato's account of ancient Greece is likewise troubling. It isn't merely that pedophilia has occurred throughout history, nor even that is has been condoned, because it has even been admired at times. If there are or have been cultures in which the good life involves the systematic sexual abuse of children, then we should not merely defer to individual cultures on the question of what the good life for a human being really is.

Conclusion

For reasons which should be clear by now, I believe the evidence favors real and objective moral values. Still, I certainly haven't proven that morality is objective. Instead, I have asked the reader to see what exactly is at stake here. Far too often, people are willing to declare morality relativistic without really thinking through the implications. That is, in a sense, cheating. The general tendency is to keep the best parts of objective morality (antidiscrimination, antiviolence, etc.) while insisting, despite all that, on a relativistic account. The result is an internally inconsistent, contradictory position. The real effect of rejecting objective morality is that you lose all of it. If there are any objective moral obligations whatsoever, then objective moral values exist. That is the choice we face.

Furthermore, a rejection of objective morality would undermine what most people have believed throughout most of history across most of the world. It is wrong to kill without cause; it is wrong to traffic in persons; it is wrong to rape. Similarly, some cultures are morally better than others; it is possible for an individual and for a culture to improve morally; it is possible for there to be moral reformers within a community. These shared intuitions are widely held to be true, and their truth is widely held to be independent of how any particular person feels about them. If our moral judgments are rightly called true or false, then there must be objective moral values to which they correspond. If there are no objective moral values, then these shared intuitions are not what they appear to be. Absent some moral reality, the best we could hope for would be societal agreement. We could agree about our emotional response to murder (Yuck!). We could collectively decree, "Do not murder!" We could hope that individuals and cultures would collectively choose to condemn murder. What we could not have, nor even hope for, would be the truth of any universal moral judgment like "Murder is wrong (for everyone)." Without objective moral values, there can be no objective moral truths. For that reason, these shared intuitions form the basis of a defense of the first premise of the moral argument. If they are true and not merely popular or emotionally appealing, then objective moral values exist.

This is, of course, not enough to show that God exists. Indeed, a surprising number of philosophers, theistic and atheistic, agree about the objectivity of morality. One of the most famous atheistic moral philosophers of our time, Peter Singer, has recently changed his position on this very topic. After decades of work in ethics trying to capture the importance of morality without relying on either a divine creator or objective moral values, Singer has finally come to believe that morality is, after all, an objective feature of reality. In a 2018 interview, he described his path through emotivism and prescriptivism. Ultimately, he found that each left the following question unanswered: "Why act morally?" After all, what power does the disgust of one person or the command of another have over someone who does not share those attitudes? Singer notes:

> And so I came to the conclusion that there is a reasonable case for saying that there are objective moral truths and this is not just a matter of our attitudes or of our preferences universalized, but there's something stronger going on and it's, in some ways, more like the objectivity of mathematical truths or perhaps of logical truths.[13]

Singer is not alone. It is entirely possible to affirm both atheism and objective moral realism. That is, it is possible to believe that objective moral values exist without thereby believing in God.

Although possible, it is neither easy nor straightforward. In the next chapter, we will consider the compatibility of atheism and moral realism. To defend the moral argument for theism, we need to defend both premises of the argument. So far, we have considered only the first premise: (1) Objective moral values exist. Our work in the next two chapters will center upon the remaining premise: (2) The best explanation for the existence of objective moral values is the existence of God. To that end, we will ask: Why does the existence of objective moral values need an explanation? What does atheism have to offer? And can theism fare any better?

---

13. "On Becoming a Moral Realist with Peter Singer."

Atheistic Moral Values

13

We can now turn to the second premise of the moral argument: "The best explanation for the existence of objective moral values is the existence of God." Why should we believe this? What does the objectivity of morality have to do with the existence of God? Robert Adams summarizes this line of defense as follows: "One of the most generally accepted reasons for believing in the existence of anything is that its existence is implied by the theory that seems to account most adequately for some subject matter."[3] For example, physics does the best job of accounting for observable reality,

---

1. J.-P. Sartre, *Existentialism Is a Humanism* (New Haven, CT: Yale University Press, 2007), 28–29.

2. R. Dawkins, *River Out of Eden: A Darwinian View of Life*, Science Masters Series (New York: Basic, 1995), 133.

3. R. M Adams, "Moral Arguments for Theistic Belief," in *Rationality and Religious Belief,* ed. C. F. Delaney, University of Notre Dame Studies in the Philosophy of Religion 1 (Notre Dame, IN: University of Notre Dame Press, 1979), 117.

and physics implies the existence of dark matter, so we accept the existence of dark matter. In the same way, a theistic metaethics—that is, a theistic system of understanding what makes something right or wrong, good or bad—does the best job of accounting for the reality of objective moral values. A theistic metaethics implies the existence of God, so Adam concludes that "my meta-ethical views provide me with a reason of some weight for believing in the existence of God."[4] The existence of God is, or seems to be, the best explanation of the objectivity of moral values.

Interestingly enough, theists are not alone in endorsing the close connection between the existence of God and the objectivity of moral values. In the introduction to *Robust Ethics*, a defense of atheistic moral realism, Erik Wielenberg notes this fact with concern. He considers the following quotation from fellow atheistic philosopher J. L. Mackie:

> [W]e might well argue . . . that objective intrinsically prescriptive features, supervening upon natural ones, constitute so odd a cluster of qualities and relations that they are most unlikely to have arisen in the ordinary course of events, without an all-powerful God to create them. If, then, there are such intrinsically prescriptive objective values, they make the existence of a god more probable than it would have been without them.[5]

Thus, Wielenberg continues, Mackie and others "who do not believe that God exists, see their arguments as posing serious challenges for moral realism."[6] Wielenberg's account is a response to this worry, and he rejects the suggestion that objective morality would serve as evidence for theism. Still, it is worth noting that the intuitive pull is there for atheists as well as theists. At face value, theism seems to be a better explanation of objective morality than atheism.

Atheistic Existentialism

But why should objective morality require an explanation in the first place? In his 1945 work *Existentialism Is a Humanism*, Jean-Paul Sartre addressed

---

4. Adams, "Moral Arguments for Theistic Belief," 117.
5. E. J. Wielenberg, *Robust Ethics: The Metaphysics and Epistemology of Godless Normative Realism* (Oxford: Oxford University Press, 2014), viii.
6. Wielenberg, *Robust Ethics*, ix.

what he took to be a persistent tendency among atheistic and agnostic philosophers to retain a notion of human nature inspired by a theistic metaethics. More plainly stated, he accused his atheistic peers of smuggling in a conception of human nature, a telos, that made little sense in a world without God. He explained:

> When we think of God the Creator, we usually conceive of him as a superlative artisan. Whatever doctrine we may be considering, say Descartes's or Leibniz's, we always agree that the will more or less follows understanding, or at the very least accompanies it, so that when God creates he knows exactly what he is creating. Thus the concept of man, in the mind of God, is comparable to the concept of the paper knife in the mind of the manufacturer: God produces man following certain techniques and a conception, just as the craftsman, following a definition and a technique, produces a paper knife. Thus each individual man is the realization of a certain concept within the divine intelligence. Eighteenth century atheistic philosophers suppressed the idea of God but not, for all that, the idea that essence precedes existence.[7]

To adopt Sartre's terminology, if God created humanity, then the essence of humanity precedes its existence. On this theistic picture, every human being is made according to a design plan with an intended purpose; mankind has a telos. Just as a hammer is created for the purpose of banging nails, and a paper knife for cutting paper, humanity was created with some divine purpose in mind. This is what it means to say that man's essence precedes their existence: if human nature was established by God prior to the creation of humankind, then it is there to be discovered, not created anew by each individual.

The trouble, according to Sartre, is that this all falls apart in the absence of a creator God. Those who endorse an atheistic worldview and yet help themselves to a theistically grounded notion of human nature are engaging in inconsistency. Sartre writes:

> Atheistic existentialism, which I represent, is more consistent. It states that if God does not exist, there is at least one being in whom existence precedes

---

7. Sartre, *Existentialism Is a Humanism*, 21.

essence—a being whose existence comes before its essence, a being who exists before he can be defined by any concept of it. That being is man. . . . What do we mean here by "existence precedes essence?" We mean that man first exists: he materializes in the world, encounters himself, and only afterward defines himself. If man as existentialists conceive of him cannot be defined, it is because to begin with he is nothing. He will not be anything until later, and then he will be what he makes of himself. Thus, there is no human nature since there is no God to conceive of it. . . . Man is nothing other than what he makes of himself.[8]

If humanity was not created by a divine mind for some preestablished purpose, then it no longer makes sense to think of human nature as something to be discovered. Instead, it is something to be invented. You can only discover something that already exists. If humanity came into existence without the help or plan of a designer, then there isn't any design to be found. Instead, Sartre maintains that it is up to each of us, as individuals, to make something of ourselves.

If there is no objective human nature, then there is no objectively good life. Some people may be better than others at creating a coherent narrative, but at the end of the day "man simply is."[9] Nothing really means anything beyond what we make of it—and it only means that for the brief duration of our lives and the lives of those who may remember us.[10] Most important for our purposes is this: Sartre was an atheistic philosopher, and he himself maintained that atheism undermines our justification for believing in the reality of objective moral values. Furthermore, he suggested that those who fail to see this are simply fooling themselves. In particular, Sartre explicitly called out those who blithely assume that "nothing will have changed if God does not exist; we will encounter the same standards of honesty, progress and humanism, and we will have turned God into an obsolete hypothesis that

---

8. Sartre, *Existentialism Is a Humanism*, 22.

9. *Existentialism Is a Humanism* began as a lecture and culminated in a novel. This quotation comes from the delivered lecture, the text of which can be found in W. Kaufmann, *Existentialism from Dostoevsky to Sartre* (San Francisco: Hauraki, 2016).

10. To be clear, Sartre's existentialism is not to be confused with the rudimentary and simplistic subjective relativism introduced in chapter 12. For a more extensive account of his position, I recommend that you read *Existentialism Is a Humanism*—a relatively brief and accessible text. For further reading, I recommend C. B. Guignon and D. Pereboom, *Existentialism: Basic Writings* (Indianapolis: Hackett, 2001).

will die out quietly on its own."[11] It was in response to this naive hope that Sartre wrote the passage in this chapter's epigraph: "Existentialists, on the other hand, find it extremely disturbing that God no longer exists, for along with his disappearance goes the possibility of finding values in an intelligible heaven."[12]

Among those values are the good life and the right action. According to Sartre, the very idea of a good life assumes that humanity was created for some particular purpose. In the absence of that creator, and in the absence of that intended purpose, there does not seem to be anything left to support the notion of a good life. If people are not intended to be anything, then it no longer makes sense to speak of individuals as succeeding or failing as persons. Likewise, there does not seem to be anything left to support the rightness or wrongness of an act—for there would be nothing for them to be right or wrong in relation to.

Evolution and Morality

If Sartre is correct, then undesigned human beings would lack an objective human nature and, with it, objective moral values. Without a designer, there is no design plan to serve as our standard of human flourishing. But what if there were a design plan of a different sort, one that did not require a designer? One common way of arguing for the existence of God is by appealing to the evidence of design in nature. In response, some atheistic philosophers point to the process of natural selection. What looks like design, they say, is really just the result of a particular evolutionary mechanism. Can an analogous move be made here?

In recent decades, a number of philosophers have defended accounts on which our shared moral values are seen as the result of Darwinian evolution.[13] We even find something of this sort in the position advanced by Richard

---

11. Sartre, *Existentialism Is a Humanism*, 28.

12. Sartre, *Existentialism Is a Humanism*, 28.

13. For example, Philip Kitcher, *The Ethical Project* (Cambridge, MA: Harvard University Press, 2011), plus the works referenced by Dawkins: R. A. Hinde, *Why Gods Persist: A Scientific Approach to Religion* (New York: Routledge, 2001): M. Shermer, *The Science of Good and Evil: Why People Cheat, Gossip, Care, Share, and Follow the Golden Rule* (New York: Holt, 2005); R. Buckman, *Can We Be Good without God?: Biology, Behavior, and the Need to Believe* (Amherst, NY: Prometheus, 2010); M. Hauser, *Moral Minds: The Nature of Right and Wrong* (New York: HarperCollins, 2009).

Dawkins in *The God Delusion*.[14] We have already read Dawkins's earlier declaration that "the universe we observe has precisely the properties we should expect if there is, at bottom, no design, no purpose, no evil and no good, nothing but blind pitiless indifference."[15] In isolation, this quotation from *River Out of Eden* seems to indicate that Dawkins dismisses the objectivity of moral obligations and values entirely. Yet in his more recent work, Dawkins acknowledges that humanity shares a broad moral code, one that favors things like kindness and generosity and condemns things like selfishness and needless violence.

In *The God Delusion*, he spends some time unpacking why it seems that humanity shares a moral code. The values widely affirmed by humanity are not, according to Dawkins, the result of a creator God or a divine notion of right and wrong. Instead, they are the result of natural selection. Our genes, as Dawkins famously notes, are selfish. They want nothing more than their own reproduction. This is not to say that *we* are selfish, but rather that we are subject to the unconscious biological imperative generated by our genetic makeup. Because our selfish genes aggressively seek their own reproduction, the organisms housing those genes—that is, our bodies—are going to act in ways that maximize their reproductive potential. As Dawkins put it in *The Selfish Gene*, "We are survival machines—robot vehicles blindly programmed to preserve the selfish molecules known as 'genes.'"[16] As a result, humanity as a species acts according to a shared set of rules designed to fulfill this shared human purpose.[17] We call these rules "morality." Thus Dawkins posits some-

---

14. R. Dawkins, *The God Delusion* (Boston: Houghton Mifflin, 2006). I am using deliberately loose language like "something of this sort" rather than claiming that this is Dawkins's stated position because Dawkins can be difficult to pin down on questions about morality. Over the past several decades, Dawkins has said a lot about morality, both explicitly and implicitly, and it can be difficult to reconcile into a single coherent account. As William Lane Craig wrote, "Although he says that there is no evil, no good, nothing but pitiless indifference, he is an unabashed moralist. He vigorously condemns such actions as the harassment and abuse of homosexuals, the religious indoctrination of children, the Incan practice of human sacrifice, and prizing cultural diversity over the interest of Amish children." W. L. Craig, *On Guard: Defending Your Faith with Reason and Precision* (Colorado Springs: David C. Cook, 2010). If Craig is correct, this inconsistency points to outright contradiction with Dawkins's own account. I think Craig may very well be correct about this! I also think it may be possible that Dawkins holds something closer to the position defended here—one which may ground something like objective morality, though not in the traditional use of that term.

15. Dawkins, *River Out of Eden*, 133.

16. R. Dawkins, *The Selfish Gene*, Oxford Landmark Science (Oxford: Oxford University Press, 2016), ix.

17. This sounds a little rosier than it actually is. If Dawkins is correct, then my genes want to maximize their own reproduction—not my reproduction, not yours, and not the reproduction of your genes. People who share my genetic makeup—close biological kin—can serve in

thing akin to objective moral values and, perhaps, even an objective human telos. In place of a designer, Dawkins offers the process of natural selection so central to Darwinian evolution.

What does this look like? Throughout the history of our species we have tended to live in community, depending upon one another for resources, guidance, and care. The person who lies, steals, and cheats is unlikely to be well-regarded by the community. Thus, the person who lies, steals, and cheats is unlikely to be helped by the community and, without the benefit of community, unlikely to live very long. As a result, lying, stealing, and cheating thwart our biological imperative whereas acts of benevolence promote it. On Dawkins's view, this is what it means to say that lying, stealing, and cheating are wrong and acts of benevolence are right; morality is a series of guiding rules largely shared by humanity and grounded in our biological impulse to ensure a future for our genes.

Of course, the promotion of our genes is not a conscious motivation; it is an unconscious biological impulse. It is neither rational nor reflective. In fact, Dawkins goes further and explicitly notes, "Selection does not favour the evolution of a cognitive awareness of what is good for your genes."[18] Goodness may be a matter of reproductive success, but *believing* goodness to be a matter of reproductive success is neither necessary nor even preferable. These guiding rules of evolution should not be understood as a series of clearly stated principles but are instead "rules of thumb, which work in practice to promote the genes that built them."[19] Like all rules of thumb, they don't always get the details right. For example, the biological impulse to reproduce generates the impulse to be sexually active, regardless of the actual fertility of your sexual partner. In the same way, Dawkins writes:

> I am suggesting that the same is true of the urge to kindness—to altruism, to generosity, to empathy, to pity. In ancestral times, we had the opportunity to be altruistic only towards close kin and potential reciprocators.

---

this regard. My genes want to reproduce themselves; they don't care whether that happens through me or through other "robot vehicles" like my children. Outsiders, those with different genetic makeup, cannot help. I call this endeavor "shared" because we are all members of the same species, but it is important that we not overstate the communal aspect of this endeavor. My genes care about themselves; yours do, as well. There is no communal benevolence here.

18. Dawkins, *The God Delusion*, 252.
19. Dawkins, *The God Delusion*, 251.

Nowadays that restriction is no longer there, but the rule of thumb persists. Why would it not? It is just like sexual desire. We can no more help ourselves feeling pity when we see a weeping unfortunate (who is unrelated and unable to reciprocate) than we can help ourselves feeling lust for a member of the opposite sex (who may be infertile or otherwise unable to reproduce). Both are misfirings, Darwinian mistakes: blessed, precious mistakes.[20]

We desire sex because our genes seek reproduction, but we often don't consciously tie sex to reproductive aims. Even when reproduction is off the table, sexual desire persists.

In the same way, we pity the weak and help the needy because our genes seek reproduction, and in the grand sweep of human history local acts of service have aided human survival. In our present era, our communities have grown so large and transient that things like kindness and generosity may not offer the evolutionary advantage that they used to. Still, like sexual desire for an infertile partner, the urge to practice kindness with those unlikely to be of much use persists. We don't take ourselves to be acting on behalf of our selfish genes, of course, and indeed our conscious motives may feel like something else altogether, but those persistently self-serving genes are ultimately responsible for our acts of moral goodness. As a result, the species of humanity with its shared evolutionary history shares a moral code.

In this way, morality could perhaps be said to be objective even in the absence of God.[21] Neither individuals nor cultures have the power to choose just what their selfish genes will decree. We are all members of the same species and therefore subject to the same biological impulses. There may be some cultural fluctuation; survival is, after all, dependent upon one's geographical and historical location. Still, on Dawkins's view, it is not up to the subject or up to the culture to decide what counts as a right action or a good life. If anything, it is up to those selfish genes. In this one small way, Dawkins's account of moral values could be said to satisfy Robert Adam's definition as being "objective in the sense that whether they obtain or not does not depend on whether any human being thinks they do."[22]

---

20. Dawkins, *The God Delusion*, 252.
21. Whether or not Dawkins would affirm the objectivity of morality, I cannot say. I can only say that in the limited way we are using this term, it seems to follow from his account.
22. Adams, "Moral Arguments for Theistic Belief," 117.

Morality as Useful Fiction

At the same time, even if they could be construed as objective, it is not at all clear that these values are rightly construed as moral. On Dawkins's account, what does it mean to say of some action or human life that it was right or wrong, good or bad? An act is right when it accords with a general rule that, historically, has tended to maximize genetic reproductive success, and an act is wrong when it accords with a general rule that, historically, has tended to undermine genetic reproductive success. Killing an innocent person, for instance, has long been a quick recipe for swift community justice and, ultimately, death. Hence, murder is wrong. Stealing from others has tended to lead to a loss of community trust, goodwill, and much-needed help. Hence, stealing is wrong. In contrast, helping others tends to earn reciprocation, so helping is good, or right. As for the good life? That one is easy! A good life is a life that tends toward genetic reproduction—either through my offspring or the offspring of my genetically similar kin. If humanity has a telos on this account (and I very much doubt that Dawkins would say that it does), it is to reproduce. And that seems to be the proper end of our genes, not of ourselves.

There is an important sense in which this is not at all what we ordinarily mean by objective morality. Morality, on this account, is not a feature of the universe; it is a convenient way of describing our genetically based tendencies to speak and act in certain ways. To use philosophical terminology, morality can be *reduced to* facts about our genetic material. The genetic materials are real, but the moral claims we have constructed in response to the activity of those genes are a useful fiction. Elsewhere, Daniel Dennett gives an excellent example of what it means for something to be a useful fiction. Consider the term *horsepower*. We use units of horsepower to accurately convey the power of an engine. Horsepower means the same thing in all engines, and it is a helpful way to quantify a complex set of measurements, but as Dennett rightly cautions, "Don't look in the engines for the horses."[23] In much the same way, Dawkins's view holds that morality is a useful way to talk about the impulses and urges that we share as a species. Still, don't look to the universe

23. D. Dennett, "Who's on First? Heterophenomenology Explained," in *Arguing about the Mind*, ed. B. Gertler and L. A. Shapiro, Arguing about Philosophy (New York: Routledge, 2007), 85.

for moral values! You are as likely to find them among the electrons and selfish genes as you are to find a horse in your car's engine.

It is easy to see why horsepower is a genuinely useful fiction. It really does correspond to the thing it purports to describe: the power of an engine. In its early usage, it also corresponded to something real and obviously relevant: the power of actual horses to perform the function that engines do now. But by using morality claims to describe reproductive advantageousness, we seem to have changed the subject entirely. Horses and engines both power vehicles. Morality and reproductive success are in wildly different categories. If this fiction is at all useful, it is so only because it is deceptive. "Santa is watching" may be a useful and effective way of saying to your children "We want you to behave!" but it doesn't point to anything real in the world. In the same way, if "stealing is wrong" maximizes genetic reproduction, it does so despite the fact that there is no such thing as wrongness. Moral values are as real as Santa on this account.

Furthermore, deceptive or not, we cannot be sure that this fiction is pragmatically useful. As Dawkins himself notes, these moral rules of thumb are rough approximations at best. After all, the traits that have maximized reproductive chances over the course of history may not be much use in the twenty-first-century Western world.[24] Instead, our residual tendencies toward pity and kindness may largely be "blessed, precious mistakes," as Dawkins wrote. Mistaken attempts at genetic propagation, blessed or precious though they may be, cannot suffice to ground objective moral values—at least, not in anything like the ordinary use of that term.

We can go further. So far, I have granted Dawkins's suggestion that altruism, pity, and kindness are genetically advantageous. It is not at all clear to me that evolutionary history would bear this out. Instead, it seems at least as likely that the violent wielding of power, racial and ethnic insularity, and sexual promiscuity were the recipe for success among our evolutionary ancestors.[25] In this vein, suppose that we were to discover today that rampant sexual promiscuity and rape coupled with racial and ethnic isolationism has

---

24. There is an easy test here. We can merely compare the birth rates of whole communities—nations, religious groups, however we chose to fix the population. Then, if we find that the communities with the highest birthrates are, in fact, the ones that seem to be the most moral, we have some reason to believe that these traits continue to increase reproductive success. I very much doubt that we will find that the results of this test favor Darwinian morality.

25. Here and throughout, I have benefitted from helpful input from Michael Morris.

been the most successful path forward for our selfish genes. We can disagree about how likely this is, but likelihood does not matter. All that matters is the question: What would follow for morality? If we one day learn that the advocate of racial purity laws who takes for himself multiple very young wives is, empirically speaking, the best robot vehicle that our genes could hope for, will we then have to conclude that this is what the morally good life calls for? Of course not. Even Dawkins himself would not advocate for that conclusion. Instead, in the face of such a discovery, it seems overwhelmingly likely that we would all persist in condemning this behavior as *morally wrong.* If I am correct, then moral rightness and wrongness is just not the same thing as genetic reproductive success. Whatever the latter is, it is not morality.

Dawkins's explanation of morality faces further difficulties. In grounding morality in wholly descriptive facts about natural selection, Dawkins fails to provide any reason why a person, who is a mere vehicle for genes, should care about morality. Instead, he leaves crucial moral questions open: Why should I act in accordance with these moral rules? Why should I care about them at all? What hold do they have on me? By what authority? This point is particularly powerful when considered alongside the fact that many people have no interest whatsoever in advancing their own genes. In fact, some people go to great lengths to prevent their genes from reproducing. Their genes may remain selfish, but their rational self is committed to overriding those impulses—whether out of specific concerns about genetic history, general concerns about overpopulation, or mere personal preference. When the question "Why be moral?" is raised against other moral theories, it often requires the introduction of an imagined figure who simply doesn't care at all about pleasure, rule-following, or divine approval. In this case, however, we need not imagine a particularly contrary person; we need only consider the countless people who do not desire to reproduce. Of course, as Dawkins clearly explained, he is not calling for us to be moral in order that we may reproduce. No, our selfish genes are to be merely unconscious motivators. Still, the problem remains: once we are made aware of what morality is, any persuasive force that moral values may have held is thereby undermined.

In the end, I think the strongest argument against Dawkins's account is this: we have no reason to expect that the right act and the good life defined in terms of genetic success rates will be right or good according to our moral intuitions. When we say that rape, torture, and violent theft are wrong, we don't mean that they are the kinds of things that are likely to block one's genes from reproducing. Should we learn they are genetically advantageous, it will remain the case that we judge them to be immoral. Likewise, when we say that benevolence is better than thievery, and honesty better than deception, we typically do not take ourselves to be evaluating among the reproductive strategies of our genes. If Dawkins is right, then our ordinary commonsense view of moral values is wrong. If we are right, if the wrongness of rape, murder, and thievery constitute actual violations of a real and objective moral code, then Dawkins's account fails.

Robust Atheistic Moral Realism

Contrary to Sartre and Dawkins, some atheistic philosophers do affirm a robust moral realism. These philosophers maintain that objective moral values must simply be understood as a fundamental feature of reality. We read in chapter 12 that Peter Singer likens moral objectivity to "the objectivity of mathematical truths or perhaps of logical truths." When we say that $2 + 2 = 4$, we mean that $2 + 2 = 4$ is true—true for everyone, regardless of their knowledge of or feelings about that truth. In her 2001 book entitled *Natural Goodness*, Philippa Foot reflects on how moral values and a human telos might be seen to be a part of nature itself.[26] In *The Moral Landscape* Sam Harris defends the view that moral truths are just as accessible to ordinary empirical science as any other domain of inquiry.[27] And in *Robust Ethics: The Metaphysics and Epistemology of Godless Normative Realism*, Erik Wielenberg defends the claim that objective moral facts are a part of fundamental reality.[28] According to each of these philosophers, objective moral values can be discovered through reflections about the empirical world, for objective morality is a part of ultimate reality.

I do not mean to say that Singer, Foot, Harris, and Wielenberg share a single theory of morality. In truth, Peter Singer devotes his efforts almost entirely to the field of applied ethics. If his extensive writings are any indication, it is far more important to him that people learn to act morally than it is that they understand where morality comes from. Harris's position is

26. P. Foot, *Natural Goodness* (Oxford: Clarendon, 2003).
27. S. Harris, *The Moral Landscape: How Science Can Determine Human Values* (New York: Free Press, 2011).
28. Wielenberg, *Robust Ethics*.

similar to Foot's, and Foot's is the philosophically stronger treatment by far. Just as I noted in our discussion of the problem of evil, moral philosophers often defend their positions with entire books. We could not do justice to the details of a specific account in a single chapter. Fortunately, for our purposes it will suffice to focus on their one shared feature. All four rely on something like the following general line of reasoning: Moral values seem to be objective. We can see the truth of our shared moral intuitions merely by reflecting on the nature of what it means to be a human being, what it means to flourish, and what it means to suffer. Some things, such as torturing a person for fun, are clearly bad. Well-being, pleasure, and other markers of human flourishing are clearly good. We should *of course* promote well-being, pleasure, and human flourishing. We should *of course* help prevent needless suffering. We should obviously not torture a person for our entertainment. No serious, morally sensitive person could dispute the truths of these moral principles. They are self-evident.

At this point, the theist can answer: Yes! Absolutely! Objective moral values are clearly a part of reality itself. There are objectively right and wrong actions, an objective human nature, and a criterion of human flourishing. The question, of course, is how this all came to be. If Sartre is correct, then every one of these shared values rests upon the long-held, difficult-to-shake conception of humankind as having been created by God, a conception which for atheism is wholly unfounded. If Dawkins is correct, then these moral intuitions are not actually indicative of normative principles about how we ought to act but are instead rules of thumb designed to foster genetic reproductive success. In light of these alternative explanations, the atheist who wishes to defend the objectivity of moral values will need to do more than merely point to their intuitive plausibility. Dawkins and Sartre have given us good reason to believe that their plausibility is not a sign of their reliability—at least not as truly normative, objective values. We would all feel the pull of shared moral norms if they were merely the by-product of natural selection. We would all feel the pull of shared moral norms if we were collectively unable to shake the notion of our species as having been created in the image of a designer God. Simply *feeling the pull* toward morality cannot, therefore, ground the objective reality of moral values.

But if God does not exist, then what is left to ground and explain the existence of these moral values? As we read in chapter 12, "The problem is not that of what will give the moral law power in men's lives, but that of a conception of the universe which will make the very existence of a moral law understandable."[29] These atheistic theories tell us that we ought to act morally, but they do so with a conception of the universe that makes it difficult to see why and how we should believe that these shared moral values have anything like true normative objectivity. Objective morality may not be impossible on an atheistic worldview, but it feels like an *ad hoc* addition. A world that is the result of blind forces and the rapid expansion of matter and energy seems unlikely to contain facts about how we ought to treat one another.

Nevertheless, atheistic moral realism claims that the universe itself contains objective moral values. What grounds and explains them? According to Wielenberg, at least, *nothing* does.[30] They are what philosophers call "brute facts" about the world. To borrow a definition from *The Stanford Encyclopedia of Philosophy*, "A brute fact is a fact that is unexplained, i.e. a fact of which there is no explanation."[31] If Wielenberg is correct, then these moral facts neither have nor need an explanation. They exist in their own right, dependent upon nothing outside of themselves. They simply are.[32] On this point, Wielenberg finds a similarity between his account and theism. He writes, "Therefore, my version of nontheistic robust normative realism has an ontological commitment shared by many theists: it implies the obtaining of substantive, metaphysically necessary, brute facts."[33] For Wielenberg, these brute facts comprise our moral reality. For theism, he notes, the fact of God's existence is similarly brute, substantive, and metaphysically necessary. Where the theist claims that God's existence is self-explanatory, that God could not fail to exist, Wielenberg says the same for objective moral values. He writes, "To ask of such facts, 'where do they come from?' or 'on what foundation do

29. D. Baggett and J. Walls, *The Moral Argument: A History* (Oxford: Oxford University Press, 2019), 198.

30. For the more philosophically experienced readers, I can give a slightly more accurate account: Wielenberg believes that moral facts supervene on natural facts, and that their supervenience relation is brute. As for the bruteness of morality, I suspect that Foot and Harris agree on this as well. Foot's work draws heavily on Elizabeth Anscombe's "Modern Moral Philosophy," in which Anscombe endorses the bruteness of some moral facts. G. E. M. Anscombe, "Modern Moral Philosophy," *Philosophy* 33, no. 124 (1958): 1–19.

31. K. Mulligan and F. Correia, "Facts," *The Stanford Encyclopedia of Philosophy*, ed. E. N. Zalta (Winter 2020 Edition), https://plato.stanford.edu/archives/win2020/entries/facts/.

32. As Michael Morris helpfully noted, this commitment to empirically unverifiable brute moral facts is very much in tension with many of the reasons given in defense of atheism.

33. Wielenberg, *Robust Ethics*, 38.

they rest?' is misguided in much the way that, according to many theists, it is misguided to ask of God, 'where does He come from?' or 'on what foundation does He rest?'"[34] These questions are misguided because brute facts neither have nor need explanation.

Wielenberg is right to note that theism includes the belief that God exists necessarily. By this we mean that the existence of God is not dependent upon anything outside of himself in the way that our contingent human lives are. A moment of reflection reveals how tenuous the life of any human individual is. Roughly one hundred years or three generations ago, four different pairs of people had to find, marry, and reproduce with one another at just the right time so that your grandparents could come into existence. Then your grandparents, all four of them, had to find one another and reproduce as well, so that your parents could come to be, followed of course by your parents. One bad case of influenza, one automobile accident, or one romantic mishap could have prevented you from ever gracing this earth. Even without considering the role of the divine in creation, we are all profoundly reliant upon persons and things outside us for existence. God, if he exists, is surely not like this. The fact of God's existence, if indeed it is a fact, cannot be explained by anything other than God, for there is nothing more fundamental, more powerful, more ultimate than God.

Does this mean that the fact of God's existence is brute? Not necessarily, if you'll pardon the pun. Many theists hold that God's existence is self-explaining, and that this is importantly different than being without explanation. On this view, it is not that God's existence doesn't require an explanation. Instead, it doesn't require an explanation that goes outside of God himself; God's existence is wholly explained by his nature.[35] Still, not too much hinges upon this distinction here. For our purposes, it is enough to ask whether Wielenberg's claim of parity really holds. That is, is it accurate to suggest that the brute fact of God's existence would be no different from the brute fact of objective moral values? It seems to me that the two are importantly different in one clear respect: it is difficult to imagine what, if anything, could be more fundamental than God such that it could ground

---

34. Wielenberg, *Robust Ethics*, 38.

35. See, for instance, T. D. Senor, "On the Tenability of Brute Naturalism and the Implications of Brute Theism," *Philosophia Christi* 12, no. 2 (2010): 273–80. And C. E. McIntosh, "Why Does God Exist?," in *Religious Studies* (2020): 1–22, doi:10.1017/S0034412520000347.

or explain his existence. In contrast, it is not at all difficult to imagine what could be more fundamental than morality, such that it could ground or explain the existence of moral facts. In the first place, Dawkins and Sartre have given us good reasons to believe that what we really have is merely the appearance of morality, and that appearance can be grounded and explained in terms of something else entirely. In the second place, theism grounds and explains the objectivity of morality in God. Clearly, it is at least conceivable that these brute facts have an explanation, and in this way their bruteness seems importantly different from that of God's existence.

The Moral Landscape

Wielenberg agrees that descriptive facts alone cannot explain moral facts. He does not deny Hume's claim that one cannot derive an *ought* from an *is*. In fact, this difficulty is largely the reason why he judges moral facts to be brute. He writes, "Any ethical fact that can be explained at all is explained at least in part by other ethical facts. . . . I take it that this is the sort of thing philosophers have in mind when they talk about a 'fact/value gap' or the impossibility of deriving an 'ought' from an 'is.'"[36] If ethical facts can only be explained by other ethical facts, and if there is no eternal standard-bearer of goodness (like God), then ethical facts must be brute facts. Perhaps the atheist who is uncomfortable with brute objective moral facts would be better served by Sam Harris's position. In *The Moral Landscape*, Harris maintains that our moral principles can, in fact, be deduced solely from empirical observations about the well-being of human beings. In other words, Harris denies that there is any gap at all between *is* and *ought*, arguing instead that "a clear boundary between facts and values simply does not exist."[37]

I want to close with Harris's account for three reasons: First, his book has been very successful and well-received among popular audiences, including my own undergraduate students. Second, he seems to be straightforwardly mistaken about this. His error has been widely noted, even by his otherwise sympathetic ally Peter Singer.[38] Finally, if I understand his error correctly,

---

36. Wielenberg, *Robust Ethics*, 43.

37. Harris, *The Moral Landscape*, 11.

38. See, also, the addendum included in more recent versions of *The Moral Landscape* where Harris includes several statements of this criticism.

it is an easy one to make, and it belies a subtler confusion that ultimately lends credence to theism. For these reasons, I thought it best to include in this chapter a brief explanation of where Harris goes wrong. As Peter Singer notes, it is easy to confuse (a) our ability to *infer* what we ought to do while drawing upon our own understanding of human flourishing with (b) our ability to *logically deduce* it on the basis of descriptive facts alone. Singer explains, "There is a fine line . . . between saying from the description, we can deduce what we ought to do and between saying when we reflect on what suffering is and when we reflect on what happiness is, we can see that it is self-evident that we ought to promote happiness and we ought to reduce suffering."[39] With Singer, I believe that Harris fails to distinguish between these two claims. As I will show, the evidence that Harris presents against the fact-value distinction—that is, against the gap between *is* and *ought*—is actually evidence of the objectivity of moral values.[40]

It is true, as Harris, Singer, Foot, and Wielenberg all note, that reflections on human suffering and flourishing make the truths of certain moral principles evident. The morally sensitive person will come to the conclusion that she ought to help the sufferer and ought not harm whenever possible.

---

39. "On Becoming a Moral Realist with Peter Singer," *AI Alignment Podcast*, hosted by Lucas Perry, October 18, 2018, https://futureoflife.org/2018/10/18/on-becoming-a-moral-realist -peter-singer/.

40. For example, Harris writes of his doctoral work using magnetic resonance imaging (fMRI) to study the brain. There, he found that "When we compared the mental states of belief and disbelief, we found that belief was associated with greater activity in the medial prefrontal cortex (MPFC.)" He went on to note that both purely factual and value-laden beliefs share this feature in common, that the content of the belief did not change the involvement of the MPFC. He thus concludes, "This finding of content-independence challenges the fact-value distinction very directly: for if, from the point of view of the brain, believing 'the sun is a star' is importantly similar to believing 'cruelty is wrong,' how can we say that scientific and ethical judgments have nothing in common?" (Harris, *The Moral Landscape: How Science Can Determine Human Values*, 120–21.)

In response, we can say: First, nobody has claimed that scientific and ethical judgments have nothing in common. In fact, everybody who believes in the objectivity of moral values agrees that they have at least this much in common: they are judgments about some feature of reality, judgments which can get things right or get things wrong, judgments which can be true or false. Second, if the brain treats these beliefs similarly (or even identically), that can only confirm the fact that we hold these beliefs to be true beliefs—not mere preferences, for example. But again, this is simply a reaffirmation of the objectivity of moral values. Perhaps what Harris means is this: We see no difference between *is* beliefs and *ought* beliefs when we observe them with an fMRI machine. Thus, there can be no important difference between them. If that is the claim, we need only note that it is simplistic and scientifically premature to suppose that the fMRI can tell us everything there is to know about the content of our beliefs.

We can even agree that the person who fails to see these truths is maladapted. What is also true, however, and what Harris alone does not seem to see, is that in coming to this conclusion the morally sensitive person will have to rely on a normative moral principle. No matter how clear the facts are concerning which acts lead to the well-being of sentient creatures, those facts alone will never include the claim "You *should* do that which advances the well-being of sentient creatures." As Hume noted, and as we observed earlier in this chapter, there is simply no way to deduce the normative claim from descriptive observations of the world.[41]

If this is the case, then why does Harris fail to see it? It may help to state the problem in terms of the moral argument: Harris mistakes evidence of the reality of objective moral values for evidence of an *explanation* of that reality; he confuses the question at stake in the first premise with that of the second. (Remember, the first premise of the moral argument states only that objective moral values exist; the second premise claims that theism is a better explanation of this fact than is atheism.) The theist and atheist can agree that there is overwhelming and deeply compelling evidence in support of this claim. Harris is absolutely right that reflections on the well-being of sentient creatures should, in a properly functioning person, reveal moral truths about how we ought to treat one another. But all that this shows is that there are in fact objective moral values. That they exist is not enough. That they exist serves only to support the first premise of the moral argument for theism.

The remaining question comes down to the second premise: Can atheism adequately explain the fact that these objective moral values exist? Even the atheistic philosopher Mackie grants that evidence of objective morality could serve as evidence of the existence of God. If atheism is to push back, if atheistic moral realists are to offer a compelling alternative explanation of how and why objective moral values came to be, they cannot do so merely by reiterating the evidence for objective moral values. The theist is already persuaded of the reality of objective moral values. What remains to be shown is that atheism can fit these values into a coherent atheistic worldview.

---

41. To be clear, there are thoughtful and reflective philosophers who reject the is/ought distinction as Hume gave it. When they do, though, they give reasons for their rejection—and those reasons are often complex and philosophically technical. (Elizabeth Anscombe, for example, in G. E. M. Anscombe, "Modern Moral Philosophy," *Philosophy: The Journal of the Royal Institute of Philosophy* 33 [1958]: 1–19.) Simply pointing to the force of moral intuitions clearly does not suffice.

Conclusion

If God does not exist, then it is difficult to see why we ought to expect our feelings about moral values to be good indicators of the truth. To finally turn our attention to the end of the quotation from *River Out of Eden* referenced throughout this chapter, consider the final lines of Dawkins's reflections:

As that unhappy poet A. E. Housman put it:

> For Nature, heartless Nature,
> > Will neither know nor care.

> DNA neither knows nor cares. DNA just is. And we dance to its music.[42]

If the atheistic scientific worldview is correct, then we live in a world of "blind physical forces and genetic replication," and we dance to the music of our DNA, unknowingly guided by our selfish genes.[43] While we could expect these moral rules of thumb to be pragmatically useful, we have no reason to suppose that they reflect any deeper, normative truth like Harris's injunction that we *ought to* maximize the well-being of sentient creatures. Likewise, as Sartre noted, if we are not the product of a Divine Artisan, we should not expect to have a coherent, shared human nature. The best we could hope for would be the radical freedom to create ourselves on our own terms.

---

42. Dawkins, *River Out of Eden*, 133.
43. Dawkins, *River Out of Eden*, 133.

Theistic Moral Values

14

And God created the human in his image, in the image of God He created him, male and female He created them.

—*Genesis 1:27[1]*

Among all human pursuits, the pursuit of wisdom is more perfect, more noble, more useful, and more full of joy.

—*St. Thomas Aquinas[2]*

D oes theism fare better than atheism with respect to objective moral values? There is good reason to believe that it can. In this chapter we will consider the claim that theism offers a better explanation of objective moral values than the explanations available if atheism is true. In the process, we will consider two paths forward for a theistic position: one focusing on the right act, and the other on the human telos and the resultant good life. Once again, keep in mind that the work in this chapter is just the beginning. As I have noted, serious work on this topic often requires book-length treatments. We will not be able to address every objection nor hash out every detail. Instead, we will do as we did for the atheistic theories and consider the overall claims of each position.[3] On the whole, theism has better resources to explain the right act and the good life than atheism does.

As some of you may have already noticed, this claim is not nearly as strong as it could be. In fact, when considering the relationship between objective

---

1. From the Robert Alter translation, *The Five Books of Moses: A Translation with Commentary* New York: Norton, 2008.
2. Thomas Aquinas, *Summa Contra Gentiles*, book 1, *God*, trans. A. C. Pegis, FRSC (Notre Dame, IN: University of Notre Dame Press, 1975), 61.
3. This need not be your final resting place for this topic. Instead, I encourage you to go further—beginning with the readings recommended at the end of this chapter.

moral values and theism, some philosophers believe that the former actually entails the latter, that it is not possible for objective moral values to exist in a world without God. Both Paul Copan and William Lane Craig, two of the most influential Christian apologists working today, offer deductive statements of the moral argument. Craig's standard statement goes as follows:

1. If God does not exist, objective moral values and duties do not exist.
2. Objective moral values and duties do exist.
3. So, God exists.[4]

This argument follows the valid argument form of *modus tollens*, or "denying the consequent." If the premises of this argument are true, it is logically impossible for the conclusion to be false. The premises of this argument entail its conclusion.

If there is a deductively valid moral argument for the existence of God available, then why have I suggested that the moral argument be stated as an inference to the best explanation? My inductive argument only renders its conclusion very likely: "God (probably) exists." In contrast, this deductive statement concludes that God does exist, and it does so with the full force of logical necessity. Why not aim higher?

Inference to the Best Explanation

The answer is, in part, pragmatic: the deductive case is hard to make. While it may feel obvious to theists that objective morality requires God, this intuition is not shared by atheists. On the contrary, as we have already seen, quite a lot of atheistic and agnostic philosophers are moral realists. Many of these philosophers have given extensive accounts detailing how objective moral values might be construed as natural features of a wholly natural world. They do not see these values as proof of the existence of God; they do not accept that the former entails the latter. For that reason, the first premise of Craig's argument, as well as the entailment at the core of any deductive moral argument, is difficult to defend. In order to defend the claim that objective morality is impossible

---

4. W. L. Craig, *On Guard: Defending Your Faith with Reason and Precision* (Colorado Springs: Cook, 2010). See also P. Copan, "Can Michael Martin Be a Moral Realist? *Sic et Non*," *Philosophia Christi* 1, no. 2, (1999): 45–72.

without God, the theist would have to show that every atheistic attempt at moral realism fails not because of *implausibility* but because of *impossibility*. Perhaps Craig and Copan are correct, and objective moral values are impossible without God, but even if that is true, it is a difficult truth to demonstrate.

Fortunately, it is also unnecessary. We do not have to show that it is impossible for there to be objective morality in an atheistic world, only that the objectivity of morality makes theism more likely than atheism. Unlike the entailment claim, this inductive case is a relatively easy one to make. Correspondingly, it is a great deal more difficult for an atheist to dispute the premises of the inductive argument than the deductive one. Think of it this way: any time that you pronounce something impossible, the merest of possibilities is enough to undermine the truth of your claim. For that reason, to reject the first premise of the deductive moral argument, the atheist need only demonstrate the barest possibility of atheistic moral realism. As we read in the previous chapter, entire books have been written in defense of this view. To reject the inductive statement, however, the atheist must show that objective moral values are better explained by atheism than theism or, at the very least, that they are no better explained by theism than atheism.

For that reason, my treatment of the moral argument will continue to center upon the argument from abduction introduced in chapter 12:

1. There are objective moral values.
2. The best explanation for the existence of objective moral values is the existence of God.
3. Therefore, God (probably) exists.

The defense of the second premise of this argument can be summarized as follows: objective moral values are a better fit in a theistic worldview than an atheistic one. A world that came about as the result of chance is not likely to be a world where we can speak truly of the right or wrong act, or the good or bad life. In the words of Sartre, it seems more likely to be a world where "man simply is." In contrast, if there is a God, and if that God designed and created the world in which we live, then we should expect to find features of the divine nature, such as goodness and rightness, in the created order. In an atheistic world, objective morality would be a surprising discovery. In a world created by a loving, perfectly good God, objective morality is exactly what we should expect to find.

Basic Moral Beliefs

Before we turn to our theories of the right act and the good life, one further advantage to theism must be noted. Theism can better explain both our ability to know moral truths and our confidence in those truths. As we saw in chapter 13, many atheistic philosophers are just as convinced of the truth and objectivity of moral intuitions as theists are. One way of explaining the confidence that we find in Harris, Singer, Foot, and Wielenberg about the objectivity of moral values is that moral beliefs seem to be what philosophers call "properly basic." In *Knowledge and Christian Belief*, Alvin Plantinga describes basic beliefs as follows: "Every train of arguments will have to start somewhere, and the ultimate premises from which it starts will not themselves be believed on the evidential basis of other propositions; they will have to be accepted in the *basic* way, that is, not on the evidential basis of other beliefs."[5] Plantinga further notes that some basic beliefs are properly basic: not only are they formed in this basic way, but they are "also such that one is *justified* in accepting them in that way."[6] In other words, it isn't simply that we hold some beliefs without grounding them in other beliefs but also that we are being reasonable in doing so. Some beliefs are reasonably held as basic beliefs.

The claim that some beliefs are properly basic is neither new nor controversial. What sets Plantinga's account apart from its predecessors is the way that he tied properly basic beliefs to the proper function of a human being. Rather than restrict the domain of properly basic beliefs to either beliefs about our conscious mental states, about which we could hardly be wrong, or mathematical and logical truths, Plantinga includes the beliefs formed through the use of a properly functioning faculty in appropriate circumstance. For example, as I stare out the window into a wooded backyard forest, I form the belief that I am observing trees, birds, and the like. I do not deduce the presence of trees from my visual experience, as I might in a logical argument; I simply come to believe that they are there through the use of my perceptual faculties. More simply stated, upon seeing them, I believe they are there. Likewise, in remembering my conversation with a friend, I thereby believe

---

5. A. Plantinga, *Knowledge and Christian Belief* (Grand Rapids: Eerdmans, 2015), 13.
6. Plantinga, *Knowledge and Christian Belief*, 14.

that the conversation occurred. Plantinga maintains that in addition to perception and memory, we also have a faculty for experiencing God—what Calvin called the *sensus divinitatis*. He writes, "The heavens declare the glory of God and the skies proclaim the work of his hands (Psalm 19): but not by way of serving as premises for an argument. In this regard the *sensus divinitatis* resembles the faculties of perception, memory, and *a priori* knowledge."[7] Just as the beliefs we form on the basis of perception and memory can be properly basic, so too can the beliefs formed as a result of the *sensus divinitatis*.[8]

With this in mind, we can see why some philosophers count moral beliefs among those that count as properly basic. Consider Paul Copan's explanation:

> Many of our moral beliefs are properly basic. That is, they are properly grounded in certain appropriate circumstances. For example, we are properly appalled at a man's adultery with his personal assistant and his abandoning his wife and children; there is no need to explain away our shock and horror at such actions. Even if it is impossible to prove in some scientific/positivistic fashion . . . that moral values exist, we probably find ourselves far more certain of the wrongness of such actions than we may be of the truth of Einstein's relativity theories or of the universe's expansion.[9]

Our intuitions about moral judgments are powerful, widely shared, and difficult to resist. We see the wrongness of infidelity and parental negligence; we see the wrongness of sexual trafficking; we see the wrongness of physical and sexual assault. We see these moral facts, and even Harris, Singer, Foot and Wielenberg would agree that the person who fails to see them is deficient in some important sense. Their deficiency is a malfunction. The question thus becomes, what does it mean for a person to malfunction in this way? In what sense can we say that the morally blind person is objectively and importantly deficient?

---

7. Plantinga, *Knowledge and Christian Belief*, 35.

8. Plantinga's account is called "Reformed epistemology." For an accessible, extensive defense of this view, I recommend his book *Knowledge and Christian Belief*. The precursor to this book is Plantinga's now-famous academic text *Warranted Christian Belief*. Students who are interested in an even more philosophically rigorous treatment of this topic may prefer to read the original: A. Plantinga, *Warranted Christian Belief* (Oxford: Oxford University Press, 2000).

9. P. Copan, "The Moral Argument," in *The Rationality of Theism*, ed. P. Copan and P. Moser (New York: Routledge, 2003), 151.

For the theist, the answer is clear: humans were created for a purpose, with a plan, and God has endowed them with the ability to see his goodness in creation and to act accordingly. We were designed to function in a certain way, and proper function in the divinely created universe reveals the truth of these moral judgments. If God exists, and if we were created by God, then we should expect the properly functioning created person to see the truths of morality as a part of objective reality. In contrast to atheism, theism offers a straightforward explanation of how and why we all come to share a set of objective moral values. How? By exercising our proper function, including the *sensus divinitatis*, and forming beliefs on that basis. Why? Because that is what we were explicitly designed to do.

In *Ethics in the Real World*, Peter Singer briefly considers (and rejects) something akin to this view. He writes, "Perhaps a divine creator handed us these universal elements at the moment of creation. But an alternative explanation, consistent with the facts of biology and geology, is that over millions of years we have evolved a moral faculty that generates intuitions about right and wrong."[10] I would not go so far as to say that Singer's proposal is impossible. Instead, I wish only to point out that if we have evolved a faculty for discerning right from wrong, then there must be such values out there in the universe to be discerned—values that are properly called "right" and "wrong." If they are there, why are they there? Where did they come from? And if they are not there at all, then what exactly is this faculty discerning? If the answer is merely reproductive advantageousness, then we should call it that. If instead these robust, objective moral values exist, and we are asked simply to accept this as a brute fact about the universe, then it seems like we can do better.

The Right Action

As I have said, some moral philosophers focus on the rightness of an act while others focus instead on the goodness of a life or person. To be clear, when

---

10. P. Singer, *Ethics in the Real World: 82 Brief Essays on Things That Matter* (Princeton University Press, 2017), 16. It is also worth noting that Singer's "alternative explanation" is wholly compatible with theism. Plenty of theists believe in evolution, and they do not necessarily construe creation as a single moment in time. There is no reason why they could not believe that God "handed us" our moral faculty through the gradual mechanisms of evolution. See, for instance: A. Plantinga, *Where the Conflict Really Lies: Science, Religion, and Naturalism* (Oxford: Oxford University Press, 2011).

it comes to philosophical treatments of the good life and the right act, far more can be said than can be explained here. The field of moral philosophy is broad, and the details can be worked out in a number of ways. Still, it will be helpful to explore a few ways of understanding these ideas, beginning with the notion of a right act.

Both Peter Singer and Sam Harris are "consequentialists." To be a consequentialist about morality is to believe that the only thing that matters in determining the rightness or wrongness of an act is the consequences it produces. There are differences among consequentialist theories—whether we ought to consider expected or actual consequences, evaluate on the basis of individual actions, or use general rules for action, and so on—but the basic idea is consistent: the end justifies the means. Most consequentialists are also "utilitarians," which means that they believe that the desired consequence is pleasure, or what Harris dubs "well-being." In *The Moral Landscape*, for example, Harris writes that "the rightness of an act depends on how it impacts the well-being of conscious creatures."[11] It is consequentialist theories like these that led Philippa Foot to construct the original "trolley car" thought experiments, which you may already have encountered in a philosophy classroom or in an episode of *The Good Place*.[12] Trolly car objections, like all objections to consequentialism, pose the following challenge: Can it be that the overall quantity of pleasure and pain is all that matters, regardless of the means of bringing those circumstances about? Even if the consequentialist can address these worries, our central line of questioning remains: What takes us from the fact of human suffering to our obligation to prevent it? What brings us from *is* to *ought*?

---

11. Harris, *The Moral Landscape*, 62.

12. P. Foot, "The Problem of Abortion and the Doctrine of the Double Effect," in *Virtues and Vices and Other Essays in Moral Philosophy*, Oxford Scholarship Online (Oxford: Clarendon Press, 2002). This essay originally appeared in the *Oxford Review* 5 in 1967. Foot's original statement goes as follows: "Suppose that a judge or magistrate is faced with rioters demanding that a culprit be found for a certain crime and threatening otherwise to take their own bloody revenge on a particular section of the community. The real culprit being unknown, the judge sees himself as able to prevent the bloodshed only by framing some innocent person and having him executed. Beside this example is placed another in which a pilot whose airplane is about to crash is deciding whether to steer from a more to a less inhabited area. To make the parallel as close as possible it may rather be supposed that he is the driver of a runaway tram which he can only steer from one narrow track on to another; five men are working on one track and one man on the other; anyone on the track he enters is bound to be killed. In the case of the riots the mob has five hostages, so that in both examples the exchange is supposed to be one man's life for the lives of five" (Foot, *Virtues and Vices*, 23). For a hilarious (but bloody) illustration, see *The Good Place*, season 2, episode 19, broadcast on NBC.

That we should promote well-being and prevent suffering is clear. I do not mean to say that it is an open question whether or not we owe one another help and consideration. Instead, the question we keep returning to is this: What generates this obligation? What feature of reality, what aspect of the world, makes moral facts true? To what exactly does the moral obligation to prevent suffering correspond?

One answer to this question can be found in a view known as "divine command theory." According to this view, actions are right or wrong in relation to a set of laws established by God. Just as legality is a matter of the community's laws, so too morality is a matter of divine law. When you are in a country, you are obliged to obey the laws of the land. It matters not at all whether you want to obey them; the obligation is a direct result of the existence of the law, bolstered and incentivized by the state's power to enforce it. In the same way, if the world really is under the authority of a creator God, then moral obligations grounded in divine commands are inescapable and universal.

Interestingly enough, Michael De Paul suggests that the eighteenth century philosopher William Paley was both a consequentialist and a divine command theorist. De Paul writes, "According to William Paley . . . we are obliged to do those things that God commands. Why then do I call him a utilitarian? Paley was a utilitarian because he thought that we can determine what God wills by considering what is most conducive to the happiness of God's creatures."[13] If De Paul is correct, then Paley offered a way to bridge the is-ought gap for consequentialism. Perhaps we are morally obligated to maximize the happiness of those we encounter, but if so, the obligation arises not simply from the fact of human happiness but instead from the will of God.

For obvious reasons, divine command theory is explicitly and inextricably theistic. As Elizabeth Anscombe wrote in "Modern Moral Philosophy," "Naturally it is not possible to have such a conception unless you believe in God as a law-giver; like Jews, Stoics, and Christians."[14] The details of such a theory

---

13. M. De Paul, "Supervenience and Moral Dependence," *Philosophical Studies* 51 (1987): 425–439. I was alerted to this paper by E. J. Wielenberg, *Robust Ethics: The Metaphysics and Epistemology of Godless Normative Realism* (Oxford: Oxford University Press, 2014), 12.

14. Anscombe, "Modern Moral Philosophy," 5. Anscombe did not endorse divine command theory, but she did note the impact that these kinds of theories have had on our moral language. Responding to the persistent tendency to speak of moral obligations in a largely atheistic philosophical framework, she wrote, "It is as if the notion 'criminal' were to remain when criminal law and criminal courts had been abolished and forgotten" (5).

vary. The Stoics, for instance, conceive of the law-giver as quite different from the God of Christianity and Judaism. Michael Austin characterizes the core feature of divine command theory when he writes, "The specific content of these divine commands varies according to the particular religion and the particular views of the individual divine command theorist, but all versions of the theory hold in common the claim that morality and moral obligations ultimately depend on God."[15] By far the most successful recent statement of this position comes from the Christian philosopher Robert Adams. In "Moral Arguments for Theistic Belief," Adams defends a view according to which "moral rightness and wrongness consist in agreement and disagreement, respectively, with the will or commands of a loving God."[16] Adams's explicit mention of the loving nature of God is not accidental. Instead, the centrality of God's love to his account explains why Adams calls his position "modified divine command theory."[17] In order to see why this modification is needed, we should consider an ancient objection to divine command theory in all its forms.

Answering Euthyphro

In Plato's dialogue entitled *Euthyphro*, the title character asks, "Is the pious loved by the gods because it is pious, or is it pious because it is loved?"[18] Nearly two thousand years later, atheistic philosopher Bertrand Russell reiterated this frequently cited objection:

> If you are quite sure there is a difference between right and wrong, you are then in this situation: Is that difference due to God's fiat or is it not? If it is due to God's fiat, then for God Himself there is no difference between right and wrong, and it is no longer a significant statement to say that God is good. If you are going to say, as theologians do, that God is good, you must then say that right and wrong have some meaning which is independent of God's fiat, because God's fiats are good and not good independently of the mere fact that he made them.[19]

15. M. W. Austin, "Divine Command Theory," *Internet Encyclopedia of Philosophy*, https://iep.utm.edu/divine-c/.

16. Adams, "Moral Arguments for Theistic Belief," 117.

17. Adams, "Moral Arguments for Theistic Belief," 119.

18. Plato, *Euthyphro*, Dialogues of Plato 1 (New Haven, CT: Yale University Press, 1984), 10a.

19. B. Russell, *Why I Am Not a Christian*, 1st ed. (London: Watts, 1927), 12.

We can state the problem more succinctly: if rightness simply means "commanded by God," then it would seem that God could command anything at all, and we would be required to call it right. Thus Adams writes, "The gravest objection to the more extreme forms of divine command theory is that they imply that if God commanded us, for example, to make it our chief end in life to inflict suffering on other human beings, for no other reason than that He commanded it, it would be *wrong* not to obey."[20] This cannot be right. Morality cannot be so arbitrary that a deity could command anything whatsoever, including recreational torture, child abuse, sexual assault, and other atrocities, and then creation would thereby be morally required to obey and call it good. If this is what morality looks like, then morality seems profoundly amoral.

For this reason Adams modifies his statement of divine command theory:

> Finding this conclusion unacceptable, I prefer a less extreme, or modified, divine command theory which identifies the ethical property of wrongness with the property of being contrary to the commands of a *loving* God. Since a God who commanded us to practice cruelty for its own sake would not be a loving God, this modified divine command theory does not imply that it would be wrong to disobey such a command.[21]

A loving God would not command us to maximize the suffering of others. A loving God could not do so while thereby remaining a loving God. Love requires and includes the promotion of the beloved's well-being. In this way, Adams invokes the perfect love of a perfect God as the ultimate grounding and explanation of rightness and wrongness. The theistic God is not morally arbitrary; the theistic God is and must be a loving God.

The Good Life

Not all theistic philosophers agree that divine commands are the best way to ground and explain objective moral values. Broadly speaking, there are

---

20. Adams, "Moral Arguments for Theistic Belief," 119.
21. Adams, "Moral Arguments for Theistic Belief," 119.

three general approaches to understanding morality. We have already been introduced to consequentialism, which looks to the consequences of an act to determine its moral status. We have also seen an example of a "deontological," or "rule-based," account in the form of divine command theory. Deontological theories define morality in terms of compliance with moral rules. The third approach is to step away from questions about the right action and focus instead on the human telos and the good life. We could call this approach an ethic of flourishing.[22]

Theism is well-equipped to ground and explain human flourishing. If humanity was created by God in the image of God, then we share an objective human nature, a telos. On this point even Sartre agrees. This nature does not rely upon individual beliefs or preferences, nor is it a matter of genetic replication. Instead, it is the implementation of a divine design. A good paper knife cuts paper. A good hammer pounds nails. No matter how beautiful the artistry, a paper knife that cannot do the task for which it was created is not a good paper knife. Neither will we find a good hammer that fails to drive nails into wood. In the same way, if humanity was created by God according to a plan and with a purpose, then it is possible to speak truly of a good and bad human life.

Crucially, this standard for a good life is radically different from most contemporary conceptions. It is not a matter of physical health nor of mental fitness. The person with Down syndrome is no less a reflection of the image of God than was Albert Einstein. Thus the theistic worldview also brings with it a notion of universal human worth. According to theism, the good life may not be the life that maximizes genetic reproduction. It likewise may not be a life of bodily well-being or earthly pleasure. It is rather something like the Westminster Catechism's affirmation that the chief end of humanity is "to glorify God and to enjoy him forever." In the wonderfully imaginative novel *The Great Divorce*, C. S. Lewis depicts an afterlife in which nearness to God brings with it increased reality, for God is reality itself. In this story, a character remarks that "there is but one good; that is God. Everything else is good when it looks to Him and bad when it turns from Him."[23] The message of this novel is clear: drawing near to God brings flourishing, and separation from God brings disintegration and death.

---

22. I am immensely thankful to Angela McKay Knobel for her helpful comments on this section.
23. C. S. Lewis, *The Great Divorce* (New York: Harper One, 1973), 97–98.

In some ways, Robert Adams's view straddles this divide between those who would emphasize what is right or obligatory and those who would emphasize the good. In *Finite and Infinite Goods*, Adams extends his response to Euthyphro. There, Adams defends the claim that God is not only superbly good but also goodness itself. Plato advanced a theory of "the forms" throughout his dialogues. The central claim of this view is that the world we observe is an impoverished, imperfect, finite representation of true reality. Earthly justice is just only insofar as it resembles true Justice, or the form of Justice. When we find something beautiful, we are seeing imperfect glimpses of Beauty itself. Whatever is good on Earth can be so only to the extent that it partakes in true Goodness, the form of the Good. On Plato's view, the forms exist eternally in a wholly immaterial realm. Contemporary Platonic philosophers construe these forms as "abstract" objects, as opposed to "concrete" ones. (For instance. "Numbers and the other objects of pure mathematics are abstract (if they exist), whereas rocks and trees and human beings are concrete."[24]) In declaring God to be the Good, Adams both draws upon and breaks from this tradition. He writes, "If God is the Good itself, then the Good is not an abstract object but a concrete (though not a physical) individual. Indeed it is a *person*, or importantly like a person."[25] In this way, earthly goodness becomes, quite literally, resemblance of the divine.

Aristotle was a student of Plato, and Thomas Aquinas a scholar of Aristotle. The most compelling aspects of Plato's works have been strengthened and enhanced by the addition of a monotheistic worldview.[26] Plato believed that the earthly human telos involves, first and foremost, the struggle of the human soul to return to the world of the forms, the world of true reality. The soul longs for union with the forms, seeks knowledge of those forms, and through reincarnation draws nearer and nearer to this eternal reality until

---

24. G. Rosen, "Abstract Objects," *The Stanford Encyclopedia of Philosophy*, revised February 13, 2017, https://plato.stanford.edu/entries/abstract-objects/.

25. R. M. Adams, *Finite and Infinite Goods a Framework for Ethics* (Oxford: Oxford University Press, 1999), 42.

26. Plato was not a monotheist, but he was a committed polytheist. He wrote often of the gods, and his view of the Good as the highest of all forms seems to foreshadow modern day monotheism. One way of expressing the oddness of Singer's, Foot's, and Wielenberg's positions is their attempt to couple a commitment to platonic forms (or something very much like them) with a robust atheism. Once you have admitted something like eternal forms into your ontology—your view of what kinds of things exist—it is difficult to see why you should rule out something like God. Correspondingly, once you have ruled out God, it is difficult to see why you should accept something like platonic forms or brute abstract moral facts.

it is, at last, freed from the trappings of its body.[27] Similarly, Eleonore Stump writes, "On Aquinas's views, for all human beings there is one and the same intrinsic upper limit to the scale of objective value—namely, God and shared union with God."[28] The very best thing for all of us, the human *telos*, is union with God. What then is the good life? It is life in pursuit of union with God.

This is not to say that everybody recognizes their desire for union with God. Instead, just as small children often fail to recognize that they are tired, hungry, or otherwise in need, so do we as a species often set our hearts upon things that do not satisfy. We value things that do not bring joy, and we fail to pursue that which leads to flourishing. If you are not convinced, ask yourself whether the wealthiest and most powerful among us, those best equipped to get everything that they want just as soon as they want it, seem to be the happiest. I submit that they do not; indeed, far from it. Fortunately, Stump continues, "For Aquinas as for Augustine, it is possible for a human person to take as her deepest heart's desire the very thing that is also her greatest flourishing—namely, God and shared union with God."[29] Our deepest heart's desire can be something temporal and earthly, or it can be God himself. When we manage to set our hearts upon God, making union with him our heart's desire, we unite our true *telos* with our earthly longings. When we do so, we will find ourselves on our way to a good life, a life of human flourishing.

A Better Explanation

Although we have only begun to scratch the surface, we have already seen three ways that theism is a better explanation of objective morality than atheism. First, theism explains why we might all come to share similar moral intuitions and hold them with confidence. If reflection on the human condition reveals clear moral principles, how and why does it do so? How did we develop the faculty for discerning these principles? And where or what are these principles, exactly, such that they are there to be discerned? Theism can answer each question. The faculty to discern moral truths is just one part of

27. For further reading, I highly recommend Plato's *Republic* (Indianapolis: Hackett, 1992).
28. E. Stump, *Wandering in Darkness: Narrative and the Problem of Suffering* (Oxford: Clarendon, 2010), 438.
29. Stump, *Wandering in Darkness*, 441.

our divinely designed human nature. As created beings, we were crafted for this purpose. The principles that we discern are likewise explained by God—through his commands or as aspects of his divine nature, or both.

Second, theism makes it easier and more sensible to speak of the right act and the wrong act. If there is a moral law like it seems, then that calls for a moral lawgiver. God is an excellent candidate for a moral lawgiver; the fundamental features of a godless universe are not.

Third, whereas atheistic commitments undermine the likelihood of a human telos and a meaningfully shared good life, theism fully explains both. The person created by a loving, divine artisan is far more likely to have a purpose than she would be were she merely the result of blind forces. To reiterate once more, I do not mean to say that those who believe in theism are more likely to live meaningful lives than those who do not. No, the point applies regardless of our personal beliefs. If God exists, then we were created according to a plan, for a purpose, under the moral authority of a perfectly good God. If God does not exist, then not one of these claims is likely to be true.

Belief in objective moral values is widely shared by theists and atheists alike. If atheism is true, then we have little reason to believe in the truth of these shared beliefs. We can affirm their usefulness, both for genetic propagation and for the orderly workings of polite society, but the further claim that they are true is harder to defend. We could follow Wielenberg and accept as a brute fact the claim that nature gives rise to these values, but this strikes many people, myself included, as oddly *ad hoc*. Sure, it is possible, but it seems implausible and unjustified. This seems especially true in light of the arguments advanced by Dawkins and Sartre, each of whom tells us that a universe not created by God is far more likely to lack ultimate values than it is to contain them. If they are correct, then our persistence in holding on to moral beliefs is either the result of our selfish genes seeking reproduction or our residual theistic trappings.

Alternatively, our keen awareness of moral truth could be the result of our status as well-designed creatures properly functioning in a universe designed by a loving God. The theistic worldview tells us that we were created, and that the creator is good. Perhaps that creator is Goodness itself. More than that, it tells us that creation serves to display the goodness of God. That is, the theistic picture tells us that moral values are real and objective parts of reality, rooted in God and present throughout our universe.

Theism is a better explanation of the objectivity of moral values than is atheism. This is the central claim of the moral argument for theism. If it is correct, and if there are objective moral values, then we ought to conclude that God—at least probably—exists. The moral argument is not a proof of the truth of Christianity; it is not even a deductive proof of theism. Still, as Paul Copan writes, "Even if we cannot move inferentially from objective moral values to the omniscient and omnipotent God of Abraham, Isaac, and Jacob, at least we can say that we live in an 'ontologically haunted universe.' Moral values serve as one of the signals of transcendence."[30] If our belief in moral values is inescapable, it may be that it is so because we live in a value-laden, morally haunted universe. The theistic worldview does a better job of explaining the objectivity of moral values than does atheism. The theistic worldview implies that God does exist. In this way, the objectivity of moral values serves as evidence of the existence of God.

Conclusion

As you may have noticed, none of this decisively proves the existence of God. Instead, the inductive moral argument challenges us to think through what we believe, why we believe it, and the consequences of those beliefs for our other beliefs. The theist and the atheist largely agree that there are moral truths. Those who would deny this claim nevertheless persist, as C. S. Lewis noted in *Mere Christianity*, in expecting moral treatment of themselves and those they love. Very few people, if any at all, live wholly amoral lives apart from moral values. The question then is what their morality tells us about ourselves and what that tells us about the world. In chapter 13, we read these words by Robert Adams: "One of the most generally accepted reasons for believing in the existence of anything is that its existence is implied by the theory that seems to account most adequately for some subject matter."[31] By that reasoning, one excellent reason for believing in the existence of God is that his existence is implied by the theory that best accounts for the objective reality of moral values. The moral law cries out for a lawgiver; the human *telos* points toward a divine designer. Real, objective moral values are evidence of the existence of a good and loving God.

30. P. Copan, "The Moral Argument," in Copan and Moser, *The Rationality of Theism*, 150.
31. Adams, "Moral Arguments for Theistic Belief," 117.

Further Readings for
Part 2

Popularly Accessible Works on the Problem of Evil

Keller, T. *Walking with God Through Pain and Suffering.* New York: Penguin, 2015.

Lewis, C. S. *A Grief Observed.* New York: HarperCollins, 2001.

Russell, M. D. *Children of God.* The Sparrow Series. New York: Random House, 2007.

———. *The Sparrow.* The Sparrow Series. New York: Random House, 2008.

Academic Works on the Problem of Evil

Adams, M. M. *Horrendous Evils and the Goodness of God.* Ithaca, NY: Cornell University Press, 2000.

Dougherty, T., and J. P. McBrayer. *Skeptical Theism: New Essays.* Oxford: Oxford University Press, 2014.

Howard-Snyder, D., ed. *The Evidential Argument from Evil.* Indiana Series in the Philosophy of Religion. Bloomington, IN: Indiana University Press, 2008.

Plantinga, A. *God, Freedom, and Evil.* Grand Rapids: Eerdmans, 1977.

Rea, M. C. *The Hiddenness of God.* Oxford: Oxford University Press, 2018.

Stump, E. *Wandering in Darkness: Narrative and the Problem of Suffering.* Oxford: Clarendon, 2010.

van Inwagen, P. *Christian Faith and the Problem of Evil.* Grand Rapids: Eerdmans, 2004.

———. *The Problem of Evil.* Oxford: Oxford University Press, 2008.

Popularly Accessible Works on Morality

Austin, M. W., and R. D. Geivett. *Being Good: Christian Virtues for Everyday Life.* Grand Rapids: Eerdmans, 2011.

Lewis, C. S. *The Great Divorce.* New York: Harper One, 1973.

Copan, P. *True for You, But Not for Me: Overcoming Objections to Christian Faith.* Grand Rapids: Baker, 2009.

MacIntyre, A. *After Virtue*. London: Bloomsbury, 2013.

Williamson, T. *Tetralogue: I'm Right, You're Wrong*. Oxford: Oxford University Press, 2015.

Philosophical Works on Morality

Adams, R. M. *A Theory of Virtue: Excellence in Being for the Good*. Oxford: Clarendon, 2008.

Baggett, D., and J. L. Walls, *Good God: The Theistic Foundations of Morality*. Oxford: Oxford University Press, 2011.

———. *The Moral Argument: A History*. Oxford: Oxford University Press, 2019.

Dawkins, R. *The God Delusion*. Boston: Houghton Mifflin, 2006.

Dennett, D. *Darwin's Dangerous Idea: Evolution and the Meanings of Life*. New York: Simon & Schuster, 1995.

Foot, P. *Natural Goodness*. Oxford: Clarendon, 2003.

Harris, S. *The Moral Landscape: How Science Can Determine Human Values*. New York: Free Press, 2011.

Kaufmann, W. *Existentialism from Dostoevsky to Sartre*. San Francisco: Hauraki, 2016.

MacIntyre, A. *A Short History of Ethics: A History of Moral Philosophy from the Homeric Age to the Twentieth Century*, 2nd ed. Notre Dame, IN: University of Notre Dame Press, 1998.

Plato. *The Republic*. Cambridge: Cambridge University Press, 2000.

Wielenberg, E. J. *Robust Ethics: The Metaphysics and Epistemology of Godless Normative Realism*. Oxford: Oxford University Press, 2014.

Plantinga's Reformed Epistemology

Plantinga, A. *Knowledge and Christian Belief*. Grand Rapids: Eerdmans, 2015.

———. *Warranted Christian Belief*. Oxford: Oxford University Press, 2000.

Also See the Online Resources Available Here

Journal of the Society of Christian Philosophers: https://place.asburyseminary.edu/faithandphilosophy/

www.believingphilosophy.com

Conclusion

In part 1 of this book, I encouraged Christians to become more philosophically minded. This means learning to think carefully about what you believe and why you believe it. It means recognizing the difference between reasonability and truth and between truth, provability, and certainty. It means being charitable to those with whom you disagree without thereby assuming that you must not really disagree after all. It means asking the hard questions, ideally before they have acquired the force generated by personal or spiritual crisis. In its more serious form, it means taking philosophy classes and reading philosophy books. Above all, it means seeking wisdom, pursuing truth. Philosophical study alone will never be enough for a full life in pursuit of wisdom, but it can be one more tool in your belt, and a very useful one at that.

In part 2, I set out to demonstrate the way that philosophy can help in the pursuit of wisdom. In a sense, all six chapters in part 2 address different aspects of the same question: What can the suffering and evil of this world tell us about God? As you may have noticed, in both cases the strongest philosophical arguments on hand were inductive, not deductive. That is, neither the atheist nor the theist will find proof of her position here. Instead, the atheistic argument from evil says that the prevalence of suffering in this world is good evidence against the existence of God. (The theist disagrees.) In contrast, the theistic moral argument says that the objective reality of good and evil is good evidence in favor of the existence of God. (The atheist disagrees.) This is, more often than not, how philosophy works. Evidence is presented, arguments are considered, and at the end of the day some disagreement remains.

If that is the case, why bother? I hope by now you have come to recognize the answer to that question. Though a philosophical argument is rarely a decisive proof, it is nevertheless immensely beneficial. The problem of evil points us to a series of important questions about God: How much can we expect to understand about the will of God? What does God's justice require? What does his love require? Should faithful believers expect suffering in life, or protection? How should the Christian respond to the suffering believer? And really, these questions just scratch the surface. The problem of evil forces the theist to think through what she believes about God, about pain and suffering, and about the world. In the same way, the moral argument points us to a series of important questions: What would it mean to say that morality is grounded in God? How would that work? What if there is no God? Why are moral values so important to us all? Can we really reject theism and keep these values? Or in doing so, would we be merely fooling ourselves? And does that even matter? Is morality really objective?

The questions are valuable. And seeking answers to these questions has value as well, even more value in community. I hope that you will take classes in philosophy, read books and listen to podcasts by Christian philosophers, and pursue a more philosophically minded faith. I hope that you will embrace the motto endorsed by St. Anselm: *fides quaerens intellectum*, faith seeking understanding.[1]

---

1. S. Anselm, *Proslogion: With the Replies of Gaunilo and Anselm*, ed. T. Williams, Hackett Classics Series (Indianapolis: Hackett, 2001).

Scripture Index

Subject Index

abduction, 124n4, 195, 234
actions
  forbidden, 198, 199, 204, 208
  obligatory, 198, 199
  permitted, 198–99, 204, 208
  right, 237–40
Adams, Marilyn McCord, 20, 157, 160, 163, 180, 189–90
Adams, Robert, 196, 213–14, 220, 240, 241, 243, 246
affirming the antecedent, 132
affluenza, 166, 166n8
Akin, Todd, 96n14
Alter, Robert, 99, 99n19
Anscombe, Elizabeth, 226n30, 230n41, 239, 239n14
antiphilosophical response, the, 6–8
apologetics, Christian, 20, 20n3
Aquinas, Thomas, 6, 79, 92, 94, 191, 192, 193, 232, 243, 244
arguments
  by analogy, 124, 125
  common types of, 132–36
  content of, 95, 118, 128–31
  criteria for good, 118, 120
  deductive, 120, 125–28, 132, 150
  evaluation of, 118–36
  form of, 118, 120–22
  finding conclusion of, 107–12
  finding the premises, 112–15
  formally stated, 105, 107, 108
  inductive, 120, 123–25, 150, 195
  reconstruction, 107–15
  role of in philosophy, 102

  well-formed, 114, 115, 125, 123–28, 195
  what are, 104–7
Aristotle, 243
Augustine, 6, 9, 79, 91, 92, 244
Austin, Michael, 240
Bacon, Francis, 17
Bartholomew, Craig G., 28
Beardsley, Elizabeth, 21
Beardsley, Monroe, 21
begging the question, fallacy of, 171–72
beliefs
  clarity of 36–38
  definition of, 37–38
  consequences of, 88–89, 121
  context of, 87–88, 89
  about the future, 50
  in God, 57–60
  justification of, 40–44
  about the past, 50
  properly basic, 235
  and propositions, 49
  reasonability of, 40–44, 105–6
  that vs. in, 38
  truth of, 44, 48–51, 65
Bennett, Tori, 144–45n5
Bergmann, Michael, 164, 164n6
Bible, the
  challenge of contextualization of, 76–78
  challenge of translation of, 72–76
  as source of wisdom, 72
  suffering in, 178–80
  sufficiency of, 72–78
biconditional, 134
brute facts, 226–28, 245

Subject Index

theistic, 232–46

Murray, Michael, 19, 20, 57

natural selection 217, 218, 219

new atheism, 3, 4, 6–8, 14, 16

noseeum inferences, 168, 169

objectivity of moral values
  atheism and, 212, 213–31
  definition of, 196–200
  and existence of God, 146, 195–96, 212,
    213–14, 227–28, 232–46
  vs. moral relativism, 203–8
  and ought vs. is, 200–203, 228–29, 238,
    239

opinions, definition of, 54–55

"ought implies can" principle, 25

ought vs. is, 200–203, 228–29, 238, 239

Paley, William, 239

Panchuk, Michelle, 158n33

perseverance, 165

Peterson, Claire Brown, 54

philosophers, Christian, 19–21

philosophy
  applying questions of, 26–29
  benefits of embracing, 13–15, 68, 69, 71,
    76, 82, 84, 90–92
  big questions of, 15, 21–26, 107
  and the Christian Church, 5–6, 27, 28,
    78–79
  Christian objections to, 67–84
  and conceptual clarity, 32–36, 69
  definition of, 5, 18, 21, 30
  and doubt, 69
  fundamentalism of questions of, 21, 22,
    26, 30
  generality of questions of, 21, 22, 26, 30
  as leading to atheism, 4, 67–68
  method of, 5
  as pursuit of wisdom, 5, 15, 18, 21,
    29–30, 67, 70
  reading, 85–102
  and rejecting falsehood, 71

Pike, Nelson, 151

Plantinga, Alvin, 20, 28, 94, 151, 181, 183,
  235–36

Plato, 210, 243, 243n26

premise indicators, 70, 95, 102

premises
  finding, 112–15
  in formally stated arguments, 105
  implicit, 113, 115
  true, 128–32
  what are, 104, 106, 107, 108

prescriptive moral theories, 197

propositions, 39–40, 49

prosperity theology, 11, 11n13, 75

provability, 60–63, 131

Pryor, Jim, 94–95

Rea, Michael, 89, 90, 92

reading
  guidelines for, 93–96, 102
  like a philosopher, 92–93, 102, 136
  philosophy, 85–102
  with charity, 96–98, 102

reasonable foreseeability, 168

reasonability, 131

reformed epistemology, 236n8

Reid, Thomas, 28

relativism
  cultural, 51–53, 203, 208–11, 209n12
  moral, 203–12, 203n11
  subjective, 53–56, 203–8

right action, the, 237–40

Rowe, William L., 80n8, 152–53, 154n26,
  154n27, 154n28, 155

Ruse, Michael, 13–14

Russell, Bertrand, 240

Sampson, Marty, 91

Sartre, Jean-Paul, 213, 214–17, 225, 228,
  231, 234, 242, 245

self-evidence, 27

sensus divinitatus, 236, 237

Singer, Peter, 212, 224, 228–29, 235, 236,
  237, 238, 243n26

skeptical theism, 160–76
  argument of, 169, 171, 172, 173, 175–76,
    178, 188
  and defense, 161
  and theodicy, 161
  as total refutation, 161, 163–67

Society of Christian Philosophers, the, 28

sovereignty, divine, 36
Sproul, R. C., 88, 103
straw man fallacy, 116
Stump, Eleonore, 20, 94, 146, 148–49, 159, 174, 177, 189, 190–93, 244
subjective realism, 53–56, 203–8
suffering
  and evil, 145–49
  and existence of God. *See* evil: and existence of God
  and fellowship with God, 191–93
  and free will, 179, 186
  and guilt, 144n4
  justification of, 189–92
  and loss, 148–49
  serious nature of, 156–58
  in Scripture, 178–80
support, 110n4, 120–23, 122n3, 136
Swinburne, Richard, 184, 189
theodicies, 161, 180–81
total refutations, 160, 161, 163
trolley car experiments, 238
truth
  of beliefs, 44, 48–51

coherence theory of, 49n1
correspondence theory of, 48–51, 52
importance of, 48
and popularity, 51–56, 60
and propositions, 49
and provability, 60–63, 131
and rationality, 40–44, 105–6
and reasonability, 131
Trueblood, David, 196
Union Theological Seminary, 36
universal generalization, 128
universal human worth, 242
utilitarians, 238, 239
Vance, J. D., 3, 9–10, 68
Wielenberg, Erik, 214, 224, 226–27, 226n30, 228, 229, 235, 236, 243n26, 245
Wisdom
  active nature of acquiring, 71
  Bible as source of, 72
  definition of, 30
  from God, 30, 31, 46, 68–71
  philosophy as pursuit of, 5, 15, 18, 21, 29–30
Wykstra, Stephen, 168, 169